WANDERLUST

The Life
of a
Globetrotting
Chef

By Joe Mannke and John DeMers

WANDERLUST
The Life of a Globetrotting Chef

Book Design by Jill Feuk

ISBN 0-9787371-0-6
ISBN 978-0-9787371-0-8

CONTENTS

ACKNOWLEDGEMENTS

First and foremost, I would like to thank my wife Connie, who encouraged me to share my story. Other encouragement and helpful comments on the manuscript came from my mother-in-law Martha Elliott, my friends Stella Hall and Bill Bosse, and our longtime cellar master from Rotisserie for Beef and Bird, Vince Baker.

Of course, taking the life I've lived and turning it into something that fit between the covers of this book was the work of two new friends: writer John DeMers, who was always there to ask me what I did or why I did it, and designer Jill Feuk, who seemed to enjoy looking at my old photos as much as I always do.

MY LIFE

WRONG PLACE
WRONG TIME

OUR LAST PICTURE OF HAPPINESS IN POMERANIA.
MY MOTHER, BROTHER, SISTER, AND ME.

*P*eople in this country love to talk about where they're from – certainly if they're from Texas, where I have lived and worked these past two-plus decades – but also if their parents or grandparents came to America from Italy or China or Latin America. They talk about their countries and customs and foods with pride, maybe with nostalgia, based on how much they really know about those things or if they've ever personally visited. In my case, I can talk in detail about the country in which I was born; but it's never easy to express my feelings only in warm and happy memories. There were lots of those, of course: I was a child in a loving family, and there's no way we ever forget how good that feels. But I came of age in a time of darkness, sadness and suffering, a time of war that robbed me of my grandparents, separated my parents for years and eventually drove me from the place I loved to the life of a refugee. Most of all, the agonies and sacrifices of World War II meant that the place I grew up, the country I would always call home would, as an official place you can find on a map, simply cease to exist.

If you look up the history of Pomerania, you will quickly discover that what you read depends on who is writing. True to its roots in the Old World, Pomerania to a Pole is a profoundly Polish country grabbed up a farm or two at a time over many centuries – taken by Germans until they could dominate and absorb it. To a German, Pomerania was an open and uncivilized stretch of low-value real estate that generations of German families developed into an agricultural powerhouse. Like similar disputes throughout Europe, the Balkans and the Middle East, neither side is willing or able to listen very well, much less grant the other any validity. To me now as an American, neither party ever seems blameless in these feuds – and the tireless talk of this king's this or that treaty's that, always in the 12th or 13th century, seems too much and too long ago. Still, in 1980, when the Polish Solidarity movement rose up against the evils of Soviet totalitarianism, those Polish shipyard workers were inspiring the world not, to me, in a place known as Gdansk but in a city from my most distant memory called Danzig.

Pomerania was a beautiful country when I was born there. It is still a beautiful country – I can tell you that, based on my visit to what is now part of Poland. It is hard for me to describe my feelings about the place, except to share with you memories of my parents and grandparents in the country, in tiny towns and villages, and once in a while in the big cities. There was lovely countryside in Pomerania, perhaps in my memory the loveliest countryside anywhere – but there was also the beauty of the Baltic Sea. This is important to me, not only for the joys of spending time on its beaches but also for the fact that my ancestors on my father's side were Vikings.

As a child, I was told these Vikings crossed the Baltic from Scandinavia to start a new life, to find new opportunities in Pomerania – setting in motion several generations willing to make any journey and bear any burden in hopes of a better life. In my case, that fabled spirit of adventure was all mixed up with the fact that the place I knew as home was taken away from me. The temptation to stay "home" was never available, whether I would have wanted it or not. Home was not only wherever we were at the time but what we were doing to feed and clothe ourselves, sometimes just to stay alive. Today, when I look back at the stories that fill this book, at the times I've faced making a new life in places I'd never known before, I feel true to the lives of my parents and grandparents. And yes, I feel true to those ancient Vikings that I, of course, never knew.

My father was proud of his heritage, and always quick to relate it to the great and formative adventure lived by his father in the wilds of southern Africa. The country now known as Namibia was called German Southwest Africa at the start of the 20th century. My grandfather was an engineer and obviously something of a pioneer, moving his family to that distant country to build the German railroad there. To build the tracks along the coast from Walvis Bay to Skagomund was easy, but things became much more

hostile as you moved inland close to the Angolan border. My father was born in a small town called Karibib between the coast and the capital of Windhoek, and these adventures formed some of the earliest memories he shared with us whenever he was home from the war. He remembered sailboats arriving on a lovely beach, for instance – so idyllic until he added that the beach was littered with gigantic whale bones. This was an important whaling station, you see. And he loved to tell a story that I'm not sure I believe or not, but one that's certainly part of our family saga.

Whenever my grandparents had to go to market, it took as much as a week with an ox pulling their cart. Because there were no babysitters in those days, they had to take my father with them. Since he was only one, they also had to take a cow along, to make sure he had fresh milk. Along the way, this story goes, a leopard came and killed the cow, making my grandparents worry that my father would have nothing to eat. Fortunately, there was also a horse, a mare nursing a little foal as they traveled. The milk from that mare, I was assured, nourished not only the mare's offspring but the baby who became my father as well.

Except for brief visits filled with wonderful stories, my father was away for much of my childhood, all through the late 1930s and early 1940s. When you are a child, the politics that later fills the history books matters not at all. What you care about is whether you have enough to eat and drink, if your family is living together or apart, if you feel safe to grow and learn and experience. It's a tribute to my mother that for so much of my childhood I felt that safe, along with my brother and my sister. We were aware, I suppose, that there was a war going on – but until it forced us to flee Pomerania forever, that war seemed, quite honestly, as though it were happening on some distant continent. The life we did live was one of the beautiful countryside, which is saying one of glorious natural abundance.

In the summer, there were tomatoes and cucumbers fresh everywhere, so many that you could never eat them all. In the fall, there were even more vegetables, especially potatoes and carrots, fresh from the harvest. At that time, Pomerania was the true bread-basket of Germany. There was never a lot of heavy industry, so that meant thousands and thousands of acres of crops waiting to be picked when their produce was at its peak. We even had ways of stretching the harvest – ancient farm cultures always do – keeping us fed until things started to grow again after the cold, cold winters. Potatoes, for instance, we'd bury right in the fields, putting them in a big hole and covering them first with straw and then with dirt. This kept them nice all the way till spring. Carrots we kept down in our basement, layering them with sand so they kept good and moist. The war had not come to visit our family yet – though it certainly would later, with a vengeance.

As is common when a woman is left alone with small children, we spent a lot of time at my mother's parents' house. This was a godsend, as they had a farm filled with horses and cows and pigs and chickens and dogs and cats. To this day, I love animals, so this was heaven for me. As a chef, I also recognize the importance of watching my grandmother cook simple, wonderful foods with whatever came in fresh from the fields and forests. My grandmother was certainly no "chef" as we know it today, but she absolutely was one of the best cooks I have ever known. There were lots of fruit trees in the back of her farmhouse – plums, peaches, cherries and apples, and I remember there was always some wonderful pastry baking in her oven. People came from everywhere to eat my grandmother's food – those fruit pastries, of course, but also the soups and stews she created with love from fresh chickens and rabbits and goats. Over the years of my life, I've worked with so many talented, carefully trained and even brilliant chefs, but no tastes have ever truly equaled those set before me by my grandmother on that farm. I've been delighted to learn that so many chefs from so many farflung parts of the world have similar memories from their childhoods – not to mention similar certainties that no food can ever taste that good again.

If you are not fighting in a war and if you are living far from the front, food becomes a strange but natural barometer of how the war is going. It certainly was that way for me and my family. The early years on my grandparents' farm were characterized by abundance, but this evolved into terrible deprivation by the end. Of course, this happens a little at a time. I guess I remember meals slowly becoming more spartan, even if on a farm you can always grow things that would never be seen in the poor cities. In the long, cold winter of 1945, I remember my grandfather telling us the army had taken much of our stored food – and even worse, had made off with his favorite horse. "How," he lamented to us and anyone else willing to listen, "am I going to plow our fields in the springtime?" As it turned out, he would never plow his fields again.

More and more families were packing up what they could all around us, trying to make their way to the safety of the west. We saw them on the roads, shivering underneath whatever blankets they could pull together as their wagon dragged along slowly behind a horse or a cow or an ox, anything that could pull. It was a trickle at first, just the occasional black smudge on the dark, wintry horizon. But finally it was a river. Almost everyone was leaving our area, saying the Russians were getting closer by the day and describing the horrors that awaited any German who dared stay behind. My grandparents felt they had to leave and tried to talk my mother into taking us with them, but she said the journey would be too long and difficult for three small children. Growing sadder by the moment, my grandparents packed what they could from the farm. One day we kissed them goodbye and they joined the river of refugees on that road. We never saw my grandparents again.

The war was coming to us. Though my mother had felt her young family would be safer staying where we were, the war – and what we now know as history – had distinctly different plans. I remember joining my mother outside gazing at the sky one night, where horrible thunder and lightning were exploding all over the place. And then I realized: this wasn't thunder and lightning. It was explosions and fighting and bombs, all mixed with the wavering red color of nearby villages burning. The thunder came closer, the lightning came closer. One enormous bombardment lasted five days, my family huddled around me in the basement. The place we had stored our carrots through the winter for so many years became the only place we now could store ourselves. When we finally felt safe enough to venture upstairs, much of the house had been destroyed - but I'll never forget that the Christmas tree was still standing. My mother and I had just walked out into our devastated backyard when a huge Soviet tank came crashing through, and I remember looking up to see its big, horrifying red star.

There was only one escape left. We gathered up my brother and sister, grabbed what blankets we could because it was so cold and made our way down to the harbor. I remember taking one last look at the crumbling house where I had so many memories, one last look at the fields where I had learned so much about life from my grandparents – and then the scene was no more. By the time we reached the waterfront, we were running, running and falling, searching everywhere for a fishing boat that might be willing to carry us away from here. We found one at last, the last fishing boat still left in Kolberg, and my mother convinced the captain to sail us out far enough to meet a freighter that was gathering refugees. As I looked back from that fishing boat, everything about my beloved city was on fire. The sky was bright red all around and above the spires of the cathedral.

It was a small fishing boat that had taken us, not the sort of vessel to attack the open and wild Baltic Sea. Yet when we reached the place to meet the freighter, all we could see was bodies and debris floating on the surface. A submarine, we realized, had torpedoed the freighter – indeed the same sub was probably still patrolling these waters. As much as he hated the idea, as much as his boat seemed unworthy, the captain took advantage of a heavy fog shrouding us and set out onto the open sea.

Somehow, the two-day voyage in that tiny boat blends in my memory with joining thousands of other refugees to catch a train west, traveling only at night to avoid dive bombers. And those three days on the train blend into our arrival at a refugee camp at the Dutch border. That was a horrible place, the kind of place you wouldn't want to walk through much less spend a single night, and I never want to think about those horrible times. My mother, my brother, my sister and I lived in that dirty, smelly, packed refugee camp for the next two years.

THE LONG WAIT FOR THE LAST TRAIN.

Imagine how it feels to me now, remembering the single image of those two years coming to an end: my mother shouting and screaming and laughing and dancing wildly, waving an opened letter in her hand. The letter had a Red Cross on it, and it told us that my father had been located - alive. It was a strange and terrible time for families on all sides of the war through all parts of Europe. So many had been separated for so long, with no way to find each other, even as the occupation forces of the Soviet Union, Great Britain and the United States struggled to make sense of it all. At last, my father came to us from where he was living in Bavaria. He was so thin, so drawn – but it was the first time I had seen my Dad in three years. After more than a little hugging and crying, he helped us begin the difficult process of arranging papers for us to join him. Finally we were able to make the long, horrible train journey from north to south, through a Germany that was bombed to pieces. We joined my father in a small Bavarian village called Achmühle. It was, for each of us and for us as a family, a new beginning.

Gravlax

Marinated
Salmon Fillet
in Dill
Yield: serves 8

3 to 3 1/2 pounds fresh salmon fillet
   skin on, but all bones removed
2 bunches fresh dill, cut into
   large pieces
1/2 cup coarse kosher salt, or sea salt
1/2 cup sugar
2 tablespoons coarse cracked
   black pepper

Wash the salmon fillet under running cold water, and pat dry with paper towels.

Cut the salmon fillet in half, and place one half of the fish into a shallow ceramic or glass-baking dish, skin down. Place the dill generously over the salmon.

In a separate bowl mix the black pepper, sugar, salt. and sprinkle the mixture evenly over the dill.

Top with the other half fillet, skin side up, and cover the dish with aluminum foil. Place a weight on top to press the salmon fillets down, and refrigerate for three days.

Turn the fish every 12 hours, and baste with liquid accumulated on the bottom of the baking dish.

When the GRAVLAX is marinated and firm, place on a cutting board and slice very thin.

Place on chilled plates, garnish with sprigs of fresh dill and serve with mayonnaise and toasted rye bread.

Pommersche Bier Suppe

Pomeranian
Beer Soup
Yield 4-6

1 cup grated Gruyere cheese
2 cups bread cubes (use hard —
   crust bread or rolls)
1/4 cup vegetable oil
2 cloves garlic, peeled and crushed
1 cup chopped onions
1 cup dry breadcrumbs
3 cups chicken or beef stock
   (canned)
1 can light beer 12 oz
1 teaspoon salt
1/2 teaspoon white pepper
1/4 cup chopped parsley
1 teaspoon Spanish paprika

Place the bread cubes on a sheet pan and toast at 400 degrees until well toasted.

Combine the oil, chopped garlic, and onions in a large saucepan, and sauté over low heat until the onions are light brown.

Stir in the bread crumbs and the bread cubes, add the beer and stock and bring to a boil. Add the salt, pepper, chopped parsley, and pour the soup into a 2 quart heatproof casserole. Sprinkle the grated cheese evenly on the top of the soup, and dust with paprika. Place under the broiler until the cheese is melted and golden brown.

Herring, Red Beets and Potato Salad

Yield: serves 4 – 6

4 large beets, trimmed
2 large Russet potatoes, peeled and
    cut into large slices
2 large carrots, peeled and
    cut into quarters
1 jar marinated herring,
    cut into small chunks
1/4 cup vegetable oil
1/4 teaspoon coarse salt
1/4 teaspoon black pepper or to taste
1 bunch scallions (white part only),
    washed and sliced
1 large sweet and sour pickle, diced
2 tablespoons cider vinegar
2 tablespoons mayonnaise
1/2 teaspoon sugar
1/4 cup chopped fresh parsley
2 tablespoons fresh dill
1/2 cup sliced radishes for garnish
1 hard-boiled egg, cut into quarters,
    for garnish
4 or 6 leaves of bibb lettuce, for serving

Place the beets on a baking dish, brush them with a little oil. Pour 1/2 cup water into the dish, cover tightly with foil and bake at 375°F for one hour, or until tender when pierced with a skewer.

Remove the beets from the oven, uncover them, and set aside to cool. Meanwhile, in a pot fitted with a steamer insert, steam the potatoes and carrots over several inches of boiling water, covered, over high heat for 25 minutes, or until tender. set aside to cool.

Cut the potatoes and carrots into 1/4 inch cubes and place in a medium size ceramic bowl. Add the scallions, pickle and herring chunks. Using a small paring knife remove the skins of the beets. Cut the beets into 1/4 inch cubes and transfer them to the bowl. In a small bowl, whisk together the vinegar, mayonnaise, a pinch each of salt and pepper, and the sugar. Whisk in the 1/4 cup oil a few drops at a time. Pour the dressing over the herring – vegetable salad and toss them gently.

Stir in the chopped parsley, dill, and taste for seasoning. Cover the salad with plastic wrap and refrigerate for several hours. Spoon the salad onto the lettuce leaves, top with the sliced radishes, garnish with hard boil eggs and serve.

Hering Salat mit Rote Bete und Kartoffel

Pomeranian Beet Soup

Yield: serves 6 –8

4 medium ripe tomatoes
4 tablespoons butter
1 cup finely chopped onions
2 cloves garlic, minced
1 tablespoon flour
1 1/2 pounds beets, peeled and coarsely grated
2 parsnips, peeled and grated
1/2 celery root, peeled and coarsely grated
3 strips bacon, chopped
2 bay leaves
1/2 teaspoon sugar
1/4 cup red wine vinegar
2 quarts beef stock (fresh or canned)
2 medium size potatoes, peeled and cut into 1/2 inch chunks
1 pound green cabbage, cored and coarsely shredded
1 pound smoked ham, cut into 1/2 inch cubes
1/2 pint sour cream
3 tablespoons finely chopped fresh parsley
A pinch of salt and black pepper to taste.

Bring 2 quarts of water to a boil over high heat; drop the tomatoes into the boiling water for 20 seconds. Remove them with a slotted spoon, and peel each tomato under cold running water. Cut out the stem, and then slice them half crosswise. With a soupspoon remove the juices, seeds, and dice the flesh, set aside.

In a heavy-duty 12-inch skillet over moderate heat melt the butter, add the chopped bacon and simmer for 3 minutes. Add the onions and garlic and, stirring frequently, cook for 8 minutes until they are lightly colored. Stir in the beets, celery root, parsnips, half of the tomatoes, the sugar, vinegar, and bay leaves.

Dust the mixture with flour, and combine well. Add 2 cups of the beef stock and simmer over low heat for 35 minutes, stirring occasionally. Meanwhile, pour the remaining stock into an 8-quart casserole, and add the potatoes and green cabbage, and bring to a boil, simmer until the potatoes are cooked, but not falling apart. When the vegetables mixture is cooked, add to the casserole with the remaining tomatoes and smoked ham. Simmer for 10 to 15 minutes until the borsch is heated. Taste for seasoning. Ladle into heated soup plates, sprinkle with chopped parsley, and place a generous scoop of sour cream into the center. Serve with crusty brown bread.

Cream of Potato Soup
Yield 6

1 1/2 pounds potatoes, peeled and sliced
1 large onion, peeled and sliced
1 small leek, cut in half,
    washed and sliced
2 small ribs of celery,
    washed and sliced
4 strips of smoked bacon
    cut into large pieces
1/4 teaspoon dried thyme
1/4 teaspoon marjoram
1 teaspoon salt
1 dash nutmeg
1 dash of white pepper
2 bay leaves
1/2 stick butter
1 tablespoon flour
1/2 pound smoked sausage, thinly sliced
1-1/2 quart rich chicken stock
1/4 cup fresh chives, washed
    and thinly sliced for garnish

In a heavy saucepan melt half the butter (1/4 stick), add the bacon and stir-fry until the bacon is cooked. Add the onions, celery, leeks, marjoram, nutmeg, and thyme; cover the pot and steam for 20 minutes over low heat. Remove and discard the bacon. Add the potatoes, chicken broth, salt, bay leaves, cover the pot and simmer over low heat for 45 minutes, until the potatoes are mushy. Puree the soup in two batches in a blender, return the soup to the saucepan, and bring to a boil.

Melt the other 1/4 stick butter over low heat, add the flour to make a light roux. Add the roux to the boiling soup and mix well. Add the smoked sausage, and simmer for 5 minutes. Taste and adjust the seasoning with salt, and pepper. Serve in hot bowls, garnish with fresh chives.

Kolberg-style Fish Sausage
Yield 6

3 pounds fresh cod
    (or any other white fish)
6 slices white bread
1 cup milk
1/2 stick butter or margarine
4 shallots minced
1/4 cup chopped parsley
1/2 teaspoon marjoram
1 lemon (the rind only, chopped)
2 whole eggs
2 tablespoons whipping cream
Salt and a dash of black pepper
    to taste
4 whole eggs
2 1/2 cups dry breadcrumbs
1/4 cup milk
1/4 teaspoon salt
3 cups vegetable oil

Clean the fish under cold water. Soak the bread in the milk, squeeze out the moisture and grind in a meat grinder along with the fish. Sauté the fish and bread mixture in the butter over moderate heat for a few minutes, then add the minced shallots, chopped lemon rind, parsley, and marjoram. Remove the mixture from the skillet or pan and place into a bowl. Season the cooked substance well and mix thoroughly with two eggs and cream.

Whip the remaining eggs, milk and salt. Form thumb-sized sausages, dip in the egg-milk mixture, and coat them with the breadcrumbs. Heat the vegetable oil in a heavy skillet and fry the sausages to a golden brown. Serve with boiled potatoes, and green salad.

Rolled Fillet of Sole with Crabmeat
Yield 6

12 fillets of sole (3 ounces each)
1 pound crabmeat
1/2 stick butter, melted
1/2 cup chopped shallots
1 cup champagne or dry white wine
1/2 cup heavy cream
3 egg yolks
Juice of 1/2 lemon
1/2 cup heavy cream for the sauce
1 teaspoon cornstarch

Rinse the fish fillets under running cold water, and place them next to each other on parchment paper, and cover each with a layer of crabmeat. Roll the fillets, and fasten with kitchen twine or a tooth pick. Melt the butter in a shallow ovenproof dish; add the shallots and the rolled fillets side by side. Mix the champagne, lemon juice, half cup cream, and pour over the fish. Cover the dish and bake in the oven (375 degrees) for 12 minutes. With a slotted spoon transfer the fillets to a serving platter and keep warm.

Beat the egg yolks lightly with half cup heavy cream, and then pour the poaching liquid in which the fillets were cooked into the egg-cream mixture. Dissolve the cornstarch with a little cold water, and bind with the egg-cream mixture. Return the fillets to the baking dish, strain the sauce over the fish, and bake for another 10 minutes. Garnish with the chopped chives and serve with boiled potatoes.

Carp in Beer Sauce (A specialty at Christmas)
Yield 4

2 carp, 2-3 pounds each
1/2 cup white vinegar
1 teaspoon salt
2 cups diced onions
1 cup diced carrots
2 tablespoons sugar
1/2 stick butter
2 tablespoons flour
4 juniper berries
2 cloves garlic
2 bay leaves
4 cans dark beer (36 ounces)
Ginger snaps or lebkuchen (6-8 ounces)
Peel from half lemon, chopped
3 cloves

Scale, wash and clean the carp under cold running water. Remove the head, tail and cut each fish into 4 pieces. Place the onion, carrots on the bottom of a heavy duty Dutch oven or casserole. Add the cloves, juniper berries, lemon peel, bay leaves, garlic, vinegar, sugar and the carp pieces. Crumble the ginger snaps, sprinkle over the fish, and add 2 cans beer. Cover the casserole and bring the liquid to a boil, reduce the heat and simmer for 15 minutes.

In the meantime melt the butter, add the flour and brown over low heat (make a light roux). Slowly add the remaining 2 cans of beer and bring to a boil. Add the mixture to the carp and simmer for another 20 minutes. Remove the carp pieces and place on a platter, keep warm. Strain the fish gravy through a sieve and bring to a boil and adjust for final taste. The sauce can be served over the carp or separate. The traditional side dish is boiled potatoes.

Gevollte Scholle

Karpfen in Biersauce

Braised Stuffed Beef Roulades
Yield 6

Rinden Rouladen

6 (4-6 ounce) rectangle sliced beef top
   round steaks
1/4 cup French mustard
1/4 cup sliced onions
2 tablespoons butter or margarine
3 slices bacon (cut in half,
    4 inches long each)
3 dill pickles cut lengthwise in half
1/2 cup vegetable oil
2 cups beef broth
3 hard-boiled eggs cut into half
2 tablespoons tomato paste
1/2 cup flour
Salt and black pepper to taste

For mirepoix (vegetable mixture)
1/2 cup chopped onions
1/2 cup chopped carrots
1/2 cup chopped celery
5 crushed cloves garlic
1 bay leaf

Melt the butter in a skillet, and sauté the sliced onion until cooked but not brown, set aside. Place a large sheet of parchment paper or foil on your kitchen counter. With a mallet pound the steaks as thin as possible, place each next to each other on the paper. Spread with mustard, season with salt and pepper. Place a strip of bacon down the center, onions, the pickle and half cooked egg across, and roll the steaks in to roulades. Tie with a kitchen twine.

In a heavy kitchen skillet heat the oil, dip the roulades in flour and brown them evenly on all sides. Transfer the meat to a platter. Add the vegetable mixture to the skillet and sauté for a few minutes until light brown, add the tomato paste and dust with the rest of the flour. Add the beef broth and bring to a boil, and simmer for a few minutes. Place the roulades in to the gravy, cover the skillet, reduce the heat and cook very slowly for one hour, turning the meat from time to time. Serve with Red Cabbage and Mashed Potatoes in a Pomeranian tradition.

Braised Rabbit
in Red Wine Sauce
Yield 6

2 rabbit (2 1/2-3 pounds each)
1/2 pound lean bacon cut fine
1/4 cup melted butter
1/2 teaspoon salt
1/2 teaspoon ground black pepper
1/8 teaspoon dried rosemary
1/8 teaspoon dried thyme
1 bay leaf
1/2 teaspoon crushed garlic
1 teaspoon currant jelly
1/2 cup flour
1/2 cup chopped onions
1/2 cup chopped carrots
1/2 cup chopped celery
1/4 cup chopped parsley
1/2 cup brandy
1 cup red wine
1 cup chicken stock
1 tablespoon tomato paste

Wash the rabbit under cold water and pat dry, cut into serving pieces. Cook the bacon in a heavy casserole over moderate heat until crisp. With a slotted spoon remove the bacon and set aside.

Sprinkle the rabbit pieces with salt, dip into the flour and sauté in the bacon fat until nice and brown on all sides. Remove the rabbit and keep warm on a serving platter. Add the butter to the bacon fat and heat, add the onions, garlic, carrots, celery and cook until transparent but not brown. Add the tomato paste, and combine well over low heat. Stir in the brandy, wine, chicken stock, black pepper, thyme, bay leaf, rosemary and bring to a boil.

Return the rabbit pieces, add the bacon, cover the casserole tightly, and simmer for 1 1/2 hour over low heat or in the oven at 350 degrees F. Place the rabbit on a serving platter, strain the sauce over it, and sprinkle with freshly chopped parsley and serve.

Suggested side orders are fresh vegetables of the season, pasta or mashed potatoes.

Potatoes
Au Gratin
Yield 10

2 1/2 pounds Idaho potatoes,
    peeled and sliced thin
1 cup cold milk
1 cup hot light cream
1/2 cup diced Gruyere cheese
1/2 cup Parmesan cheese
1/2 cup melted butter
1/2 cup dry breadcrumbs
1/2 teaspoon salt
Nutmeg and white pepper
    to taste

Bring the milk and cream to a boil, add the sliced potatoes and simmer slowly for 5 minutes. Add the seasoning. Layer the potatoes in a buttered ceramic pan, alternating them with the cheeses. Finish with cheese on top. Top with the milk and cream. Sprinkle with bread crumbs and dot with the melted butter. Bake the potatoes in a slow oven at 300 F for about 45 minutes until the top is golden brown.

Roasted Goose
Yield 8

Gänsebraten

1 goose (13 pounds)
1 pound dried prunes
2 medium sized apples
1 medium sized onion
1 teaspoon dried thyme
3 cloves garlic
1/4 teaspoon cinnamon
1 cup chicken stock for deglazing

Mirepoix:
1 carrot diced, 1 onion diced,
   and 1 bay leaf
1/4 cup cornstarch
   dissolved in a little water
Pepper and salt

Preheat the oven to 350 F. Rinse the goose under cold water inside and outside, and pat dry with paper towel. Combine all ingredients, (except the corn starch and mirepoix) and place into the carcass of the goose. Using a needle and twine close the front and back, then season well with a seasoning salt. Place the bird into a roasting pan breast up, add a cup of water and roast for about 2 hours, basting from time to time.

Turn the goose over, add the mirepoix and roast another 45 minutes until golden brown.

Place the goose on a fireproof platter and keep warm.

Make the gravy by deglazing the roasting pan with chicken stock, skim off the goose fat and thicken with cornstarch. Remove the legs first, then portion the rest of the bird, serve with bread or potato dumpling and red cabbage.

Potato Dumplings
Yield: serves 6

Kartoffel Klosse

2 pounds baking potatoes
1 teaspoon salt
2 whole eggs
1 1/2 cups flour
3 tablespoons butter, cut into bits
1/2 cup toasted bread croutons
A dash of nutmeg

Place the potatoes unpeeled into a soup pot, cover with water and boil for about 40 minutes, or until fully cooked, drain and let cool completely. Peel the potatoes and mash them with a masher or a ricer.

In a large bowl, stir together the potatoes, salt, nutmeg, eggs and flour. Transfer the dough to a well-floured surface and knead with your hands until the mixture is smooth. Add a little more flour if the dough becomes sticky.

Cut the dough into 6 equal pieces. Flour your hands roll each piece into a thin sausage, about 18 inches long and 3/4 inch in diameter. Cut each strip into 1 1/2 inch pieces. In the palm of your hand, flatten the dough with a soupspoon, insert a few bread croutons in the center, and seal the dumpling securely. Set aside.

In a large saucepan, bring 4 quarts salt water to a boil over high heat. Add one third of the dumplings to the boiling water.

After the dumplings rise to the surface reduce the heat and simmer for 4 minutes longer. Transfer with a slotted spoon to a colander and drain. Dot with one third of the butter and toss so they won't stick together. Repeat in 2 more batches with the remaining dumpling batter. Serve with any stew or roast.

Almond Bread

Mandelbrot

2 cups whole unblanched almonds,
 with skin
1 teaspoon baking powder
4 large eggs
3/4 cup vegetable oil
2 teaspoons vanilla extract
3 cups flour
1 cup sugar
1/4 teaspoon salt
1/2 cup whole milk or cream
 for brushing

Set the oven to 375°F. Toast the almonds in the oven until light brown, stirring occasionally. Transfer to a plate and let cool. In a food processor chop the almonds coarsely. In a bowl beat the eggs with a whisk or electric mixer for 1 minute, add the sugar and continue beating. Slowly whisk in the oil and vanilla until combined well. In another bowl sift together the flour, baking powder and salt, add the almonds and mix well.

With your hands knead together the flour and egg mixture until the dough is thick and sticky. Divide the dough into two parts and roll into logs, 2 1/2 inches wide by 12 inches long. With a metal palette lift each log onto a well-greased cookie baking dish, spacing it 4 inches from the first log. Brush with milk or cream. Bake in the center of the oven for 30 minutes, or until the logs are light brown and firm in the center. Remove from the oven and let cool for one hour. Turn the oven down to 300°F.

With a wide spatula remove the logs from the cookie pan, and transfer them to a cutting board. With a serrated knife, cut the logs on a diagonal into 3/4 inch thick slices. Return each slice on to the cookie pan and bake until light brown and crisp. Let cool, and serve with coffee or tea.

Scrambled Eggs with Bacon, Onions and Potatoes

Hoppelpoppel

Yield 6

4 medium potatoes (about 2 pounds)
2 1/2 cups coarsely diced bacon
1 1/2 cups chopped onions
1/2 cup green scallions
12 eggs
1/2 cup finely chopped parsley
Freshly ground black pepper

Boil the potatoes with the peel in plenty of lightly salted water until cooked, but not overcooked.

In the meantime, in a heavy skilled cook the bacon over low heat until brown and crisp. Remove the bacon with a slotted spoon and place on paper towel. Remove one third of the bacon fat from the skillet and add the onions and scallions, sauté for 5 minutes.

Remove the potatoes from the boiling water, and place on a cutting board to cool, then cut into slices. Add them to the onions-scallions and sauté until light brown on both sides. Then beat the eggs in a porcelain or stainless steel bowl with the parsley, salt and a dash of black pepper. Add the bacon to the potatoes and pour the eggs evenly over the skillet. With a wooden spoon or spatula, combine the mixture over low heat until the eggs are cooked, but still moist. Shape the Hoppelpoppel like an omelet and place on a preheated platter and serve.

Pomeranian Ham Cutlets
Yield 4 servings

4 slices Westphalian or Black Forest
    ham (1/2 inch thick,
    about 1 pound)
1 1/2 cups milk
1/2 cup flour for dredging

Batter:
    1 cup all-purpose flour
    1/2 cup milk
    1 large egg
    1 1/2 teaspoons sugar
    1/2 teaspoon salt
    1 dash of nutmeg
    3/4 cup corn oil for frying

Pound the sliced ham with a mallet between plastic sheets to tenderize. Place in a shallow baking dish and cover with the milk to marinate for two hours in the refrigerator. Remove the ham, and pat dry, reserving 1/2 cup of milk to make the batter. Place the dredging flour on a large plate and set aside.

Make the batter: Place the flour in a small mixing bowl, add the sugar, salt, egg, nutmeg, and whisk to a smooth paste. Dust the cutlets in the dredging flour, then dip into the batter, make sure each side is well coated. Fry in the corn oil on both sides until golden brown. Remove the ham and drain on paper towel. (you may have to fry the ham in two batches). Serve with boiled new potatoes and crisp summer salad

Yeast Crumb Cake
Yield 12 X 15 inch cake

3 1/2 cups flour, sifted
1/2 cup sugar
3/4 cup warm milk
1 teaspoon grated lemon peel
2 whole eggs
3 egg yolks
1 stick butter, softened
1 package dry yeast
1/4 cup lukewarm water

Streusel Topping:
    2 sticks of butter at room temperature
    1/4 cup melted butter
    2 cups sifted flour
    1 cup sugar

Pour the water into a small mixing bowl and sprinkle it with the yeast, add a little sugar, and stir until completely dissolved, add 1 tablespoon of flour, mix well, cover with a towel and set aside in a warm, draft free place. In a large mixing bowl beat the remaining sugar, eggs, egg yolks, and butter until creamy. Add the flour, milk, lemon peel, yeast mixture, combine well and place the dough on a floured board, knead for about ten minutes until smooth and elastic. Place in a buttered bowl, cover with a towel and let the dough rise until double in bulk.

When the dough has risen, punch down and knead again for a few minutes. With a rolling pin stretch the dough until it fits into the cake pan, top with the streusel and bake in the middle of the oven for 45 minutes at 350 Fahrenheit until the top is light brown and crisp.

Mix all topping ingredients, working quickly with your fingertips by rubbing the flour, butter and sugar. The streusel should be coarse.

Spread over the cake.

Braised Red Cabbage
with Green Apples
Yield 10

3 ounces smoked bacon
  cut into small strips
1 cup diced onions
1 cup diced green apples (Granny Smith)
1/2 cup melted butter
1 cup water
1/4 cup red wine
1/4 cup red wine vinegar
1/4 cup brown sugar
1/8 cup red currant jelly
2 bay leaves
1 stick cinnamon
2 whole cloves
3 juniper berries
2 1/2 pounds sliced red cabbage
1/2 teaspoon Cornstarch
  (dissolved in a little water)
1/2 teaspoon salt to taste
1 dash black pepper to taste

In a heavy casserole or flat pot melt the butter, add the bacon, onions, and cook slowly for 10 minutes, but do not brown the onions. Add the sliced red cabbage, diced apples, and top with the water, vinegar, and red wine, combine very well. Stir in the rest of the ingredients (except the corn starch) mix well, cover the pot and simmer for 20 minutes over low heat.

Check occasionally to make sure the liquid does not completely evaporate.

When the cabbage and apples are cooked, mix the cornstarch with a little cold water, and stir into the cabbage to thicken the liquid. Taste for proper seasoning.

Potato Pancakes with
Applesauce
Yield 10 pancakes

6 medium sized potatoes
  (about 3 pounds)
2 large eggs
1/4 cup grated onions
1/3 cup cake flour
1/2 teaspoon salt
1 dash of nutmeg
3 cups of vegetable oil

Peel and grate the potatoes coarsely. Place in a sieve or colander and squeeze out as much moisture as possible.

In a large mixing bowl, beat the eggs, add the onions and gradually beat in the flour, salt and nutmeg. Add the potatoes to the batter and mix well.

In a heavy, preferably iron skillet heat the vegetable oil until it splatters. Pour 1/4 cup of the potato mixture into the hot oil and flatten with a spatula to form a 3 inch pancake. Repeat this procedure until the pan is full.

Fry the pancakes over medium heat for about 2 minutes until golden brown and crisp on both sides. Place on an ovenproof plate and keep warm in the oven. Continue to make pancakes with the remaining mix, adding more oil to the skillet as necessary. Serve the pancakes as soon as possible with applesauce, plus sour cream to your liking.

BAVARIA
AND BEYOND

My brother Klaus and I (standing) help father build our house.

To many of my American friends now, Bavaria pretty much is Germany – a land of beautiful mountain valleys, men in lederhosen and pink-cheeked Fräuleins who deliver steins of beer for Oktoberfest. That, obviously, is the Bavaria that most people know today and that is just fine for the German tourism industry. But it is not quite the Bavaria I knew in those dreadful years right after the defeat of Germany in World War II.

There were many happy aspects, of course. We were all alive, which was the main thing after two years in the refugee camp. My father had reappeared, as though from the dead, for a joyous reunion that promised to last for the rest of our lives. But there were many challenges.

As a little boy, I knew the road from being a child to being an adult able to support himself would be long and hard. After all, keeping our family fed was hard enough. As we began a new chapter in our lives in the tiny Bavarian village, the first thing I had to deal with was discrimination. Discrimination was a fact of life that existed in Europe at that time and, I have learned, exists almost everywhere in the world to this day.

My family was Prussian. That meant that we refugees were Protestants in a community of Catholics who had always lived there. In those days, they were none too happy to admit us into village life, much less let us play with their children. Sadly perhaps, our differences were hard to miss. The Bavarians were usually short, stocky and rather dark, while we Prussians were tall, thin (especially after starving) and light-skinned, with hair as white as snow.

We can all learn much from children. To this day, I love to see how they interact. I love to see the way they hesitate under pressure from the grownups, but in the end they hop right over some puddle that those much older have decided is a wide, wide river. So it was with the religious and regional prejudice that existed.

Luckily, there were a couple of things that caused things to change for the better. One was necessity to do so on both sides. The other was soccer. These diverse forces combined to quickly evolve our situation into one that was happier than we first found.

Our necessity was obvious. We had to build a new life in a place far from our home. For the Bavarians, the necessity was almost as strong. The local mayor was under orders to work with us, get us resettled and start providing an education for all of the new children. He had no choice in the matter, but he didn't have to like it.

Soccer, as you may know, was an incredibly popular game in Bavaria back then, as it is now. There were many teams around the villages and the local kids quickly realized that if they had these long-legged, tall Prussians on their teams, they would win. The youngsters went to their parents and, despite initial refusals, talked them into inviting us to lunch and then asking us to join them to play soccer.

Years later, as a parent, many times my daughters would work their same magic on me and I would think back to the Bavarian children who managed to look past hundreds of years of bitterness and strife. Some of them became my very best friends and we share a warmth that has lasted more than half a century. Every two or three years, wherever we happen to be in our lives, we go home to hold a reunion in the foothills of the Bavarian Alps. We love to laugh about all of those days.

One night I was sitting with my family after dinner – we called it dinner anyway, even though it was just a couple potatoes, maybe some spinach. We lived in this tiny three-room house, with a little annex that my father built which was where my sister lived, and also a little attic that he built as the bedroom for my brother Klaus and me. There really wasn't enough space, and of course no luxury at all. So at the table after dinner that night, my father announced something very important. We, he said, were going to build a house. Everybody was very happy.

My father was very handy, very good at building things, and we all believed in him and trusted him. And we believed in him even more the following weekend, when we drove up to the piece of land he had chosen for our new home. It was beautiful, about eight acres in the forest with this little brook flowing through. We're going to have a beautiful home, he said, right here in the foothills of the Bavarian Alps.

With the help of a loan we could get as refugees, part of the U.S. Marshall Plan aimed at spurring the rebirth of Europe, my father did buy the land, and that was the first chapter. But the reality was very different from the dreams we were all having by this time. And believe me, it wasn't always fun. My father bought a Volkswagen – well, actually I believe he bought it at some point during the war and had been hiding it in the woods. But at least we had a car, a motorized vehicle for which my father soon built a trailer for carrying building materials, starting with gravel we all gathered from down by that brook.

Klaus and I had the job of putting in the foundation for our new house, which meant using shovels and a couple of wheelbarrows to dig out this big hole. We dug and we dug, even enlisting friends whenever we could talk someone into helping us for a day or two. But this was such backbreaking work that it was hard to keep anyone helping us for long. It took us a full year, which meant dealing with winter right up to when it got too cold to keep on digging. At that point my father went to the local farmers and purchased the trees, chopping down maybe three dozen trees and renting an ox to pull them to the mill. There was definitely no Home Depot to buy lumber in those days!

When spring came, we mixed cement and all that gravel then poured the mixture into molds to make stones. It took about an hour to make each stone, but when it was ready we could open up the nuts and bolts and there was a stone for our house. All that spring and summer, my brother and I made stones, building up these huge piles. We made thousands and thousands of stones.

The third year we were able to start building – the foundation and the basement first – and then by the fourth year we were able to put up the walls and the roof, with the windows, doors and floors going in by the fifth year, along with the electrical and the plumbing. It was a very hard job, and it took five years away from my youth. My father always told us that if you really wanted to do something, you could.

If you want to climb a mountain, he told us, and if you looked only from the bottom, it would always look too tall and difficult and dangerous to climb. Almost impossible. But once you start climbing, and then once you're halfway up, you almost always can make the rest of the way. My father taught us so many lessons during those five years, but what he wanted most was to create what that house is to me: a monument to persistence and sacrifice and dedication.

It was around this time – perhaps I was turning 11 – that I discovered something that would form the rest of my life. I discovered, without really thinking about it at the time, that I was something of an entrepreneur. There was very little food around our village, and even less money to buy it even if it had been available. Technically, it was an economic dead end. But when this happens, people always find ways of bonding together, bringing different things to the table and living on, one day at a time.

I worked, for instance, on a small farm for a man named Herr Berkman. He had goats and chickens, plus a donkey by the name of Max. Since I've always loved animals, I went over to the farm a lot. Before I knew it, I had learned how to put a harness on the donkey, and Herr Berkman would ask me to deliver some flowers here, a tree over there, maybe some peat moss someplace else. I made all the deliveries for him, and believe me, I was in my glory.

He had no money to pay me, even though he always insisted he wanted to. One day he came to me and said, "How about if I give you two goats?" That's what he did and very soon those goats had baby goats. By the time I had about 35 goats, he gave me a chicken and a rooster, also as my pay. My father built a chicken coop for me and before long I had about 60 chickens. Then …well, he gave me a couple of rabbits that multiplied to about 50 rabbits. And, as you can imagine, that didn't take long. Needless to say, by this time, we had plenty of food. And I would sell something to get money, and I would barter to get other things we needed. It wasn't long before I bought myself a bicycle. Even way back then, I was an independent businessman.

In 1951, I suffered one of the saddest days of my entire life. My mother died of cancer. My father took on the responsibility of raising the three of us. If you've seen The Sound of Music, about the von Trapp family, that is the way our father raised us. He was a military man, very disciplined, and every day there was an inspection. We had to shine our shoes, make our beds, and we always had to have clean clothes. We had to sew our own things together, put buttons on, everything.

There were many times, in case you are wondering, that I didn't like my father very much. However, I must admit and have to say that he gave me a lot of gifts for the rest of my life. He taught me to be disciplined, to be orderly and honest, and to always live and work with integrity. That, you see, was my father.

By the time I was 15, I knew it was time to seek some kind of higher education. For me, that meant looking for an apprenticeship. I wanted eventually to be an electrical engineer, so I figured I would start by becoming an apprentice to an electrician. The only way I could think to do this was to climb onto my bike every morning and peddle the 20 miles from our village into Munich, where I figured any apprenticeship would have to be.

My plan was much easier said than done. It was 1953 and Germany was still in rubble. As winter came on, the trip to look for work got harder and harder.

Ultimately, I decided that the whole idea of coming home each night to my goats and chickens just wasn't going to work. I had to live in Munich, whether I could stay with an aunt or at the YMCA.

I sold all my animals and then had a little bit of money to start my future. When finally I told my Dad I was leaving for Munich, I'm sure he didn't really think I had the courage to leave my family and our village for such a strange life in the big city. To this day, I remember him asking me when I'd be coming back. "Dad," I said, "I'll come back when I can be somebody." At that time, I had no idea it would take 23 years before I could come back to my village in Bavaria in the way I had described.

In Munich, all the money I'd made selling my chickens, goats and rabbits certainly didn't last very long. And that apprenticeship as an electrician never materialized, so I did the next best thing. I worked as a pin boy in a bowling alley. Don't laugh. In those days, somebody had to run and jump back and forth setting up the pins that all those bowling balls kept knocking over. Believe it or not, this job put me in the place I needed to be to discover my true calling.

Every Thursday afternoon a group of gentlemen came in to bowl. I had only been working there a few weeks when one of the gentlemen, Herr Ernst Knappe, came to me and said, "Young man, don't you have any-

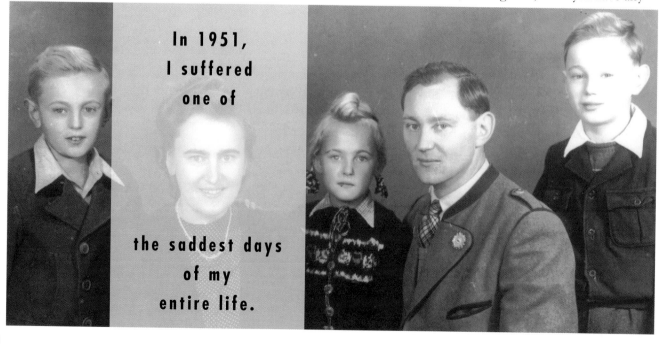

In 1951, I suffered one of

the saddest days of my entire life.

thing better to do than setting up these pins?" In a sense, having failed in my apprenticeship efforts, the answer was an obvious no. "I would like to be somebody someday," I told him, "and I would like to learn a trade. In fact, I would like to be an electrician."

The gentleman thought for a moment and said, "Well, there's nothing I can do to help you with that, but would you be interested in a being a chef in a fine hotel?" Being honest and since I knew nothing about cooking, I said I had no idea. "Why don't you come see me at my hotel," he said. "You can watch what goes on there for a day or two. If you like what you see, I'll sign you up as an apprentice in the kitchen. If you don't like it, you can always come back here to the bowling alley."

I was at that man's hotel the very next day. It was the Bayerischer Hof, one of the finest hotels in Munich and it remains so today, almost 60 years later. I'll never forget all the things I saw and heard and learned that day as they opened the door to an entirely unexpected future.

I saw all the chefs running around in their white

Bayerischer Hof, 1955, with Fritz Sonnenschmidt, future teacher and culinary dean of the Culinary Institute of America

suits and their high hats. I was fascinated by the pastry shop, where the hotel baked all its own breads and made cakes and pastries of every kind, with just about every filling you could imagine. In the main kitchen, I watched the chefs making all types of soups. And over here was the poissonier cooking fish from all over, and here was the saucier preparing every style and color and flavor of sauce, a handful of basic traditions used to build dozens of others by knowing just how to blend them. And it all happened, everything that really mattered, around this big old coal stove right in the middle of the kitchen.

It turns out that the Shah of Iran was dining at the hotel that night with his beautiful wife Sorya and his entire entourage. Everybody was working in a kind of crazy frenzy. To me, it felt good. It felt right. Finally, the head chef, Herr Knappe, called me aside and said, "Why don't I show you the dining room."

The Shah's party was enjoying dinner at that moment, so I had to be very careful as I looked out from the kitchen, so as not to disturb anybody. Yet even

With 1956 crew at Bayerischer Hof

through that crack in the kitchen door, I could see all the things that these chefs had accomplished. It was wonderful – the service, the white gloves, the glistening gold and silver of each table setting. I took one look at the wonders of this dining room, turned to Herr Knappe and said, "Yes, I want to be part of this life."

For all the elegance and pampering I remember from gazing out into the dining room that first night at the Bayerischer Hof, the apprenticeship that awaited me was anything but elegant or pampered. In fact, the apprenticeship system that existed, the only real system that gave the world European chefs generation after generation, was more difficult than anything I could have imagined.

In the course of each week, I worked four days in the kitchen and spent two more in the classroom, studying every aspect of food preparation and presentation. These lessons could have been frozen in ice or carved in stone, so little had they changed over the centuries. The idea was not to change, not to create as so many young American chefs can't wait to do today – the idea was to obey. Only by obeying your masters could you hope to someday become a master yourself.

The days and nights were grueling in every way. Even in this most revered of hotels, the kitchen was very primitive. Stainless steel hadn't arrived yet, so

there were all these galvanized steel pots, ancient and almost black, needing to be scrubbed within an inch of their lives at the end of every night. Almost everything that wasn't galvanized steel in our kitchen was wooden. That meant that we had to make our own soap with lye and scrub everything down constantly – under very watchful eyes.

Chickens still arrived with all their feathers, so when 50 chickens were delivered we had to go down into the basement and pull out the feathers and clean them. There were buckets and buckets of escargots, rushed right in from the field and stinking so bad. We had to get in there with our bare hands and clean them. The worst thing was the frog legs that the old French chefs always loved so much. Those frogs, I remember, would show up with some of them still alive. After that, I promised myself I'd never eat frog legs and I have kept that vow to this day. It was, you must know, a horrible time for me.

Also, since we were just apprentices, there was every form of hazing. Sometimes, it was simply cruelty – being told to do something alone that any experienced chef would call in two or three helpers to help him with the task. Other times there was violence. Since a professional kitchen can be a high-stress place, beating somebody up for no good reason is one way to let off a little steam. Sometimes the hazing got so weird that when I remem-

28

ber, it makes me laugh in a really painful way – laughing at myself, mostly. One day one of the chefs gave me the assignment of going down into the basement to "dry the sauerkraut." I told him quite frankly I had no idea how that was done, so he said, "Just put out some string and hang the sauerkraut to dry." What he had in mind, of course, was something like what a good German Hausfrau would do with her laundry.

Well, I was obedient. I was disciplined. I was my father's son. I went down into that basement, strung out string all over the place and set about hanging the sauerkraut out to dry. By the time the head chef needed me for something, the others were laughing up a storm. They said, "Oh Ekkehard … (my German name) he's down in the basement, just playing around." The chef came downstairs like an army inspector, yelling and screaming at me. I explained what I was doing, and assured him I'd been told by the sous chef to do it. But all he kept saying was, "How in the world can you dry sauerkraut?" Apparently, he was not all that interested in having me show him!

Considering the nature of my training and whatever natural talents I possessed, it should come as no surprise that I passed all my exams with flying colors and became a real chef. In fact, even though I was only 18, the head chef actually called me in and said, "Listen, Ekkehard, you did a wonderful job. I want to help you further your education." What he proposed was a series of jobs at some of the most legendary hotels in Europe and Great Britain, from the Plaza-Athenee in Paris to the Savoy and Claridge's in London.

You're a young man, he told me, and this will give you solid work experience. It will also give you the opportunity to learn another language at the same time. All the time he was talking, I was smiling and after a while, he wondered out loud what I was thinking. I assured Herr Knappe I appreciated his willingness to help, using his contacts at these great hotels, and that I was touched by his faith in my skills. "But," I told him simply, "I have my own plans." Not only did I have my own plans, I had my own job as well. I'd always wanted to see the world, not just the inside of one kitchen. I was going to cook on a train.

That I did, and within a few short months I'd been promoted from serving breakfast with another chef to serving as executive chef on the Rheingold Express to Bremerhaven – in charge of all the food on this huge train winding through the beautiful castles and vineyards of the Rhinegau. The next step from there was the luxurious Mozart, which traveled from Munich to the composer's fairy-tale city of Salzburg, then on to Paris, then all the way back to Vienna. My job had me crossing from one capital of old Europe to the other, each region more beautiful than the one before. I was on top of the world.

Or at least, that's what I thought, until one day on my train I met a man whose last name was Gelardi, presumably Italian, but in fact, British.

"Are you the chef?" he asked.

Yes.

"How old are you?"

I'm 18.

"Oh my," he said, "I could use a couple of guys like you."

Where can you use me?

"We," the man said, "have some wonderful hotels in Africa."

Bavarian Cheese and Ham Tart
Yield 6

1 frozen pie shell (9 1/2 inch)
1/2 pound cooked ham, diced
1/2 pound Emmentaler or
     Swiss cheese (diced)
1/2 cup fresh mushrooms, sliced
1/4 cup chopped fresh parsley
4 strips bacon, finely sliced
1 large onion, peeled and coarsely diced
1/2 stick butter or margarine
2 scallions, thinly sliced (the white part only)
1 medium – size green pepper,
     cored, seeded and diced
1 dash of fresh nutmeg,
     and ground black pepper
6 whole eggs
3/4 cup light cream
1 teaspoon salt

Heat a heavy casserole, add the bacon and sauté over high heat until light brown, add the butter, onions, scallions, pepper, and fresh mushrooms. Lower the heat and sauté the mixture until most of the juices have evaporated. Remove from the stove and cool for ten minutes. Place the ham, parsley and cheese in a mixing bowl. In a separate bowl whisk the eggs, cream, salt, black pepper and nutmeg until smooth.

Add the bacon, vegetable mixture to the ham and cheese mixture, then pour the egg, cream mixture over it and combine well with a rubber spatula. Pour the filling into the pie shell, and bake uncovered for one hour at 300 degrees until cooked and golden brown. Serve with green salad or watercress.

Beefsteak Tartar
Yield: serves 4

1 1/2 pounds very lean
     freshly ground top round
3 egg yolks
2 tablespoons salt
1/4 cup vegetable oil
1/4 cup finely chopped onions
1/2 teaspoon Spanish paprika
1/2 teaspoon ground black pepper
2 tablespoons capers, thoroughly
     drained and chopped
3 tablespoons finely chopped parsley
6 flat anchovy fillets, drained
     and chopped (optional)
4 large leaves of Boston lettuce
Crusty dark bread and butter

Beefsteak Tartar is made traditional from fresh ground beef, and served as soon as possible to maintain a nice red color and freshness. Place the meat in a chilled stainless steel bowl, add the egg yolks, oil and combine gently, add the rest of the ingredients and combine well. Shape the steak Tartar like a hamburger, place on Boston lettuce and serve with additional chopped onions and crusty dark bread.

Allgäuer Käse und Schinkenkuchen

Beefsteak tartar

Bavarian Goulash Soup

Yield: 16 cups

2 pounds boneless chuck,
   cut into 1/4 inch cubes
3 medium onions, diced
2 carrots, diced
1/4 stick butter
1/4 cup all purpose flour
1/4 cup vegetable oil
4 teaspoons Hungarian paprika
3 teaspoons tomato paste
3 tablespoons cider vinegar
4 cloves garlic, crushed
1 teaspoon salt
1/4 teaspoon dried marjoram
1/2 teaspoon caraway seeds
10 cups beef broth
5 medium potatoes, peeled and diced

Heat the butter in a 5-quart kettle, add the chopped onions, carrots and sauté until golden brown, stirring occasionally, set aside. In a bowl toss the beef cubes and flour until coated evenly. Heat the vegetable oil in a frying pan over high heat; add the beef cubes and brown on all sides. Add the beef to the onions, carrots and cook over slow fire for 5 minutes, add first the paprika, then the tomato paste, caraway seeds, garlic, marjoram, salt, and pepper, mix well with a wooden spoon, then add the beef broth, and vinegar.

Bring the soup to a boil, cover the pot and simmer for 45 minutes. Add the cubed potatoes and simmer for another 30 minutes, or until the potatoes, and the meat are tender. Serve in hot bowls with crusty artisan bread.

Haddock in Dill Sauce

Yield 8

4 pounds fresh haddock or cod fillets
1 teaspoon salt
1 medium size onion chopped
2 bay leaves
8 crushed black peppercorns
1 large leek, cut in half, washed and sliced
1 cup milk
1/4 cup white vinegar
4 cups cold water
1/2 cup dry white wine
1/2 cup heavy cream
1/2 cup chopped fresh dill
8 fresh parsley sprigs
1/2 stick butter, cut into bits,
   at room temperature

Place the water, white wine, milk, vinegar, bay leaves, peppercorns, leeks, and onion in a stockpot, and bring to a boil. Boil the court bouillon for 10 minutes to reduce the liquid in half. Wash the haddock under cold running water and cut into 8 portions. Place the fish into a shallow baking dish, season with a little salt and strain the fish stock over it. Seal the pan with aluminum foil and bake in the oven for 15 minutes at 350 degrees. With a spatula, carefully remove the haddock to a heated serving platter, and keep warm.

Pour the poaching liquid into a saucepan and bring to a boil until reduced to one cup. Add the heavy cream, chopped dill, and boil for two minutes, then whisk in the butter bit by bit. The sauce should have a nice thick texture. Ladle over the fish fillets, garnish with fresh parsley, and serve with seasonal vegetables and boiled new potatoes.

Bayerischer Sauerbraten

Yield: serves 6-8

4 pounds boneless beef roast
1/2 cup dry red wine
1/2 cup wine vinegar
2 cups cold water
1 tablespoon brown sugar
1 medium size onion, peeled and sliced
6 black pepper corns crushed
5 juniper berries crushed
3 cloves garlic, crushed
3 bay leaves
1/4 cup vegetable oil
1 cup diced onions
1/2 cup diced celery
1/2 cup diced carrots
1/4 cup flour
2 tablespoons tomato paste
1/2 cup beef broth
1/2 cup gingersnap crumbs

Speiseraum − Dining room

In a 3-quart stockpot, combine the wine, brown sugar, vinegar, water, sliced onions, crushed peppercorns, garlic, juniper berries, and bay leaves. Bring the marinade to a boil, simmer for 5 minutes, then remove from the heat and let cool. Place the beef into a deep crock and pour the marinade over it. (The meat should be covered, if necessary add more red wine) Cover the crock with plastic wrap and refrigerate for two to three days, turning the meat from time to time.

Remove the meat from the marinade and pat dry with a paper towel. Strain the marinade through a fine sieve and set aside. Discard the spices and onions. In a heavy-duty 5 quart flameproof casserole heat the vegetable oil. Add the meat and brown gently on all sides. Transfer the meat on to a platter. Add the diced carrots, onions, and celery to the oil in the casserole and cook them over moderate heat, stirring constantly until cooked but not brown.

Add the tomato paste, dust with the flour and cook a few more minutes until well combined. Add the marinade, bring to a boil, whisk until smooth. Return the meat to the casserole. Cover tightly, and bring to a boil, then place the casserole in the oven and cook for 2 hours at 350°F. Transfer the meat to a platter, cover with foil and keep warm

Add the gingersnaps to the sauce and simmer for 10 minutes to vaporize some of the liquid and to thicken the sauce. Strain the sauce through a sieve, and season to your liking. Slice the meat and ladle the sauce over it. Serve with dumplings or pasta, and red cabbage.

Oxtail Ragout
Yield 4

5 pounds oxtail, cut into 2-inch lengths
10 cups water
1 cup red wine
2 teaspoons salt
1 large onion, peeled and diced
2 carrots, peeled and diced
3 ribs celery, washed and diced
10 black peppercorns, crushed
2 cloves
5 cloves garlic
3 bay leaves
1 cup vegetable oil
1/2 cup flour
1 teaspoon Spanish paprika
3 tablespoons tomato paste

Mix the flour, salt, and paprika in a large bowl. Heat the vegetable oil in a heavy-duty casserole over high heat. Dip the oxtails into the flour mixture (a few at a time), then roast in the hot oil until brown on all sides, and remove from the casserole. Continue this procedure in several batches. Place the onions, celery, carrots, garlic, peppercorns, bay leaves, and tomato paste into the casserole and sauté for 5 minutes over low heat.

Add the oxtail, cover with water, and bring to a boil. Cover the casserole tightly with a lid, place into the oven at 350 degrees and bake for about 4 hours. Remove the meat with a slotted spoon to a serving platter. Season the sauce to your liking and thickness, add the red wine and strain over the oxtail, serve with egg noodles or homemade spätzle.

Bavarian Sausage Hot Pot
Makes 8 servings

1/2 pound knockwurst, sliced 1/4 inch thick
4 cups rich beef broth (home made)
1 1/2 pounds green cabbage,
    cored and cut into large pieces
1 medium onion, diced
1 stick butter
2 medium size carrots, peeled and sliced
1 cup green beans, tipped and
    snapped into halves
1 pound potatoes, peeled and
    diced into 1/2 inch cubes
1 pound rutabagas or parsnips, peeled
    and cut into 1/2 inch cubes
2 cups frozen green peas
1/2 teaspoon caraway seeds
1/2 teaspoon dried marjoram
1 bay leaf
2 tablespoons freshly chopped parsley
Black pepper and salt to taste

Melt the butter in a heavy casserole or kettle, add the vegetables, (except the frozen peas), marjoram, bay leaf, caraway seeds and sauté over low heat. (do not brown). Cover with beef broth and simmer for 20 minutes over moderate heat. Add the peas and sausage, and chopped parsley, bring to a boil. Adjust the flavor with salt and black pepper, and serve in a soup plate with crusty dark bread.

Boiled Beef with Horseradish Sauce and Steamed Cabbage

Serves 6

2 1/2 quarts water
3 pounds boneless beef rump
1 medium size carrot, peeled and sliced
2 leeks, cut in half, washed and sliced
2 turnips, peeled and sliced
1/2 cup chopped parsley
1 bay leaf
10 peppercorns
2 teaspoons salt
1 medium head of white cabbage

Horseradish Sauce:
1/2 stick of butter
1/4 cup flour
2 cups beef stock
1/2 cup heavy cream
1/4 cup prepared horseradish
1 bay leaf
Salt and pepper to taste

Place the water in a medium size pot or Dutch oven; add the meat, carrots, leeks, parsnips, peppercorns, bay leaf and salt. Bring the broth to a boil, lower the heat and simmer uncovered for about two hours. Skimming the top occasionally to remove any scum. When cooked (the meat should be fork tender) remove the meat, vegetables, and place on a platter, cover with foil and keep warm. Reserve the beef stock.

Cut the cabbage in half, and remove the core. Slice each half into 3 wedges and place in a shallow casserole; strain 3 cups of the reserved beef stock over it. Cover the casserole and steam over low heat for 30 minutes, or until the cabbage is tender.

To make the sauce, melt the butter in a small saucepan over low heat. Blend in the flour and cook the roux for two minutes. Mix in two cups of hot beef stock and cook for 5 minutes, stirring constantly until the sauce is smooth and thickened. Combine with the horseradish and cream, mix well, add salt and pepper to taste. To serve, place the steamed cabbage wedges on a heated serving platter, slice the beef across the grain about 1/4 inch thick, and arrange the slices over the cabbage. Arrange the vegetables around the beef, top with a little broth, sprinkle with chopped parsley, and serve with the horseradish sauce.

Veal Cutlets in Cream Sauce
Yield 4

1 1/2 pounds veal scallops
   (cut from the top round or loin)
1 teaspoon salt
1/4 teaspoon black pepper
1/2 cup flour
1/2 cup melted butter
1/2 cup heavy cream
1/4 cup dry sherry
1/4 cup chopped shallots.
1/2 cup chicken stock
1 cup sliced fresh mushrooms
1 dill pickle thinly sliced
Freshly chopped parsley for garnish

Heat the butter in a heavy 12 inch frying pan. Season the scallops with salt and pepper, and then dust with flour. Place the scallops into the hot butter and sauté over high heat on both sides until golden brown.

Remove the meat, place on a serving platter and keep hot. Add the shallots, mushroom and pickles to the remaining butter, and sauté for a few minutes. Deglaze the pan with the sherry, add the cream, chicken stock, and simmer for two minutes, stirring continually.

Pour the sauce over the schnitzel, sprinkle with parsley and serve with Bavarian spätzle and fresh vegetables of the season.

Ragout of Venison with Wild Mushrooms
Yield 8

3 pounds venison shoulder, trimmed
   and cut into cubes
1/2 stick butter
1/2 cup vegetable oil
1/2 cup minced shallots or onions
1/2 cup flour
1 teaspoon Spanish paprika
2 medium size yellow onions, peeled and diced
1 1/2 pounds fresh wild mushrooms, washed and sliced
1/2 pound lean bacon strips, cut into juliennes
1/2 teaspoon dried thyme
1/4 teaspoon rosemary
1/2 teaspoon salt
8 black peppercorns, crushed
2 bay leaves
1 teaspoon tomato paste
1 cup whole cranberry sauce
1 cup heavy cream
2 cups beef broth
2 cups dry red wine

Spread the cubed venison on a large serving platter. Mix the flour, paprika, salt, and dust the cubed venison generously. Heat a heavy duty casserole, and brown one fourth of the venison in one tablespoon each of the butter and oil over high heat, transfer to a bowl. Brown the remaining venison in three batches, adding more butter as needed.

Stir-fry the onions, shallots, and bacon with the remaining butter and oil. Return the browned venison to the casserole, add thyme, rosemary, tomato paste, bay leaves, peppercorns, and mix well. Add red wine, beef broth, cranberry sauce, cover the casserole and simmer for 2 hours over low heat, or until the venison is tender. With a slotted spoon remove the venison and place in a serving bowl. Strain the sauce into another pot, add the mushrooms, cream and simmer for five minutes. Adjust the thickness and taste. Pour the gravy over the venison; serve with pasta or traditional spätzle.

German Egg Noodles

Serves 8

Eierspätzle

2 cups flour
1/8 teaspoon nutmeg
2 large eggs
1/2 cup milk
1/4 cup melted butter
3 tablespoons vegetable oil

Sift together the flour, salt, nutmeg, and pour the mixture into a mixing bowl. Make a well in the center, whisk the milk and eggs together and pour into the well. With a wooden spoon beat for 5 minutes until the dough is smooth and elastic. (You also can use an electric mixer, set at medium speed)

In a 4-quart stockpot bring the water to a boil, add 1-teaspoon salt. Using a spätzle maker, (or a colander with large holes), force the batter through the holes into the boiling water. Simmer for five minutes over low heat, stirring occasionally. With a slotted spoon lift the spätzle to a large bowl of ice water, and let stand until chilled. Drain the spätzle well, melt the butter in a frying pan and sauté until hot. Taste for seasoning with salt and white pepper, and serve at once. You also can sprinkle the spätzle with your favorite cheese, Gruyere or Parmesan.

Sauerkraut with Pineapple

Serves 8

Sauerkraut mit Ananas

2 pounds sauerkraut
  (preferably imported)
1 can (12 ounces)
  chopped pineapples
1 cup chopped onion
4 strips smoked bacon,
  sliced in julienne strips
2 bay leaves
6 juniper berries
2 cups champagne
1 raw potato

Soak the sauerkraut in cold running water. A handful at a time, squeeze the sauerkraut until it is completely dry. Sauté the bacon in a heavy casserole until light brown, add the chopped onions and cook until glazed. Add all the ingredients, cover the casserole and simmer over low heat for 1 1/2 hours.

Grate the raw potato directly into the casserole and mix well. The starch will thicken the sauerkraut. Cook the sauerkraut a few more minutes until most of the liquid is evaporated. Taste for seasonings and serve on a hot platter with smoked meats or sausages.

Apple Pancakes

Yield: 4 pancakes

Pancake Batter;
- 1 1/2 cups flour
- 1/4 cup sugar
- 1 teaspoon baking powder
- 1/4 teaspoon salt
- 1/4 teaspoon vanilla extract
- 1 cup milk
- 2 eggs
- 2 tablespoon melted butter
- 1 dash of nutmeg
- 1/2 cup sugar and 1/4 cup melted butter
    for caramelizing the pancakes
- 1/2 cup vegetable oil

Apple topping:
- 3 medium-size Golden Delicious apples
- 3 tablespoons sugar, mixed
    with 1 teaspoon cinnamon
- 1 tablespoon lemon juice

Peel and core the apples, cut the apple in quarters, then slice each quarter into thin slices. Place apples in a ceramic bowl and combine with cinnamon-sugar and lemon juice, set aside. Sift the flour, sugar, baking powder and salt into a mixing bowl, and make a well in the center. Whisk the eggs, butter, milk and vanilla, pour into the well and whisk until smooth and creamy.

Generously oil a 10-inch Teflon sauté pan and heat over moderate heat, pour a quarter of the pancake mix into the pan. Tilt the pan first to one side, then to the other side, until the batter coats the bottom of the pan. Arrange the sliced apples into the batter and cook the pancake, first on one side, then by using a spatula to turn on the other side. The pancakes should be golden brown, place on a heated serving platter and keep warm. Just before serving heat the melted butter, add the sugar and return each pancake for a few seconds into the butter – sugar mixture. Serve with vanilla ice cream.

Bavarian Apple Strudel

Yield: serves 6

- 4 cups peeled, and sliced
    Granny Smith apples
- 1/3 cup raisins
- 3 tablespoons Kirschwasser (Cherry Brandy)
- 1/2 cup sugar
- 1/2 cup dried breadcrumbs
- 3 tablespoons cornstarch
- 1/4 teaspoon ground cinnamon
- 1 dash ground cloves
- 8 sheets frozen phyllo dough, thawed
- 1/2 cup melted butter
- 3 cups vanilla ice cream
- 1/2 cup powdered sugar, for dusting
- 6 ripe strawberries, and fresh mint

Combine brandy and raisins in a bowl. Microwave on high for one minute to soften the raisins. In a large bowl combine apples, raisins, sugar, cornstarch, cinnamon and cloves. Toss well and set aside.

Place phyllo sheet on work surface (cover remaining dough with a damp towel to keep from drying) lightly brush with melted butter. Working with one phyllo sheet at a time, brush the remaining seven sheets with butter, placing one on top of the other. Place a sheet of plastic wrap over phyllo, pressing gently to seal sheets together, discard plastic wrap.

Spread apple mixture over the phyllo sheets, leaving a 1/2 inch border. Sprinkle the breadcrumbs over the apples, and start rolling the strudel in a jellyroll fashion (do not roll tightly, or the strudel may split).

Place strudel, seam down, on a cookie sheet, brush with butter and bake for 35-40 minutes until golden brown at 350°F. dust with powdered sugar. Serve hot with ice cream, garnish with strawberry and a sprig of fresh mint.

Bavarian Nusstorte

Yield: one 11 inch cake

1 cup softened butter
4 1/2 cups sifted cake flour
1 cup sugar
1/4 cup dark rum
2 whole eggs
1 egg yolk
1 egg yolk, 1 tablespoon cream,
    use to glaze the torte
1 grated lemon zest
1 dash salt

Walnut Filling:
1 1/3 cups sugar
1/3 cup water
1 cup whipping cream
3 cups coarsely chopped walnuts
1/3 cup honey
2 tablespoon Kirsch (clear cherry brandy)

Soften the butter in a stainless steel bowl at room temperature. Add the sugar, rum, egg, egg yolks, salt, lemon zest, the sifted flour, and work with the fingers until all particles combine and form a ball. Wrap in plastic and chill the dough for half hour, then divide the dough in three parts. Press one part into the bottom of an 11 inch spring-form, use the second part to line the sides about 1 inch high.

To make the walnut filling, place the sugar and water in a large skillet, cook over low heat until sugar is dissolved and becomes light brown. Gradually add the cream, scrape the bottom of the skillet to loosen the sugar, simmer over low heat until ingredients are combined to a smooth sauce. Stir in the honey, Kirsch and combine with the chopped walnuts. Cool slightly and spread filling in pastry lined pan.

Roll the third part of the dough and cut into strips, place over the filling about one inch apart. Brush the lattice with egg yolk-cream mixture and bake in pre-heated oven at 350 degrees for about 45 minutes, until baked and golden brown. Serve with vanilla ice cream, fresh berries and a sprig of fresh mint.

Bavarian Plum Cake with Whipped Cream

Yield: makes one 11 inch tart
Serves 8 to 10

2 pounds Italian plums (washed, pitted,
    then quartered, but not cut all the
    way so the quarters can be spread
    like flower petals)
1 cup apricot glaze or jelly
1/2 cup sliced almonds (toasted)
1-cup heavy cream (whipped)
    with 2 teaspoons of sugar

Pastry:
2 1/4 cups sifted flour
1/3 cup cold milk
1/4 cup granulated sugar
1 tablespoon baking powder
1/4 teaspoon salt
1/2 stick cold butter
1/3 cup sugar mixed
    with 1/2 teaspoon ground cinnamon

Preheat oven to 350 degrees, generously butter an 11-inch tart pan on the bottom and sides. Cream the butter and sugar in a small bowl with an electric mixer at high speed. Sift the flour and baking powder together, add the salt and combine by hand with the butter-sugar mixture. Press the dough smoothly over the bottom and up the sides of the prepared tin. Arrange the plums skin down in the pastry shell in rows, fanning the plums. Sprinkle generously with the cinnamon sugar, and bake for about 45 minutes.

Cool the tart at room temperature. Heat the apricot glaze with two teaspoons cold water in a saucepan, and glaze the plums with a pastry brush. Sprinkle the toasted almonds evenly over the plums. Cut in wedges and serve with whipped cream.

Raised Dumplings with Vanilla Sauce

Yield 6-8

2 cups sifted flour
1 1/2 teaspoons dry yeast (1 envelope)
1/2 cup sugar
1/4 cup lukewarm water
1 cup lukewarm milk
4 tablespoons melted butter
2 whole eggs
2 egg yolks
1/4 teaspoon salt
Grated lemon rind from 1/2 lemon

Baking liquid:
Blend together:
1/4 cup melted butter
1/4 cup sugar
1 cup light cream

Kitchen on my train in 1956

In a small bowl dissolve the yeast with 1/4 cup warm water, add a little sugar and flour to make a light paste. Cover the bowl with a towel and set aside in a warm place for 5 minutes until the yeast bubbles.

In a larger bowl mix the sugar, salt, lemon rind, whole eggs, egg yolks, warm milk, butter, flour and starter dough. Beat the dough vigorously until smooth. The dough should be firm, form into egg-size pieces and round them slightly on a floured board. Place them in a covered casserole or flat pot, leaving a small space between each.

Brush the dumplings with a little baking liquid, cover the casserole and allow the dumplings to rise in a warm place. When the dumplings are doubled in size, pour the baking liquid over it, close the casserole tight, and bake for 45 minutes at 300 degrees. Separate the dumplings before placing on a serving dish, and serve with vanilla sauce (recipe below). Garnish with fresh mint and a fresh strawberry.

Vanilla sauce:
8 egg yolks
1 cup sugar
4 cups milk or light cream
1 teaspoon vanilla extract

Beat the egg yolks and sugar with a wire whisk. Bring the milk to a boil, stirring constantly, and pour the boiling milk in a stream over the egg yolks. Over low heat, stirring the egg-milk mixture, simmer slowly until the sauce is thick enough to coat a spoon. Do not boil the sauce or it may curdle. Add the vanilla extract and strain through a strainer.

Christmas Stollen
Yield 2 each 12-inch Stollen

8 cups sifted flour
2 sticks butter at room temperature
3/4 cup warm milk
3/4 cup dry currants or raisins
3/4 cup diced, candied orange peels
1/4 cup diced, candied citron
3/4 cup chopped walnuts
1 cup dark rum or brandy
1 cup sugar
2 whole eggs
4 packages dried yeast
1/2 cup warm water
1/4 teaspoon salt
1 teaspoon vanilla extract

Topping:

1 stick butter, melted
1 cup confectioners sugar

Place the currants, diced fruit and nuts in a ceramic bowl, add the brandy, mix well, cover the bowl and let rest over night at room temperature. When ready to proceed, sprinkle the yeast over the warm milk, add a little sugar and two-teaspoons flour, mix well with a wire whisk, cover the bowl and let rise for 15 minutes.

Use one cup of flour and mix with the candied fruits to coat them. If your mixing bowl of your electric mixer is large enough to hold all the ingredients proceed, if not knead your dough on the kitchen counter.

Cream the butter, sugar, vanilla and eggs at high speed for 5 minutes, add the flour, yeast mixture, and milk, mix at low speed with the dough hook for 5 to 8 minutes, until the dough is smooth and elastic. Add the candied fruit, and knead until well combined. Do not over mix to avoid crushing the fruit. Cover the dough and let rest at a warm place for 45 minutes to one hour.

Punch the dough down and divide into two parts. If the dough still seems sticky, knead in another 1/4 cup flour or so. Now roll the dough, one part at a time into a 12 X 6 inch oval. (Proceed with the second part the same way) Lay your rolling pin the length of the oval and press down to make a crease. Fold the dough over so that the top portion is slightly smaller than the bottom. Place the stollen on a baking sheet, cover with a kitchen towel and let rise in a draft free area for about 45 minutes or one hour.

Preheat the oven to 375 degrees and bake 40 to 45 minutes. Brush the stollen generously with the melted butter, and then sift the confectioner's sugar lavishly over the stollen until snow white. Bavarian stollen tastes the best after one day at room temperature.

Joe's Weihnachtsstollen

Salzburger Nockerl
Yield: serves 6

3 egg yolks
1 teaspoon vanilla extract
1/2 teaspoon grated lemon peel
1 tablespoon flour
4 egg whites
2 tablespoons sugar
3 tablespoons confectioner's sugar

Preheat the oven to 350°F. Separate the eggs, place the whites in a mixing bowl and the yolk in a medium size stainless steel bowl. Combine the egg yolks with the flour and lemon peel. With an electric rotary whisk beat the egg whites, add the sugar, and continue to beat until whites are nice and stiff. Blend the egg whites with the yolks, using an over-under motion, instead of mixing.

Generously butter an oval 8-by 10-by 2 inch fireproof baking dish, Place three mounds of the mixture in the dish, using a rubber spatula. Bake the nockerl in the middle of the oven for about 10 minutes or until light brown. Sift the confectioners sugar over the nockerl and serve immediately, perhaps with vanilla or raspberry sauce.

Lemon Créme Dessert
Serves 6

1/4 cup cold water
1 envelope plain gelatin
3 egg yolks
3 egg whites
1/2 cup sugar
1/4 fresh lemon juice
2 teaspoons grated lemon peel
1 cup whipping cream
3 tablespoons sugar
Fresh mint, strawberries,
        and whipped cream for garnish

Place the gelatin in a small stainless steel bowl, add the cold water, and set in a small skillet of simmering water. Stir until the gelatin is dissolved completely. Beat the egg yolks, and 1/2 cup of sugar with an electric beater until pale yellow and stiff. In a different chilled bowl whip the heavy cream until firm. With a rubber spatula gently combine the egg mixture with the cream, lemon peels and gelatin.

Rinse the mixing bowl well with cold water and dry with a paper towel. Beat the remaining egg whites with the 3 table-spoons sugar until stiff, and then fold into the lemon – cream mixture. Spoon the lemon cream into 6 wine glasses and refrigerate for at least four hours. Garnish with a dab of whipping cream, fresh strawberry and a sprig of fresh mint.

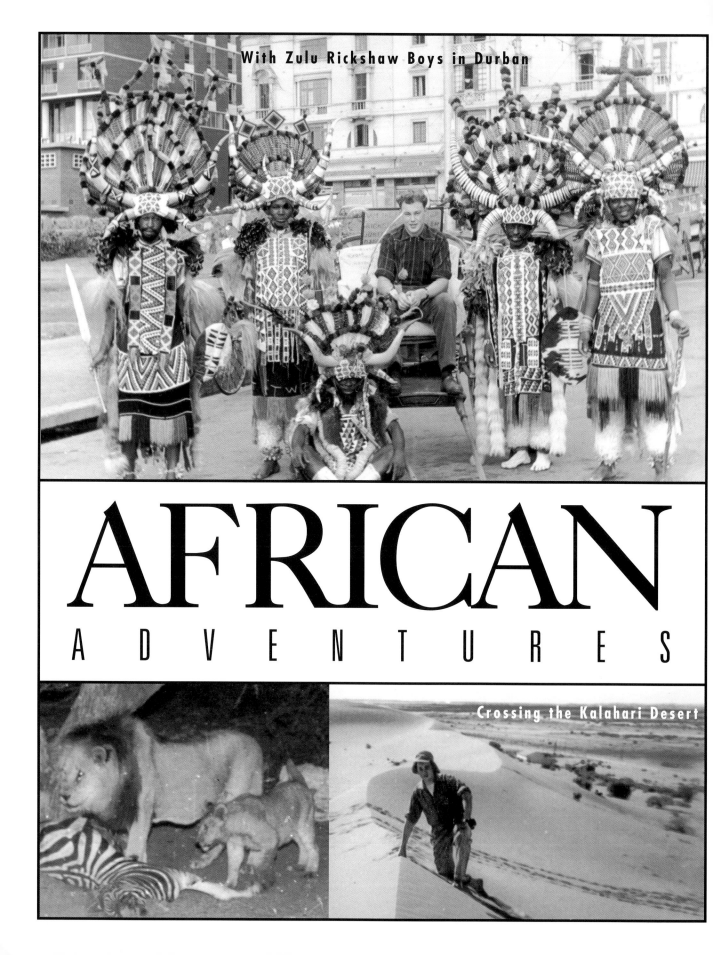

With Zulu Rickshaw Boys in Durban

AFRICAN
ADVENTURES

Crossing the Kalahari Desert

Sometimes, when I tell friends and customers about my first great journey from Germany to the southernmost tip of the African continent, I suspect they are thinking, "Geez, Joe might just as well have walked!" Even to me, the trip I recall seems to come from a different world, considering that today Johannesburg, Cape Town and Durban are nonstop flights from many of the world's cities – not short flights, mind you, but at least direct ones. And if you are comfortable in a nice airline seat, enjoying lots of great food and wine and watching movie after movie, it's not such a painful experience.

There were no movies on my first trip to South Africa, except maybe the one I was starring in. There was food and wine, but we had to land each time we wanted some. And the whole trip took no less than five days. It was a young man's adventure in a young man's life. It was the kind of experience that forms you, toughens you, and reveals to you that life need not be lived within the strict confines of where you were raised or how you thought your life had to be.

In a sense, the flights that carried me south in 1956 were like a movie – except that the intermissions were every bit as fascinating as the film. Of course, when you are the one living the story, the intermissions are part of the film. Each exotic person you meet, each dazzlingly different vista carries you farther from the people and places that were comforting and familiar.

For all the difficulties of my still-young life, from war to the refugee camp, I had still been a European living in Europe. I had been surrounded primarily by people who spoke German, and who had at least suffered through many of the same experiences my family and I had. As the film that was Africa began to unroll before my eyes, I understood (and have spent the rest of my life understanding more deeply) that there were people of many different skin tones and languages and religions, formed by experiences that were not my own. I've always been blessed, I suppose, by having a feel for differences in people – differences that nonetheless still let us live and work together as colleagues, as comrades.

I was certainly excited about my trip. I had been given a three-year contract to cook in South Africa, and they would pay for my expenses to get there. Over several weeks in Munich, I gathered up my plane tickets, my South African visa and work permits, plus many other pieces of paper that accomplished many other things. At last my packet was in order. I said goodbye to my dad in Munich and traveled by train to Frankfurt.

Carrying my one little suitcase, I made my way to an airport that felt more like a train station. I looked all over for a place to check-in before learning that I had to wait at the Alitalia desk. I watched with anticipation, gazing out at all the large planes taking off or landing, until someone changed the sign at the desk from ALITALIA to TREK AIRWAYS. There was a pretty stewardess who counted us passengers, from 1 to 18, and then announced, "I think we're all here." As a group, we went downstairs and boarded a bus that took us out onto the tarmac. Waiting there for the very first flight of my life was this very small airplane, a twin-engine DC-3. The stewardess waved to the captain in the cockpit and, using a rope, he let this crazy-looking ladder down. We all climbed up into the plane.

During the next few days, I discovered that flying in such a small plane is a mixed blessing. Such a

flight can take a long time, considering the slower speed, the lesser altitude and the need to refuel at intervals that seem ridiculous today. But it also meant being more involved with the places over which you are flying. We were, for instance, unable to fly over the Alps – we had to fly through them. The time was just before Christmas and that meant following long valleys and crossing between peaks turned white with snow and ice. We dropped in for lunch at Nice, since by that time the winter scenes had given way to the bright sun of the French Riviera. Then, we headed out across the Mediterranean till we landed on Malta. That island, so famous for its involvement with the Knights who fought the Crusades, was our stopping place for the night. We slept, as I recall, at the Phoenix Hotel.

Our destination right after breakfast was Cairo but we were forced to detour for a lunch stop in Benghazi, Libya. Things were none too peaceful in Egypt at that time because Egypt's President Nasser was virtually at war with Britain and France over the Suez Canal. Bits of history, all seen looking out a window of a DC-3. After lunch, there was only desert through my window, as we worked our way across southeast Libya to an oasis called Wadi Halfa. This strange name would become better known years later, when the Russians built a huge dam there to generate electricity. At that time, there was absolutely nothing but this little runway, and I remember the plane landing with only miles and miles of sand around us.

Shortly after leaving Wadi Halfa, the desert started giving way to the wild plains and hills and jungles of the Africa that is in all of our dreams. Highlights of the journey included stops in Khartoum, an entire city made out of mud, and in Entebbe on Lake Victoria. Years later, when the Israeli special forces staged a daring rescue of a highjacked jetliner being held with the blessing of dictator Idi Amin, I could know in my heart that I had once landed on that same strip. We made our way slowly south to Boulawayo, then finally onward to the largest city of South Africa, Johannesburg.

Joburg, as the locals call it, was a cosmopolitan city with well-dressed people scurrying everywhere, lots of hustle and bustle and busy streets with double-decker buses the same as those I had read about in London. This time, I was not staying. I went straight to the train station and bought a ticket to reach my first work assignment in the dramatic city of Durban on the Indian Ocean.

I can't express how exotic, how foreign, how exciting Durban seemed to me then, especially after two days of crossing the open desert in an old train pulled by a steam engine locomotive. Fact is, I was too excited to close the window in my compartment. I wanted to feel more completely a part of the terrain. I awoke the next morning after sleeping the entire night with the window open. I was covered in soot from the engine. Everything in my compartment was black. That took some serious cleanup in order to get ready for my first looks at my new home. Some of those first looks were from the passenger seat of a rickshaw that met me at the station. It was pulled through the streets by Zulus done up in wild headdresses and full warrior garb.

Over the days that followed, I learned to surf in the Indian Ocean, enjoying the summer weather that was Christmas south of the Equator. I learned my way around my new kitchen and also around the open market where we shopped for the hotel. There were huge fish just off the boats, many weighing 100 pounds or more. One day there was even a 200-pound sea turtle, which we took back and turned into a wonderful turtle soup. And there were all of these rainbow-colored tropical fruits and vegetables that I, of course, had never seen before, even in some of the most sophisticated kitchens in Europe.

The staff at the Edwards Hotel was a rainbow as well. The head chef, Werner Trosch, was Swiss and the pastry chef, Alfredo Porccini, was Italian – two nationalities I already knew well. There were also many colleagues from India. I'll never forget the wonderful aromas arising from the spicy curries they cooked for themselves. The rest of the kitchen staff was Zulu. Yes, Zulu. They all worked in short pants and had bare feet all the time. This was certainly different from what I'd taken for granted back in Germany!

Actually, I have always prided myself on being able to work with anyone in any kitchen, no matter what his or her nationality. I suppose I learned a lot of those skills early on in Durban. The challenge, as you can understand, is not only the high-stress nature of cooking for hundreds of paying customers but the fact that so many in any kitchen are new immigrants, men and women working hard a long way from home to send money back to their families.

It was that way in Durban then and in Texas now. These are, quite frankly, people without a lot of security. It would be incredibly easy to disrespect and exploit them. I really hope my staff feels I've been a good boss. It matters to me that many have been with me for 20 years or more. I'm grateful for those lessons learned long ago and far away, at the southern tip of the world. There are days now that I look around my kitchen and think, compared with curry-ladling Indians and barefoot Zulus, my coworkers in Texas aren't very exotic at all!

What can I say? South Africa was a great adventure and a great education for a very young chef who was also a very young man. I actually had to learn three new languages at the same time: English of course, since the British had a long colonial history in that part of the world, Zulu to communicate with the bulk of my kitchen staff and finally Afrikaans. Afrikaans was an important language in South Africa, a Dutch-based language spoken and, in a sense, created locally by some of the area's earliest settlers.

All of us, the young men working in that kitchen, went to the beaches of Durban often. Most of us were single, so there was no reason not to spend our days off surfing the big waves that rolled in from far out. Other days, we traveled to an area called the Thousand Hills, where they filmed the movie "Zulu." To this day, it's the place where many Zulus

live. I loved learning about the Zulus, and came to respect their spirit and their pride and their culture. There was a racial divide between us, naturally at that time, between their dark faces and my very light one. But that didn't mean we couldn't respect each other – yes, even respect our differences - and learn important lessons about life from each other.

The Edward was a great hotel, offering many opportunities to cook for some of the wealthiest people from Europe and Great Britain. At that time, they'd come to South Africa for the entire season – November, December, January – escaping the unpleasant winter weather up north. They would travel with these huge retinues of servants. Some would even have a Rolls Royce or two shipped down, letting them truly lord it over us "locals." But we in the kitchen cooked wonderful meals for these guests every day and night, enjoying the experience, the challenge and the occasional private joke about this one or that one. We were only cooks in the kitchen, after all!

As fine a place as the Edward was, I got restless after a couple years. Durban was a resort city, and that meant the same people came every year and the same things tended to happen, in season and out of season, like clockwork. I longed for a bit more excitement, something not so predictable. In South Africa, that meant Johannesburg. After putting my boss on notice that I was interested in any openings at their Joburg property, he at last told me yes. A sous chef was needed there, and I grabbed at the job with my usual silly enthusiasm. Perhaps I grabbed every bit as much at the chance to travel the thousand or so miles from Durban to Johannesburg on my motorcycle.

I suppose I was foolish to attempt such a thing,

45

but I really didn't want to sell my motorbike, and what young man hasn't done something foolish? The trip wasn't at all comfortable, and it wasn't at all safe. Among other challenges, there were steep mountains of the Drakensberg with treacherous winding roads going up and around. About halfway between my two cities, in the absolute middle of nowhere, the transmission of the motorbike said "Enough!"

I was trapped. There was nobody around. I thought maybe a car would come if I waited by the side of that road long enough, but I was kidding myself. Apparently, not many people were silly enough to even drive a car where I was driving a motorcycle. Finally, far in the distance, I spotted a railroad track – and I reasoned that if there was a track, there would be a train passing by. I walked my bike to the side of the track and waited. Eventually, starting as just a speck on the horizon, a

**With Longer and Shorty
at the Dawsons Hotel in Johannesburg**

freight train appeared on that desolate stretch of track and it was heading in the direction of Johannesburg. I took off my shirt and started waving it wildly above my head, shouting like a crazy person till the engineer stopped the train. He turned out to be a pretty nice guy, helping me lift up my bike and find a place to settle in. With much hissing and coughing, the train started up again. Thirteen hours later, I was in Johannesburg.

Working at the Dawson's Hotel was an incredible experience. It allowed me to live, explore and grow in a terrific and sophisticated metropolis. But my heart, I came to realize after a time, was on the water. I'd been born on the Baltic. And even though Pomerania was

gone as a country, my memories of picnics on its pristine beaches only grew more intense with each passing year. So I convinced my friend Wolfgang to join me in applying for work in the seaside town of Port Elizabeth, near Cape Town. Both of us got jobs there at the Marine Hotel, me as the executive chef. This time, we traveled to our new jobs by train. It didn't occur to me to ride my motorcycle.

In retrospect, the single greatest highlight of the time spent in Port Elizabeth was the month I wasn't there. In the way that young men do, Wolfgang and I conspired to stash as much money as we could, devise ways to make money on the road, take a month off from work and travel to visit my great-uncle in Namibia, which we still knew as German Southwest Africa. He was living there, on a farm a million miles from anywhere. He was in his late 70s, and it really seemed my last chance to see and feel some part of those stories I'd grown up hearing my father tell about my adventurous grandfather. Of course, to have such an experience, Wolfgang and I would have to be a little adventurous ourselves.

We pooled our savings and bought an old American Buick. That Buick became our transportation, our dining room, our housing – and considering the nature of two weeks travel across the Kalahari Desert, our time machine. Time, in fact, seemed to stand still through day after day of sand, stretching as far in every direction as we could see. Once in a while, we'd spot an African bushman making his way, though we never saw where anyone might reasonably come from or head to. Just nothing, and lots of it.

We'd packed a bit of food, but we relied mostly on wild game we shot with a rifle we kept handy at all times – springbok, kudu, élan. We'd shoot them in those wide open spaces and cook them over a fire. Seldom in my life has any meal tasted so good to me.

As we traveled, Wolfgang and I also set in motion our "brilliant" plan to bankroll the trip. Before leaving Port Elizabeth, we'd invested in about 20 cookbooks and maybe 20 more books of medical treatments. These we sold to farmers along the way, for about three times what we paid, naturally. Besides, the two of us were professional chefs. We cooked great meals to encourage people to purchase our books. I guess they believed that if they owned these cookbooks, they would cook as well as we did. Wolfgang and I were happy to let them believe that.

We spent several days visiting my great-uncle, who tried his best to convince me that what I really wanted to do with my life was be a farmer in Africa, just like him. He didn't know – in fact, even Wolfgang didn't really know - that just as several times previously in my life, I was making other plans.

The trip back to Port Elizabeth was a nightmare, leaving behind the last vestiges of my family's African past. The money was going faster than Wolfgang and

I had expected. We ran through the gasoline, driving hundreds and hundreds of miles through desert each day. And all the sand tore away at our tires, forcing us to purchase four new ones. That was an entirely unplanned expense. For two days, driving a different route from Windhoek through country that had no game, we had nothing to eat at all. Things were starting to feel desperate, considering the days still between us and Port Elizabeth. By the time we spot-

ted a few natives (Hottentots, they were called) keeping an eye on some scraggly goats, maybe my good sense had grown a little shaky.

"Quick, stop the car," I told Wolfgang, grabbing up the rifle.

"What are you going to do?"

"Shoot us some dinner."

"You can't do that. They'll kill us!"

"It's going to go so fast, you just watch me."

In a matter of moments, I had aimed the rifle at a goat and pulled the trigger. I'm a pretty good shot, but the goat moved and the shot wasn't fatal. Mah! Mah! That goat was making such a racket. The Hottentots came running toward us with their spears. For a fleeting instant I feared Wolfgang would be proven right. But I jumped out of the Buick, tossed the goat into the trunk and ordered Wolfgang to floor it even before I was back in my seat. The Hottentots had no car, so happily they weren't able to follow us.

Today, I know shooting that goat wasn't a nice thing to do. But we were very, very hungry. About 20 miles farther along the dirt road we spotted a windmill that had water. We washed the goat, cooked it over an open fire and enjoyed a very nice dinner. We spent the night by that windmill, feeling safer than we'd felt in quite some time, perhaps feeling the structure rising above our heads meant civilization had been here at least in a small way.

In the end, Port Elizabeth was not for me. There were temptations, of course, to stay there and cook in our hotel until there might be an opportunity to open a restaurant. And there were other jobs possible - running an inn, operating a fishing boat, heading inland to farm. Looking back, I can say that the concept of creating a business appealed to the entrepreneurial part of my brain. But another setting had taken over all such dreams, all such huge ambitions. One day, when Wolfgang was going on and on about all the businesses we could start in Port Elizabeth, I listened as long as I could and then waved him to silence.

"No," I said calmly. "We have to go to America. We have to go to America and become millionaires!"

Malaysian Pickled Fish

Yield: serves 6-8 as an appetizer

2 pounds halibut or king fish,
   sliced about in inch thick
1/2 cup vegetable oil for the marinade
1/2 cup vegetable oil for pan roasting the fish
2 large onions, peeled and cut in half,
   then sliced 1/8 inch thick
4 cloves garlic, peeled and crushed
1/2 cup brown sugar
3 teaspoons finely chopped chilies
3 tablespoons Madras type curry powder
1 tablespoon scraped, finely chopped
   fresh ginger root
4 large bay leaves
1 teaspoon ground coriander
2 teaspoons salt
2 cups white vinegar (preferable malt vinegar)
1 cup water

Starting at least two days ahead, heat 1/2 cup of oil in a frying pan. Pat the fish steaks of your choice completely dry with a paper towel, and pan roast on both sides for about 4 minutes until light brown. Remove the fish from the pan, let cool, cut into one inch long strips and place into a ceramic dish.

Discard the oil from the frying pan, clean with paper towel and heat the other 1/2 cup oil over moderate heat. Sauté sliced onions and garlic until cooked and golden brown stirring constantly. Add the sugar, chilies, curry powder, ginger root, coriander, bay leaves and salt. Cook over low heat for a few minutes. Stirring slowly add the vinegar and water, and bring to a boil, simmer for 10 minutes.

Ladle the marinade over the fish, cover tightly with plastic wrap and refrigerate for two days.

Serving suggestion: Serve each portion on a leaf of lettuce, top with the marinated onions and moisten with the liquid. Garnish with a sprig of fresh dill.

Cape Meat Pie

Serves 4-6

2 pounds ground lamb or beef
4 slices white bread
   soaked in 1/2 cup milk
2 whole eggs
1/2 teaspoon black pepper
1 1/2 teaspoons salt
1/4 cup chopped parsley
1 stick butter (4 ounces)
   or margarine
1 medium size onion chopped
2 cloves crushed garlic
1/2 teaspoon curry powder
1/2 teaspoon turmeric powder

Topping:
3 whole eggs
1/2 cup light cream
1 dash of nutmeg and salt
4 bay leaves

In a heavy duty sauté pan melt the butter, add the onions, garlic and simmer for a few minutes, but do not brown. Combine with the turmeric and curry powder, place in a bowl and mix well with the rest of the ingredients. Place the mixture in a well-greased fireproof dish and bake in the oven at 350 degrees for 10 minutes. When the bobotie mixture begins to take color remove from the oven. Place the bay leaves on top, beat the 3 eggs with 1/2 cup light cream and pour over the meat. Continue to bake the bobotie until nice and brown, but do not overcook. Serve with boiled rice and chutney. Garnish with fresh mint.

Curried Meat Pastries

Yield: 25 pastries

1 pound ground lean beef or lamb
1/4 cup vegetable oil
1 medium onion, chopped
1 tart green apple, peeled, cored and finely chopped
2 cloves garlic, mashed
2 teaspoons ground cumin
2 teaspoons gingerroot, finely minced
1 teaspoon turmeric powder
1/2 teaspoon ground coriander
1 1/2 teaspoons salt
1/8 teaspoon cayenne pepper
1/8 teaspoon ground black pepper
1/2 cup fruit chutney
1/4 cup raisins
1/2 cup cashew nuts, finely chopped
1/4 cup yogurt
Pastry Dough (recipe below)

In a frying pan, brown the meat over high heat until it loses its pink color. Drain thoroughly and set aside.

In a large frying pan, heat the vegetable oil over low heat. Add the onions, apple, garlic, and sauté just until tender. Add the cumin, gingerroot, turmeric, coriander, salt, pepper, and cayenne; sauté stirring for 5 minutes. Add the browned meat, chutney, raisins, cashews, and blend well together. Remove from heat and add enough yogurt so that the mixture holds together but is not too mushy. Chill in the refrigerator for 2 hours.

Pastry Dough

3 cups cake flour
1/2 teaspoon salt
1/2 cup melted butter
1/2 cup yogurt
1/4 cup chilled water

Sift the flour with the salt into a large bowl. Stir in the melted butter, then the yogurt, and the water. With your hands knead together to make a firm dough. Cut off a piece of dough the size of a small walnut. Roll between the palms to form a ball. On a well-floured board roll out the ball of dough to form a thin circle 3 - 4 inches in diameter. Place one tablespoon chilled meat filling on the dough circle. Moisten edges with a little water or milk, then fold over to form a half moon, use a fork to seal the edges. Trim off any rough edges with a paring knife. Repeat rolling and filling, using the remaining dough and filling.

Place 2 cups vegetable oil in a large frying pan and heat over high heat. Fry pastries 4 to 5 at a time, turning once, until they turn to a deep golden brown. Drain on paper towels, and serve hot.

Samosas

Boerewors

Mulligatawny Soup
Yield: Serves 8

1 cup lentils (soaked over night
    in cold water)
3 tablespoons butter
1 medium onion, chopped
1/2 cup diced celery
1/2 teaspoon ground ginger
2 cloves garlic, mashed
1/8 teaspoon cayenne pepper
1/2 teaspoon coriander
3 teaspoons curry powder
1 tablespoon flour
1/2 teaspoon English mustard
1 1/2 teaspoons salt
8 cups strong chicken stock
1 cup cooked diced chicken meat
1/4 cup lemon juice

*Melt the butter in a heavy-duty
casserole over low heat. Add the
onions, celery, garlic and cook until
the onions are glazed but not brown.
Add all the spices and combine well,
dust with flour, add the drained
lentils and chicken stock. Simmer
gently for about 2 hours, stirring
from time to time. Purée the soup in
a food processor, add the lemon
juice, diced chicken and bring to a
boil. If too thick, add a little more
chicken stock, and season to your
liking. Serve with toasted garlic
croutons in heated soup plates.*

South African
Homemade Sausage
Yield: serves 8

3 pounds lean boneless beef
    cut into 1/2 inch cubes
1 pound boneless pork,
    cut into 1/2 inch pieces
2 tablespoons ground coriander
2 tablespoons ground cloves
1 teaspoon ground nutmeg
2 tablespoons salt
1 teaspoon freshly ground black pepper
1 pound fresh pork belly fat, finely ground
1/4 cup South African brandy
2 sausage casing, each about 30 inches long

*Soak the casing for about 2 to 3 hours in
warm water, or until the casings are soft and pli-
able. Grind the meat through a meat grinder, using
a very fine blade. In a mixing bowl combine the
ground meats, brandy, salt and all the spices.
Knead the mixture vigorously with both hands,
and then beat with a wooden spoon until combined
well. Cover the bowl, and let the meat rest in the
refrigerator for one hour. Wash the sausage casing
thoroughly under running cold water to remove all
traces of salt in which it was preserved.*

*To make each sausage, tie a knot about 3 to 4
inches from one end of one length of the casing. Fit
the casing to the open end over the funnel on the
sausage attachment of the meat grinder. Carefully
push the casing up to the funnel, just like an accor-
dion. Place the sausage mixture into the mouth of
the grinder, start the motor, and with a plunger
push the meat into the grinder, and into the casing.
Once the casing is filled, slip the sausage off the
funnel and knot the open end. Sauté the sausage in
a frying pan or under the broiler until light brown
and until no trace of pink remains.*

Pan-Roasted Shrimp Piri-Piri
Yield: 6-8

3 pounds large shrimp
   (12 to the pound if possible)
1 cup dry white wine
1/4 cup olive oil
2 tablespoons Chinese oyster sauce
5 shallots, peeled and chopped
6 crushed garlic cloves
5 small hot red peppers,
   seeded and chopped
1/4 cup olive oil for sautéing
   the shrimp
1/4 cup chopped cilantro

Wash the shrimp under cold running water, and peel, leaving the tail intact. Starting at the tail end, butterfly each shrimp, cutting to, but not through, backside of shrimp. Place all ingredients but sautéing oil and cilantro in a large glass or stainless steel bowl, cover with plastic wrap, and refrigerate for about 3 hours.

In a large sauté pan heat 1/4 cup olive oil, remove the shrimp from the marinade, and cook for 10 minutes over high heat. In a separate pan bring the marinade to a boil, reduce the liquid. Place the shrimp Piri-Piri on a hot serving platter, pour the sauce over it and sprinkle with the chopped cilantro, serve with rice pilaf.

Curried Seafood with Pineapple
Yield: serves 4

2 ripe pineapples
1/2 pound small shrimp
4 ounces canned tuna fish
1/2 pound crabmeat
1/4 cup coarsely chopped peanuts
1 tablespoon curry powder
1 cup mayonnaise
2 tablespoons pimentos, diced
1 tablespoon chives, finely chopped
2 tablespoons tomato ketchup
1 tablespoon A1 sauce
1 teaspoon prepared mustard
Pinch of salt and a few drops
   Tabasco sauce

Peel and cook the shrimp in boiling water for 6 minutes. Chill the shrimp in cold water, drain and dry the shrimp with a paper towel, then place them in a large mixing bowl. Flake the tuna, crabmeat, and add to the shrimp. Sprinkle with curry powder, add all the other ingredients and mix well. Set aside in the refrigerator.

Cut off the top of each pineapple and split in half from top to bottom. With a small sharp knife cut along both sides of the core at an angle, pull out the core and discard. Carefully cut out the ripe pineapple flesh and cut into thin strips. Combine with the seafood salad and mix thoroughly. Fill each pineapple shell with the mixture and chill before serving. Serve on a bed of Boston lettuce and garnish with fresh cilantro and a wedge of lemon.

Baked Haddock
Yield: serves 6

2 pounds haddock or cod fillets
1 1/2 pounds potatoes, peeled and sliced
6 medium size tomatoes
3/4 cup olive oil
1/4 cup melted butter (to grease
    the fireproof dish)
2 medium onions, peeled, cut in half and sliced
1 teaspoon finely chopped fresh chilies
    (without the seeds)
6 cloves of garlic, peeled and crushed
1/4 teaspoon sea salt
1 teaspoon brown sugar
1/3 teaspoon dried thyme
2 bay leaves

Drop the sliced potatoes into enough lightly salted boiling water to cover them completely and cook briskly, uncovered, until almost tender. Drain the water and chill the potatoes under cold water and set aside. With a paring knife cut a small cross at the end of each tomato, and place in a pot of boiling water. Simmer for 15 seconds, remove from the pot and peel under cold water. Cut the peeled tomatoes into large chunks.

In a heavy duty skillet heat the oil, drop in the onions, garlic and sauté for 8 – 10 minutes stirring frequently over medium heat. Watch carefully for any sign of burning, regulate the heat accordingly. Add the tomatoes, chilies, brown sugar, thyme, bay leaves, and cook uncovered until most of the liquid in the skillet has evaporated. Place the cod fillets into a well-buttered fireproof dish, place the sliced potatoes over the fillets, and spoon the tomato sauce over the fish. Cover with foil and cook in the oven at 350° F for 25 to 30 minutes, or until the fish flakes easily when prodded gently with a fork. Sprinkle with freshly chopped parsley, and serve with fresh vegetables of your choice.

African Guinea Hen
Yield: serves 4

2 guinea hens or pheasant
1 teaspoon seasoning salt
1/2 cup flour
1/4 cup butter
1/2 cup vegetable oil
8 slices bacon coarsely cut
12 large mushrooms
    cut in quarters
1 cup light red wine
2 medium size potatoes, boiled,
    peeled and cut into
      1/8 inch cubes
1/2 cup pearl onions
1 tablespoon chopped
    fresh parsley

With a sharp knife remove the four breasts, legs and thighs from the two guinea hens. Pull off the skin and discard. Separate the thighs from the drumstick. (The drumstick can be used for soup). With a mallet pound the breasts and thighs lightly, season with salt and dust with flour. In a frying pan heat the oil and sauté the guinea hens over high heat for four minutes on each side until golden brown. Discard the oil, add the butter and sauté for another few minutes.

Add bacon and mushrooms and sauté a few minutes longer, until bacon is cooked but not crisp. Add wine, potatoes, and onions. Cover and simmer slowly for 25 minutes. Place the birds on a heated platter, sprinkle with chopped parsley, and serve with seasonal vegetables of your choice.

Natal Indian Chicken Biryani

Yield: serves 4

1 whole chicken (2 pounds)
1/2 teaspoon salt
1 1/2 cups basmati rice
2 tablespoons vegetable oil
1 medium size onion, thinly sliced
3 cloves garlic, crushed
1 green chili, seeded and finely chopped
2 teaspoons finely chopped fresh ginger
3 teaspoons curry powder
1/4 teaspoon turmeric powder
1/4 teaspoon garam masala (North India spice blend)
3 Roma tomatoes cut into wedges
2 bay leaves
4 green cardamom pods
4 whole cloves
1/4 teaspoon saffron strands
1 tablespoon flour
1/4 cup chopped cilantro

Wash the chicken under cold running water. With a sharp knife separate the legs, thighs and breasts from the carcass. Discard the skin, and cut the meat into medium size chunks. Wash the rice with several changes cold water. Put into a large bowl, cover with plenty of water and leave to soak for half hour. Meanwhile, heat the vegetable oil in a large frying pan and sauté the onions for 8 minutes. Add the garlic, chili, garam masala, and ginger, fry over low heat for 2 minutes. Season the chicken with salt, dust with flour and add to the frying pan. Stirring occasionally pan fry the chicken until light brown, add the curry powder, and gently stir in the tomato wedges. Continue cooking for 5 minutes, then remove from the stove and set aside.

Preheat the oven to 375°F. Drain the rice, and in a large saucepan bring 1 1/2 quarts water to a boil, add the turmeric powder, bay leaves and rice. Cook for about 10 minutes, or until the rice is almost cooked. Drain the rice and toss together with cardamoms, cloves and saffron. Layer the rice and chicken in a shallow ovenproof dish until all the mixture has been used. Seal the dish with aluminum foil and bake in the oven for 20 minutes, or until the chicken is tender. Remove the foil, sprinkle with freshly chopped cilantro and serve with your favorite chutney.

Grilled Medallions of Pork Tenderloin with Curried Peach Relish

Yield: serves 6

2 pork tenderloin (total about 2 1/2 pounds)
3 scallions, white parts only
1 tablespoon fresh or dried thyme
1/2 tablespoon ground allspice
1/4 teaspoon black pepper
6 cloves garlic, peeled and crushed
1/4 cup light soy sauce
1/4 cup honey
1 teaspoon Tabasco sauce
3 tablespoons vegetable oil for basting

Relish:
2 pounds firm-ripe peaches
1 pound tomatoes
1/2 cup chopped red onions
1 tablespoon peeled, minced fresh ginger
1 teaspoon salt
2 tablespoons vegetable oil
2 tablespoons sugar
1 tablespoon fresh lime juice
1 tablespoon curry powder
1 tablespoon turmeric powder

Trim the pork tenderloin of the silver skin, and all excess fat. Slice into 1 inch thick slices, and pound gently between two sheets of plastic wrap. In a ceramic or stainless steel bowl combine scallions, thyme, soy sauce, honey, garlic, allspices, pepper, and Tabasco sauce. Place the pork medallions into the marinade, cover and refrigerate for 5 hours, or over night.

To prepare the relish, cut a shallow X in bottom of each peach and tomato with a sharp knife and blanch in two batches in a 4-quart saucepan of boiling water for 10 seconds. Remove with a slotted spoon to a bowl of ice water. Peel peaches and tomatoes, then cut peaches in half and remove the pit. Dice the peaches into 1 inch cubes. Coarsely chop the tomatoes.

Heat the oil in a frying pan, add the onions, ginger, and sauté for 3 minutes, stirring constantly. Add the curry and turmeric powder, combine well, then add the sugar, lime juice, peaches, tomatoes, and simmer for 8 minutes over low heat. Transfer to a bowl and cool, then chill for 6 hours. Prepare a grill for cooking over medium-hot charcoal; remove the pork medallions from the marinade, brush with oil and grill on both sides until well done. Place on a serving platter and serve with the relish.

Indian Kofta

Indian Meatballs Stuffed with Almonds, served in Curry Sauce

Yield: 4

1 1/2 pounds lean boneless lamb, finely ground
16 whole blanched almonds
1 egg
1/4 cup breadcrumbs
3 tablespoons besan (chick-pea flour)
1/2 teaspoon salt
1/2 cup clarified butter
1/8 teaspoon black pepper
1/2 cup finely chopped onions
3 cloves garlic finely chopped
1 tablespoon finely chopped fresh ginger
1/2 teaspoon ground coriander
1/2 teaspoon cumin powder
1/2 teaspoon turmeric powder
1/4 teaspoon chili powder
1 1/2 cups unflavored yogurt
1/2 cup coarsely chopped cilantro
2 cups vegetable oil for frying

Place the almonds in boiling water and soak them for two hours. Remove the almonds and discard the water. In a deep bowl, combine the ground lamb, egg, chickpea flour, salt, black pepper, and breadcrumbs. Knead vigorously with both hands, and then beat with a wooden spoon until the mixture is smooth. Divide the lamb into 16 equal portions and shape each one into a meatball. Pat the meatballs into a flat circle, place an almond in the center, and close the ball completely.

Pour the vegetable oil into deep fry pot and heat to 375°F, fry 4 meatballs at a time for about 5 minutes or until they are golden brown. Remove with a slotted spoon and place in a fire-proof ceramic dish.

In a 4 quart saucepan, heat the clarified butter, add onions, garlic, ginger, and simmer for 2 minutes, then add coriander, cumin, turmeric and chili powder.

Stirring constantly, cook over moderate heat for 5 minutes until the onions are golden brown, add the yogurt and bring to a boil. Spoon the sauce over the meatballs, cover the ceramic dish and place in the oven for 20 minutes at 350°F. Sprinkle with chopped cilantro and serve with steamed rice.

Indian Lamb Curry

Yield: serves 6

2 1/2 pounds lean boneless lamb, cut in 1-inch cubes
1/2 cup vegetable oil
2 medium size potatoes, peeled and cut into quarters
2 medium size onions, sliced
2 medium size tomatoes cut into quarters
2 tablespoons curry powder
1 teaspoon fresh ground ginger
4 cloves garlic, peeled and crushed
1 pinch nutmeg
1 teaspoon salt
1/2 teaspoon turmeric powder
1/2 teaspoon coriander seeds
1/4 teaspoon red hot pepper
1/2 cup course chopped cilantro
1 cup water

Place the cubed lamb in a large shallow bowl, and sprinkle with salt and hot red pepper, cover and marinate for 2 hours. In a heavy-duty 12-inch skillet heat the vegetable oil over moderate heat, add onions and garlic, simmer until light brown. Add the curry, turmeric powder, nutmeg, coriander seeds, and combine well, add the meat, tomatoes, and the water. Cover the skillet and simmer for 45 minutes, stirring occasionally. Add the potatoes and simmer for another 30 minutes, or until the meat is tender, sprinkle with freshly course chopped cilantro and serve with steamed rice.

Lamb Stew
Yield: serves 4

2 pounds boneless lamb, cut into 1-inch cubes
1/4 cup vegetable oil
2 tablespoons flour
1 tablespoon Spanish paprika
1 large onion, peeled, cut in half
    and sliced very thin
1 medium size potato, peeled and diced
    into 1/2 inch cubes
6 cloves garlic, minced
6 medium size ripe tomatoes,
    cut in half and sliced
2 chilies, seeded and chopped
2 whole cloves
1 teaspoon salt
2 bay leaves
1/4 teaspoon rosemary

In a heavy-duty frying pan heat the oil over moderate heat. Mix the flour, salt, and paprika in a mixing bowl. Add the lamb cubes and coat with the flour mixture, then transfer a few pieces at a time into the hot oil. Turn the pieces frequently with a slotted spoon so that they color richly and evenly without burning. Transfer the meat to a casserole and keep warm.

Add the sliced onions and garlic to the frying pan, and sauté in the same grease until light brown. Deglaze the pan with a 1/2 cup of water, stir in the tomatoes, cloves, chilies, bay leaves, and rosemary. Pour the mixture over the meat cubes, cover the casserole, reduce the heat to very low and simmer the bredie for 1 hour; stirring it from time to time.

Remove the cover, mash the tomatoes and onions with a wooden spoon, add the potatoes, close the casserole and simmer for another 40 minutes, or until the meat is very tender and most of the liquid has evaporated. Depending on the meat, your may have to degrease some of the fat with a spoon.

Taste for seasoning, discard the cloves and bay leaves, and serve the bredie from the casserole, accompanied by hot boiled rice.

Lamb Brochettes
Serves 4 to 6

2 pounds lamb,
    cut in 1-inch cubes
1/2 cup olive oil
4 crushed cloves of garlic
1 medium size onion diced
1/4 teaspoon turmeric powder
1/2 teaspoon curry powder
1 tablespoon apricot jam
1 tablespoon brown sugar
1 teaspoon crushed
    fresh ginger
2 sprig fresh rosemary

Place all the ingredients in a porcelain or stainless steel dish, combine well and marinate over night. Place the meat on a bamboo skewer, season with a little seasoning salt and grill over a hot grill to your liking.

To make the sauce, use the remaining marinade and combine with 1 cup beef broth, bring to a boil. Make a smooth paste with 1 teaspoon corn starch and 1/4 cup cold water, and with a wire whisk stir in gradually into the simmering marinade. Taste for seasoning. The brochettes should be served over rice or pasta and topped with the gravy.

Venison Boere Stew

Yield: serves 6

3 pounds venison, cut into cubes
1/4 cup vegetable oil
1 cup marinade, strained
1 teaspoon salt
1/2 cup dry red wine
1/4 teaspoon black pepper
1 cup beef broth (fresh or canned)
1/4 cup flour
1 tablespoon red currant jelly
1 tablespoon Spanish paprika
1/4 cup heavy cream
1 onion, coarsely chopped
4 slices bacon, diced
1 stalk celery, coarsely chopped
1/2 pound fresh mushrooms, sliced
1 carrot coarsely chopped
12 pearl onions, parboiled
2 tablespoons tomato paste

Marinade:
2 cups dry red wine
2 cloves garlic, crushed
1 cup wine vinegar
1 teaspoon peppercorns, crushed
1 cup water
12 juniper berries
1 carrot, coarsely chopped
4 bay leaves
1 stalk celery, coarsely chopped
1 teaspoon dried thyme
1 large onion coarsely chopped
2 oranges, sliced

Cooking staff at Marine Hotel, Port Elizabeth

Combine all marinade ingredients and marinate the venison two days in the refrigerator. Drain and pat dry. Strain and reserve the marinade. Spread the meat onto a platter, season with salt, pepper and dust with flour and paprika. Heat the oil in a skillet, and brown the venison cubes, and bacon, (you may have to sauté the meat in 2-3 batches), and transfer to a casserole. Deglaze the skillet with the beef consommé, add to the meat. Add the vegetables, red wine, and marinade. Bring the stew to a boil, cover the casserole and bake in the oven at 350°F for 1 1/2 hours or until the meat is tender.

With a slotted spoon remove the meat to a serving dish, and keep warm. Strain the gravy through a sieve, then return to the casserole. Stir in the red currant jelly, heavy cream, fresh mushrooms, pearl onions and bring to a boil. Simmer for 5 minutes and serve with any kind of pasta and fresh vegetables.

Monkey Gland Steak
Yield: serves 6

2 1/2 pounds beef tenderloin, cut into 6 steaks
1/4 cup vegetable oil
1 tablespoon seasoning salt
1/8 teaspoon black pepper
1 teaspoon prepared English mustard
2 tablespoons butter
1/2 cup sliced small mushrooms
1/2 cup finely chopped shallots or onions
1/4 cup chopped pickled cucumbers
1 teaspoon capers chopped
2 cloves crushed garlic
3 tablespoons Worcestershire sauce
3 tablespoons A-1 sauce
1/2 cup brown sauce, or canned mushroom soup
1/4 cup port wine or sweet sherry
1 tomato, peeled, seeded and diced
2 tablespoons chopped parsley

Pound the individual steaks with a mallet or heavy pan thin like a steak Diane. Season with salt and spread mustard on both sides. Heat the oil in a large sauté pan and brown on both sides, fry 3 steaks at a time, and place steaks on a serving platter.

To make the Monkey Gland sauce, add the butter, mushrooms, shallots, garlic, cucumbers, and capers to the same pan in which the steaks were sautéed in and cook over low heat for 5 minutes, but do not brown. Add the Worcestershire, A 1 sauce, brown sauce, chopped tomatoes, sweet sherry, chopped parsley, and black pepper. Bring to a boil and ladle over the steaks. Serve at once with potatoes or pasta.

Gingered Tomato Chutney
Yield: 4 cups

3 pounds ripe Roma tomatoes, peeled and chopped
2 fresh jalapeno chilies, seeded and chopped
1 1/2 cups white vinegar
2 cups sugar
1 1/2 cups golden raisins
1 cup finely chopped onions
2 cloves garlic, crushed
3/4 cup peeled, finely chopped fresh ginger
2 tablespoons dry English mustard powder
1/4 teaspoon ground cloves

In a heavy-duty saucepan bring vinegar and sugar to a boil until the sugar is dissolved. Add the remaining ingredients and simmer the mixture for 2 hours over low heat, stirring occasionally. The chutney should be thick in texture, transfer into a heatproof dish and cool. Chutney will keep for up to 3 weeks.

Tamatar Chanti

Melk Tert

Soetkoekies

Milk Pudding Tart
To serve 6

Pie crust:
 1/2 cup soft butter
 1/2 cup sugar
 2 cups sifted flour
 1 dash of salt
 1 egg

Filling:
 4 cups milk
 1 tablespoon butter
 1 cup sugar
 3 whole eggs
 3 tablespoons flour
 3 tablespoons cornstarch
 1 tablespoon vanilla essence

Cream the butter and sugar together and beat in the egg. Add the flour and salt, knead until soft dough is formed. Press the mixture into a 9-inch pie pan and bake at 350 degrees for 15 minutes until golden brown.

Bring the milk and butter to a boil. In a large bowl cream the sugar, eggs cornstarch, vanilla essence. With a wire whisk stirring constantly pour the hot milk gently into the mixture. Return the mixture to the pot and heat slowly until thickens. (Do not boil) Pour the pudding into the piecrust and let cool. Refrigerate overnight, sprinkle with sugar, cinnamon and serve with whipped cream. Garnish with fresh mint and a ripe strawberry.

Almond-spice Cookies
Yield: 30 cookies

2 cups flour
5 tablespoons soft butter
1 teaspoon baking powder
1 teaspoon ground cinnamon
1/2 teaspoon ground ginger powder
1/4 teaspoon ground cloves
1/4 teaspoon salt
1 1/4 cups brown sugar
1 whole egg, lightly beaten
1/4 cup sweet sherry
1/2 cup blanched almonds, chopped in a blender
16 whole blanched almonds split lengthwise
 into half
1 egg white combined with
 2 teaspoons of water, beaten to froth

Preheat the oven to 350 °. Grease a cookie pan with a tablespoon of soft butter. Sift flour, baking powder, cloves, salt and ginger together. In a separate bowl, cream the remaining butter and brown sugar, add the egg and cream for another 2 minutes. Add the flour mixture, sherry wine, and chopped almonds, and knead vigorously with your hands until it can be gathered into a firm ball. If the dough is too soft, add another 1/4 cup flour.

On a floured surface roll the dough into a 1/4 inch thick circle and with a round cookie cutter or the rim of a glass cut into 2 inch rounds. Arrange the cookies about 1 inch apart on the buttered baking sheet. Then gather the scraps of dough into a ball, and cut again into circles. Press a blanched almond half gently into the center of each soetkoekie, brush with the egg white-water mixture and bake for 15 minutes, or until they are crisp and firm. Remove with a metal spatula and serve.

coming to AMERICA

Aboard the S.S. Bremen

Port Elizabeth was a beautiful little town, and I had a wonderful job there. I was the chef in the supper club "Skyroof" on top of the Marine Hotel, and the hotel was right on the Indian Ocean. I lived at the hotel, with an incredible view of the water dotted with little islands. I had another friend there, Manfred Kirstein, and he was our general manager. He was from Prussia, better educated than I was, and he always was a gentle, positive person. Actually, he was the one who taught me how to drive a car. But one of the most valuable things he did was taking me to the bank and helping me open checking and savings accounts. He taught me how to save money. He taught me that if you take a little bit of your earnings each time and save it, when you get old you will be wealthy. He said this was just a principle of money. Most of the time, I did manage to follow his suggestion.

Of course, Wolfgang and I had decided to go to America and become millionaires. We were all excited to go, but life was wonderful in Port Elizabeth with a great job and great friends. It became more and more difficult to even think about going. As it turned out, I met another nice man named Fritz Bulbring, who had a hardware and feed store – his grandfather came from Germany in the late 1800s and started this small business. By the time I met Fritz, the place was enormous and they sold everything. They also invited me out to their farm, with orchards of oranges and grapefruit. I met Fritz' father, and he told me all about his father. They had, I think, about 35,000 acres of prime land. It was a great life, and I went to the farm many, many times.

At Marine Hotel with my friends Wolfgang Mälzer and Manfred Kirstein

One morning Manfred and I had breakfast together. You see, he wanted to talk to me. He said, "Here you are, Ekkehard (my real German name), you're 21 years old. I can see you being very comfortable here and I'm very happy for you, but don't get stuck in Port Elizabeth. There's a big, wide world out there, with lots of things to do. You have to go on and see the world." That made sense, but I just didn't know how to do it. And Manfred went on: "Look at the political situation. You don't want to put all your heart and all your work into South Africa, when the whole world is positioned against it because of apartheid. The world is not going to stand by and let this happen, so there's going to be a lot of political changes in the future. Everything's going to change, and nobody knows what's going to happen."

Things happen sometimes in life, and I'd always believed in God – especially after all the bombs and rockets I experienced in my childhood. I always had a feeling that somebody was looking out for me, whenever I was in trouble. And this has helped me for more than 67 years. So it happened that, since I liked to surf, I went out with my surfboard into the Indian Ocean, and there were big waves. One big wave took me right off my surfboard and my surfboard almost hit me in the head. It hit me on my left arm, and I could really feel the pain. As I was swimming back to shore, feeling kind of woozy, I looked at my watch, and my watch was smashed. That afternoon, I went to our local jeweler, who was a regular customer at our supper club.

"Max Goldberg," I said, "I need a new watch or

can you fix this?" He picked out a real nice watch, and I told him I'd like it but I just didn't have that kind of money. He told me I could pay it on time. We started talking about money, and Max said, "You know I may have a job for you. I have a strawberry farm, about 15 acres outside Port Elizabeth, and I might need you to be my foreman during the day, since you are a chef at night."

Well, I knew about farming. The harvest was coming up, and as Max explained, I would have to harvest the strawberries – and then I'd have to sell them. He took me out to his farm, and there were all these beautiful, big strawberries. Lots and lots of them.

There was a man, his name was Umfondizi, a Zulu with four wives and about 16 children, living out there, and since I'd learned how to speak Zulu in Durban, we could communicate. So I said, "Max, I'll take the job." As it turned out, my job would be to market the strawberries. Of the money I took in, one-third went to Max, one-third went to me, and one-third went back to the farm for salaries and food. Two days later, I drove out in my Audi and packed it with strawberries. Hundreds and hundreds of pounds. I took them to local supermarkets, bakeries, and very soon I had a nice thriving business.

Still, as the high season really came around, I experienced something I'd never experienced before – competition. There were so many strawberries around, there was no way Port Elizabeth could eat them all. The price went down, down, down. So one morning I realized I had to come up with a system so I could compete and sell all my strawberries. I was thinking about how I could do this when again something unusual happened. I had to take my Audi in for service, and there was Hans

Weber, the foreman for the repair shop. He fixed my steering. And I met another guy, this one named Klaus, also a German immigrant, who was there to design a new logo for the repair shop. I asked Klaus to design me a pretty label to put on jars, and I told him I'd need 5,000 or 6,000.

A week later, I got my labels and I was very excited, and I went to the Bulbring hardware store and bought myself a couple of hundred jars. My system was that if stores took my strawberries and didn't sell them in a day or so, when they'd started to look less beautiful, I told them I'd come by to replace them at no additional charge. And my customers said, "If you pick up all the strawberries we don't sell, how are you going to make money?" I said, "Leave that to me."

Sometimes I'd pick up as much as 50-60 pounds of old strawberries and take them back to the farm. I bought a field kitchen from a local army surplus store – and I made strawberry jam. I put the jam in all those jars and put on the label that Klaus had designed. And in the end, I made more money with my strawberry jam than I ever made selling fresh strawberries. I'd always had a good relationship with the food editor of the newspaper in Port Elizabeth, so I talked her into writing an article about how much better it would be to have my strawberry jam with traditional afternoon tea than the orange marmalade that was so customary. Before long, it seemed like everybody in Port Elizabeth was eating my strawberry jam. And my bank account was growing.

Finally, by the middle of May 1960, I looked at the balance in my account. And I said to myself, "Now I am ready to go to America."

In 1957, a few months after my departure from

Munich, my brother Klaus also had the wanderlust and immigrated to the United States. As a professional die maker, he settled in Michigan to build automobiles. After serving in the U.S. Army, he became an American citizen and was able to speed up my visa and green card. I had to get a certificate from my local police that I was not a criminal and a certificate from my local church that I was not a communist. I went to Thomas Cook's international travel agency and bought a plane ticket from Port Elizabeth to Johannesburg, a plane ticket from Johannesburg to Munich by way of Rome, a train ticket from Munich to the port of Bremerhaven and a ship ticket from Bremerhaven to New York. Even though a check would have been appropriate to buy all those tickets, I opened my suitcase and paid the lady at the travel agency in cash - with my strawberry money.

"You must have worked very hard for this," she said.

And I said, "Yes, I did."

When I saw the plane in Johannesburg to take me back home, I was so impressed. Even in 1960, most planes still had propellers. But besides being very elegant, the "Comet" was a British design for something quite new – a jet. I was looking forward to my flight – only nine hours to Rome, the lady at Thomas Cook's had told me – and after my long trip down with Trek Airways to South Africa in the first place, that sounded great to me. Just nine hours with BOAC and I'd be home on my own continent, home in the heart of Europe. As it turned out, my trip home to Munich took ten days.

We got on our way in the morning and had a very nice breakfast, but it wasn't long before the captain announced there was something wrong with the engine and we would have to land in Bulawayo / South Rhodesia (Zimbabwe). We had some cocktails there and then took off again, but two hours later the captain came on the microphone again and said there was still a problem. Our plane, he told us, would land in Nairobi in Kenya and then fly back to London with only the crew. I was one of the people who were very happy with this adventure; some people were

upset because they needed to get back to London or to Rome. The New Stanley Hotel, where they put us up in Nairobi, was very nice, with everything done in an African zebra skin design. The head stewardess asked all the passengers who needed to get going right away. I told her I had all the time in the world. My ship didn't leave Bremerhaven for about four weeks and I'd be happy as long as I got to spend a little time with my father in Bavaria.

Every day they took us somewhere, and I was able to feel like a tourist. By bus, they took us out to a wild game reserve, where I saw elephants, giraffes, lions and monkey's and they took us to a plantation where they grew tobacco, and coffee. In Nairobi, of course, everything was with compliments of British Overseas Airways Corporation. Finally, one morning the stewardess knocked on my door and said, "Mr. Mannke, in about three hours another plane is going to come and take you to Rome. It's going to be another Comet."

Within a few hours we were in Rome, and I caught a Swiss Air plane onward to Geneva. We had a layover in Geneva and I didn't want to just stay at the airport so I took a taxi into town, enjoying the beautiful city and the lake and the mountains with snow still on them, even though it was May. And as I walked along the lake, all of a sudden, somebody says, "Hey Ekkehard, what are you doing here?" And I realized it was an old friend of mine from the hotel school in Munich, Horst Manhard. I told him I was leaving for New York and then heading on to Miami, and he said he was going to Cairo to open up the new Hilton hotel there. We shook hands and said our goodbyes. We had no idea that 14 years later we'd meet again in Houston, Texas – and even live in the same neighborhood.

We went to Munich and I visited with my Dad and my stepmother and my younger half-brother and half-sister. I went back to my little village Achmühle in Bavaria, and all I could think of was how I just didn't belong there anymore.

While I was in Munich, my father asked me if I would help him build a swimming pool. Actually, it wasn't like a question, it was more like an order – that was just the way he was. So I helped him for the next eight days. The day came, though, and I caught the train to Bremerhaven – the same train I'd been a cook on, the Rheingold Express. The next day I took a taxi to the pier and there she was, the S.S. Bremen, a very modern ship, a beautiful ship. I'd never been on an ocean liner before, so this was a whole new experience. We were about 1,200 passengers, and there was a band, streamers and laughter as the tugboat took us away from that pier in Bremerhaven. I had gazed out at oceans before, of course, at the Indian Ocean from Port Elizabeth. But I had no idea what to expect on the other side of the Atlantic.

I remember it was early, maybe 6 o'clock in the morning when I heard someone shouting that land was in sight. By the time I stepped out onto the deck, I could see it was so much more than land. There, almost seeming to loom above me, was the Statue of Liberty. And there was the beautiful skyline of New York – my new home. I had one more look at the German flag. I knew that the ship would go home, and I would stay in New York City. I was happy with myself. I knew I'd had to sell lots and lots of strawberries to get here.

The question now was: What's the next step? I had no destination, and I didn't know anybody. I said to myself: So far, so good.

I know that in Paris, there had been many little hotels – very economical, very pretty and very French. And on Broadway not too far from Times Square, it looked much the same. There was one little hotel I noticed, and it had a flashing light that kept saying, "$7… $7… $7…" Well, I had $7.00, so I went to this hotel. I knew right away this was not a

**Sherman Billingsley
Owner of The Stork Club**

first-class place. The man out front asked me how long I wanted to stay and I said, "Maybe a couple of days." He told me most people don't stay that long. We took an elevator that was like a rabbit cage up to the third floor, the man opened up the door and the room was vacant. There was graffiti on the walls, and the bed wasn't made. "What do you expect for $7?" the man asked.

This was my first experience in the hospitality industry in America.

I kept on walking. I saw the Empire State Building, and the top just disappeared in the clouds. I'd never seen big buildings like this in my life. I found a nice room at the Sheraton Atlantic Hotel, on the 28th floor for $28.00 and I was full of joy. Before long, I was pushing all these buttons – I had never seen television before.

Plan A was catching the Greyhound bus to Miami. I came from warm weather in South Africa, and I wanted to go there again. I had some contacts down there, at the Fontainebleau and the Americana hotels. But I said to myself, you know what: Miami can wait. I'm staying in New York. So I went down to the gift shop to get a newspaper, which must have weighed 10 or 15 pounds. I said to the man, "Excuse me, sir, I just want one newspaper." And he said: "That's the Sunday edition of The New York Times – either you want it or you don't want it!" So I took this big, thick newspaper back up to my room, and yes, there were lots of openings for chefs in restaurants. One ad said "Morning Chef," and coming from a farm family, it's part of my heritage that I like to get up early. That sounded just fine to me.

Monday morning, I woke up and went down to the coffee shop for eggs and some sausage. By 9-

9:30, I figured that was a good time to call for a job. I started calling. People kept asking and asking me all kinds of questions, about my residence and my phone number, and it was so complicated. Eventually, I got on the phone with a man described as "The Boss," talking about one of those "Morning Chef" positions. There was a connection: I was interested in him and he was interested in me. I agreed to meet him at his place in an hour.

I looked on my map, and I figured that since it was only 20 blocks from 32nd Street to 53rd, I could walk. I went along Fifth Avenue, and I was amazed. I finally came to 53rd Street and Fifth Avenue, and I looked all around. I was looking for a restaurant. I hadn't asked the name of the restaurant. I went east, as instructed, and there was only this one thing called "The Stork Club". There was a picture of a stork, standing on one leg. I figured the place had something to do with babies, maybe with maternity leave. I had no idea that back in the late 1930s, about the time I was born, The Stork Club was the most famous nightclub in the world.

The Boss, when I met him and sat down to talk over a cup of coffee, had steel-clear eyes. And right from the beginning, I knew that if I wanted this job I was going to have this job.

There were pictures of people I recognized all over the walls, people like Bob Hope and John F. Kennedy, and I said, "All those people have been here?" And he said, "Oh yes, all those and many, many, many more." The Boss eventually told me he was going to hire me as morning chef and pay me $195 a week, which was three times more than I'd ever made before. Of course I'd come to America to be a millionaire. I decided this was going to go faster than I thought!

As I was about to leave the Stork Club with a promise to start work the next morning at 8:00, The Boss asked me, "Now what was that name again?" And I said, "Well, you know, my Mom had a very classic Germanic name for me – Ekkehard – and my middle names are Wolfgang-Henning, and my last name is Mannke." And he looked at me a moment

and said, "That's very complicated. Do you mind if I just call you Joe?" So "Joe" is not my real name, but it has been how people have known me for the past 46 years.

"Sir," I said, "now what's your name."

"My name is Sherman Billingsley. But most people call me Mr. B."

I rented a room at 72nd and Broadway from a widow named Mrs. Ostrovsky, who had lived in Poland for about 20 years before coming to New York. Her late husband, I gathered, had left her some money. So here she was renting me a very nice spare room for $15 a week. I got my suitcase and checked out of the Sheraton Atlantic hotel, and I had a real address in New York City at last.

My new friend, Sherman Billingsley, was waiting for me on my first day of work. "You're right on time," he said. "I like that." So he took me down to the kitchen to introduce me to the other cooks. The kitchen wasn't much, and it was in the basement. To my surprise, every single cook was Chinese, and I thought, this will certainly be something different! Though I was officially in charge, I could see there

With Papa Lee in the kitchen at the Stork Club

was another chain of command. And with the cooks all being Chinese, their leader among them was the elder, Mr. Lee. They called him Papa Lee, and I knew I had to be nice to Papa Lee. I knew he was the spokesman and, among them, he called the shots.

Mr. Lee had been in New York for maybe 15 years, but as he lived and worked among his own people, he spoke mostly Chinese. Still, he could communicate very, very well. It only took me a couple hours to know there was a connection there, and that we would get along well. Mr. Lee said, "Just tell us what you want us to do." Of course, in 1960, the Stork Club had already started going downhill. Times had certainly changed from the club's wild glory days in the 1930s and through the war years of the 1940s, when political, show business and sports celebrities filled every table every night. Now, there were all those family values formed after the war during the Eisenhower era, values that would certainly be challenged during the decade of the 1960s ahead – but we certainly didn't see all that coming. We started cooking for lunch that first day, and then it was lunch time and service got under way in the dining room. At some point, I remember, Mr. B. came down into the kitchen and said, "Joe, I want you to put a clean apron on and come up. I want to introduce you to some of my customers."

It was a beautiful dining room. It was full and there was a lot of laughing and champagne. Mr. B. went over to one table, where there was a man with a round face who didn't look very friendly. He said, "Joe, I want to introduce you to Mr. Hoover. This is Mr. Hoover." I was polite, of course, but when I didn't seem to understand, Mr. B. said, "This is J. Edgar Hoover." At another table, I was introduced to Arthur Godfrey and Walter Winchell, and I had no idea who these men were either but they shook my hand. Then I looked to the right and I couldn't believe it. There was this very handsome man with dark hair sitting with several beautiful ladies. One of the ladies I recognized because she played in "Gone With the Wind." Her name was Vivian Leigh. And I definitely recognized the man. I was so excited, so I looked at Mr. B and I said, "I know this man over there." "Yes," he said, "that's Tyrone Power." And I said, "He may be Tyrone Power to you, but to me he's Mr. Zorro!" (from my favorite Disney movie).

When I came down into the kitchen, I bubbled, bubbled, bubbled to Papa Lee about how excited I was to meet all these famous and important people on my first day cooking at the Stork Club. He made a little sign with his mouth, touching his finger to it and leading me over to the side.

At another table, I was introduced to Arthur Godfrey and Walter Winchell.

"Listen, Joe," he said, "one thing you have to understand about the Stork Club is that everything is bugged. Mr. B has microphones everywhere. So whatever you say in the kitchen, whether it's bad or if it's good, he can listen every day. There's a microphone on every table in the dining room, and whatever customers say, he can listen in." I thought a moment and asked, "Is that legal?" And Papa Lee said, "I don't think so, but not all the things Mr. B. does are legal. He has his own rules."

At some point, the story goes, J. Edgar Hoover found out about all these microphones and had a confrontation with Mr. Billingsley. In fact, they got so angry, Hoover stayed away from the Stork Club for more than a year. The part of the story I enjoyed most was the picture of J. Edgar Hoover telling Sherman Billingsley that listening secretly to other people's conversations was his job.

New York was my first experience with labor unions, something so different from anything we'd had in Europe and incredibly different from South Africa – where if someone didn't like the way you did something they'd just send you to work down in the diamond mines. America, of course, was a democracy, so there was much new for me to understand. One day we received a notice there would be a staff meeting, and I as the chef was instructed to make some nice sandwiches for about 50 people. There was beer, cognac, whiskey, gin and Scotch. Sherman Billingsley finally addressed the staff, telling everybody what a wonderful job they did and what a wonderful job they had. Was everybody happy here, he asked us. Considering all the alcohol we'd consumed with our lunch, everybody was very, very happy here indeed.

But then, two days later, I read in the newspaper that the union was suing Mr. Billingsley for bribing the employees in a way that would keep them from voting to go union. I read the article and understood that, by some logic or other, Mr. Billingsley was breaking the law – handing out money to this or that employee who needed it for some personal or family emergency. I really couldn't have cared less.

I really loved my job. I was so happy, working in the morning and exploring every neighborhood in New York once I got off work at 4:00 in the afternoon. I went to Chinatown, Central Park, the Empire State Building, Grand Central Station. Everything was in Grand Central Station; it was a whole city by itself. One day I decided to go see the Brooklyn Bridge, so I walked out on the bridge and stopped at the center, gazing out over the water and to all the wonders of my new life in America. They stretched beyond these buildings and streets and trees, they stretched out farther than anything I could think of, want or even dream. That's exactly what I was thinking when somebody raced up to me all upset. "Are you all right?" he kept asking. "Are you all right?" He thought I was about to jump. I assured him that was the farthest thing from my mind.

It didn't take me long at the Stork Club to figure out that the food was just horrible. There was no creativity, and I don't think Sherman Billingsley knew the whole world was changing around him. One day I had a meeting with Mr. B and told him we had to make changes in the kitchen – come up with some new dishes and rewrite the whole menu. He just looked at me and said, "Joe, this is a very successful club and we've been doing the same thing for 30

years, and there's absolutely no reason to change." That was the end of the story, even though I knew it was 1960 and a lot of things needed to change.

About four days later, Mr. B came to me and said we should go have lunch somewhere and talk about our kitchen. We'd go, he said, to La Grenouille on 52nd street, since that place was getting a lot of publicity in The New York Times and all over our area in different publications. He said maybe we could learn a thing or two. I was happy.

The next day we went over to La Grenouille. Mr. B insisted on sitting in the corner, and he was quick to explain that he had been a bootlegger at one time. That meant that even though it had been many years in the past, he still had enemies. He said he never forgot that even when he was walking down the street, always staying right up against the wall in case he had to duck in when he heard a fast-moving car scream around corner.

"Sir," I said. "I really don't know what a bootlegger is."

So Mr. B explained to me all about Prohibition, which made no sense to me as a European at all. He described how one way around the no-alcohol amendment was to open up a drugstore and sell booze as a medicine. Another way was to buy whiskey that arrived from Canada and sell it only to customers he knew very well – since federal agents often went around and ordered drinks from restaurant and nightclubs, then arrested those who gave them what they'd asked for. It was very lucrative, and there were no taxes to pay either. You couldn't exactly offer to pay taxes on money that was illegal to make in the first place, even if you wanted to.

As we were sitting at La Grenouille, I slowly realized Mr. B didn't really want to talk with me about food at all. He didn't really want to discuss new dishes for the Stork Club or any of the fresh culinary ideas that were turning up on plates in some other restaurants around New York. He just wanted to talk, to share, maybe to unburden himself of his general sense of hard times. I thought he was very human, though as eccentric as he could be.

Somehow this man became my mentor. I never wanted to totally be like Sherman Billingsley, because there were lots of things he did that I didn't agree with. But I said to myself, "I want to be like him in some ways. I want to be well known, I want to be famous. I want to have my own business. And of course I want to drive a Cadillac." In my life, all that came true. But it took years and years and years.

Over the weeks and months, I developed mixed feelings about Mr. B. Sometimes he was very nice, and sometimes he was very strange. In most restaurants, for example, there is always some writing on a blackboard in the kitchen, usually about that day's special dishes or other things concerning the menu. But Mr. B always wrote his own kind of notes. Sometimes we read, "Heat is not needed, cut it off." Other times the note was "Air conditioning is not needed, cut it off." Once in a while we saw his hand-scribbled mantra, "When lights are not needed, cut them off." All signed "SB." In our paychecks, we usually received little notes as well, things like "Keep a smile on your face" and "Please every customer." It may sound silly, but to him this was very important.

I'm sure Mr. Billingsley had something to do with it when one day a photographer came into the kitchen and took a bunch of pictures of me at my post and also interviewed me, asked me a lot of questions about what we were serving at the Stork Club and why. A couple days later, there was a big article about this "Chef Joe Mannke" in the New York World-Telegram. This was quite exciting, considering that I was just some guy who was just off the boat, a guy from far away in Pomerania.

By the late fall, a friend of mine who was the maitre d' at Luchow's, one of the true old-line German restaurants in New York, told me that one of his friends was moving down to Florida, and that meant I could move from 72nd and Broadway to join him in a house on Sunnyside in Queens. It was a whole different world from Manhattan, but it was still only about 20 minutes by train from the Stork Club. Perhaps best of all, this meant that I could write to my old friend Manfred in South Africa and tell him,

"Don't waste your time down there. America is the place to be."

Initially, after I picked him up at LaGuardia Airport, Manfred went to work in the Stork Club; but his experience there was not a happy one. Manfred was a great maitre d', but Mr. B didn't like what Manfred was doing – and Manfred didn't like what Mr. B was doing. One night, one of the richest men in New York was in the club, a guy who had made lots of big deals in real estate. He had too much to drink, so at one point this man gets up from his seat and simply relieves himself behind the curtains. Manfred was very upset about this and told the gentleman this was the kind of thing he shouldn't do in a fine restaurant.

Still, when word of this reached Mr. B, it was Manfred that he chose to reprimand. "He just does that," the boss explained, "every once in a while!" The next day, Mr. B said, he would replace all the curtains and all the carpets, and this wealthy gentleman would pay for it. This was just too much for Manfred, something he would never understand about America. He resigned as maitre d' of the Stork Club.

This proved to be a good move for Manfred – and, as I later realized, one he'd been planning and pursuing for some time. He was hired immediately as the maitre d' at the new Four Seasons restaurant in the Seagram's building on Park Avenue, one of the restaurants that led the charge toward changing the tired old foods long enjoyed by New York's upper-crust into the creative, exciting, fresh and seasonal cuisine that most restaurants in America feel compelled to serve today. Someone had to point the way and not lose their shirt doing it. The Four Seasons did it, and became one of the most successful restaurants even a success-crazed city like New York would ever know.

Manfred was so happy there. Every time I saw him, he looked so happy. He talked about the food and service so much that one day I just had to go over. He introduced me to the head chef Albert Stockli who was Swiss, and showed me around the bright, shimmering kitchen that matched the dramatic, elegant dining room. This was so different from the old, weary Stork Club with its chicken potpies and beef stew. This was the place that would set the tone for the whole next generation of restaurants in New York City.

I would have loved to work there, but I was too young and too inexperienced. But it did implant in me one thing. I realized by watching and hearing about the Four Seasons that if you really want to be somebody in America, you couldn't do it by yourself. You have to be part of a great team.

As it turned out, my roommate Mike Walter quit Luchow's and joined the Plaza Hotel as banquet manager. He told me about all the fancy parties the Plaza was always hosting, and he assured me I could make lots and lots of money if I'd be willing to work nights as a banquet waiter. I told him I didn't know if I could learn to carry one of those big hotel trays full of plates, but all Mike said was "Learn." Since I wanted to be a millionaire eventually, I figured here was the start. The Plaza was a fantastic hotel, a real heartbeat of New York social life with sometimes 40 or 50 different functions each day. And it was only a six-block walk from the Stork Club to the Plaza overlooking the southern edge of Central Park.

The winter of 1960-61 was one of the coldest on record up until that time, as some might remember from the icy inauguration of President John F. Kennedy. And that was in Washington – way down south! I decided I really couldn't see myself spending another winter in New York, especially since my heart was always in the south. And for all the great things happening with Manfred at the Four Seasons, he was always talking about his mom and his dad back in Hamburg. One day, he said, "Joe, we really need to stick together, and I hope that one day we will have a restaurant business together. But I want to go home to Hamburg in Germany"."

It was different for me. I knew America was my country. I liked the whole thing, and it was inside me somehow, inside in ways that made me think I was meant to be here all along. Even as I understood what Manfred was saying, even as I remembered more than enough stories (like that rich man behind the curtains at the Stork Club) to know he was right, I also knew that nothing in that Old World he longed for so much was calling out to me. Within a certain amount of time, Manfred opened two very successful restaurants in Germany, then sold them and went into the Mercedes-Benz business. His only return to the United States would be as a tourist. So for all our talk over all those years about going to America to become millionaires, Manfred actually became a millionaire back where we started in Germany.

By the time I'd completed 18 months in New York, even though I was content with my life in Sunnyside / Queens and my job at the Stork Club, I felt it was time for a change. And in my life, so often, one door opens even as another door is closing. One day in the late fall, I was watching the ice skaters in Rockefeller Center, and just like a bird about to head south, I was ready to fly. All of a sudden I looked around and there was a travel agency, and in this travel agency there were many, many pictures: luxury cruises, new hotels, all kinds of wonderful experience and places. Still, what really caught my eye was an artist's rendering of a new hotel in Bermuda. I looked at this sketch of this lovely hotel sitting on a rock, and somehow I knew that was where I had to go.

There was a pretty young woman in the travel agency – I remember her name was Sally – and I walked up to her and said, "Sally, I need some help. I would like to work at that hotel in Bermuda, the one in the artist's rendering. The Carlton Beach Hotel." With some disappointment, Sally said she couldn't help me with that, though she would be happy to book me a room or a suite at the resort, since she had all the information on rates and when the place would be opening.

"I don't need a room," I told her, my own disappointment far greater than hers. "And I don't need a suite. What I need is a job in Bermuda."

Fresh Lump Crabmeat Ravigote
Yield: Serves 4

1 pound fresh crabmeat
1/2 green pepper, finely chopped
    with ribs and seeds removed
1/2 red pepper, finely chopped
1 celery rib, finely chopped
1/2 teaspoon English mustard
1/4 teaspoon salt
Juice from 2 lemons
1 cup mayonnaise
3 drops Tabasco sauce, and
    white pepper to taste
Boston lettuce leaves
1 hard boiled egg, quartered
1 Italian tomato cut into wedges
2 teaspoons fresh chives
4 black olives
Capers

Pick over the crabmeat to remove shells and place in a mixing bowl. Add the chopped peppers, celery, lemon juice, mustard, and salt. Mix in 1-cup mayonnaise, and Tabasco sauce. Arrange the lettuce leaves on a serving plate, place the crabmeat salad into the center, sprinkle with chives and garnish with boiled egg, tomato, olive, and capers.

Waldorf Salad
Yield: serves 6

4 large firm ripe apples,
    peeled, cored and cut
    into juliennes (3 cups)
3 tablespoons fresh lemon juice
3 medium-size celery stalks,
    washed and cut into juliennes
    1 1/2 inches long
1 cup coarsely chopped walnuts
1 cup mayonnaise
2 tablespoons corn syrup
1/2 cup heavy cream
1/3 cup chopped chives
6 Bibb lettuce leaves

Combine the apples and lemon juice, corn syrup in a deep bowl and combine gently. Stir in the celery and walnuts.

In another bowl whisk together the cream and mayonnaise until smooth. Pour over the apples and toss well. Shape the lettuce leaves into cups on 6 inch chilled individual plates. Mound the Waldorf salad in the cups, dividing it evenly among them. Sprinkle with chopped chives and serve.

Lump Crabmeat and Avocado Salad
Yield: Serves 6

1 1/2 pounds fresh lump or
    Dungeness crabmeat
1 1/2 cups mayonnaise
1/4 cup bottled chili sauce
1/2 cup diced celery
1/4 cup diced green bell peppers
1/4 cup diced red bell peppers
1 tablespoon fresh lemon juice
1 1/2 teaspoons Worcestershire sauce
1/2 teaspoon English dry mustard,
    dissolved with a little water
4 drops Tabasco sauce
1/2 teaspoon salt
3 large firm ripe avocados
12 bibb lettuce leaves
2 large ripe tomatoes, stemmed and
    cut into wedges
3 hard cooked eggs, cut lengthwise
    into quarters
8 radishes sliced thin
2 tablespoons chopped fresh chive

Combine the mayonnaise, chili sauce, celery, peppers, lemon juice, Worcestershire sauce, Tabasco and salt in a deep mixing bowl. Whisk until all ingredients are well blended. Add the crabmeat and toss gently with a rubber spatula until the crabmeat is evenly coated. Cut the avocado in half, and with the tip of a paring knife loosen each seed. With a large soupspoon scoop out the flesh from each avocado half and place on 6 individual chilled salad plates.

Spoon the crabmeat mixture into the cavities and arrange the bibb lettuce around the avocado.

Garnish the leaves with the tomato wedges and hard cooked eggs. Sprinkle the sliced radishes and chives on top. Serve at once.

Root Celery Pancake with Smoked Salmon
Yield: 6 appetizers

3 pounds celery root, peeled
    and coarsely grated
1/2 cup chopped onions
2 tablespoons flour
2 large eggs
1/3 cup chopped chive
2 cups vegetable oil for frying
12 thinly sliced smoked salmon
2/3 cup sour cream
3 tablespoons prepared horseradish
6 leaves of bibb lettuce
    (Boston lettuce)
6 pickled beets, sliced
18 snipped chives

In a small bowl combine sour cream, horseradish, cover and refrigerate. In a large bowl combine the grated celery roots, onions, chives, eggs and flour. Season with salt and pepper to your taste. In a skillet over medium heat fry small portions of the celery mix (you should make 12 fritters) in hot cooking oil. Cook on both sides until crisp and golden brown. Remove from the skillet and drain on paper towels.

Place the bib lettuce on the side of a 6-inch plate and garnish with sliced beet. In the center place two small pancakes, top with smoked salmon. Ladle a generous spoon of sour cream horseradish on the salmon, and garnish with 3 sniped chives.

Fried Oysters on the Half Shell Rémoulade

Yield: serves 6 as an appetizer

2 dozen oysters on the half shell
2 cups corn meal
1 cup milk
1 whole egg
Salt and pepper to taste
1 cup mayonnaise
3 tablespoons fresh chopped parsley
1 tablespoon tomato paste
1/2 teaspoon Tabasco sauce
1 teaspoon Worcestershire sauce
1 tablespoon fresh lemon juice
1/4 cup chopped cornichons or dill pickles
1 1/2 tablespoons minced shallots
2 tablespoons sour cream
2 cup finely shredded lettuce
2 quarts vegetable oil for deep-frying

Remove the oysters from the shells and transfer to a bowl, cover with plastic wrap and chill.

Wash the shells under running cold water, and place upside down on paper towels to dry.

Line a baking pan with double layer of paper towels.

Make the rémoulade sauce: Place all the ingredients into a ceramic or stainless steel bowl, add the mayonnaise, sour cream, and whisk together, set aside. Preheat the oven to 200°F. In a 4-quart heavy saucepan heat the oil over moderate heat until the deep-fat thermometer registers 375°F.

In a small bowl whisk together milk and egg, dip the oysters one by one first into the egg-wash then in the corn meal, transfer to a plate.

Working in batches of 6, fry oyster until golden brown. (About 2 minutes) With a slotted spoon transfer the fried oysters onto the paper lined baking pan and keep warm in the oven. Set the oyster shells on a serving plate covered with shredded lettuce. Spoon 1 tablespoon of rémoulade sauce into each oyster shell, place a fried oyster on top, and serve piping hot.

Baked Oysters Rockefeller
Yield: serves 6

1 pound fresh spinach
1/2 cup fresh chopped shallots
1/2 cup chopped celery
1/2 cup chopped fresh parsley
2 cloves garlic, crushed
2 anchovy fillets, chopped
4 tablespoons melted butter
1/2 cup dry bread crumbs
1 teaspoon Worcestershire sauce
1 tablespoon anise-flavored liqueur (Pernod or Ouzo)
1/2 teaspoon salt
2 drops Tabasco sauce
36 fresh Oysters
3 cups Mornay sauce (recipe below)
1 cup grated Parmesan cheese

Wash the spinach well in cold water. Drain, and place in a heavy saucepan with 1/4 cup of water. Cover and steam over low heat until just wilted. Remove from the heat. When the spinach is cool enough to handle, squeeze out the excessive water. Place the spinach, shallots, celery, parsley, garlic, and anchovy fillets in a food processor and process coarsely. Heat the butter in a skillet add the spinach mixture, liqueur, Worcestershire sauce, Tabasco sauce, salt, bread crumbs, and simmer over low heat for a few minutes.

Open the oysters and remove the top shell. Arrange oyster halves side by side on a sheet pan covered with rock salt or foil, and spoon the spinach mixture over the oysters, smoothing the tops with the back of the spoon. Cover each oyster with a generous portion of Mornay sauce, sprinkle with Parmesan cheese and bake in the oven until golden brown.

Mornay Sauce

3 cups milk, heated
1/2 cup butter
1/2 cup flour
1/2 cup grated Gruyere cheese
5 egg yolks
Salt and pepper to taste

Melt the butter in a skillet; add flour to make a light roux. Bring milk to a boil and whisk vigorously into the roux to make a smooth sauce. Add the Gruyere cheese and simmer for 10 minutes. Slowly pour the sauce over the egg yolks whisking constantly.

Beef Carpaccio

Yield: serves 4 as an appetizer

4 (3-ounce) slices beef tenderloin
1/2 teaspoon salt
1/4 teaspoon black pepper
1/2 medium size onion,
    chopped very fine
10 large basil leaves,
    shredded into thin strips
3 ounces Parmesan cheese
    (in a chunk)
5 tablespoon extra virgin olive oil

Pound the beef slices between two pieces of plastic wrap until very thin and 7 inches in diameter. Arrange one piece on each of the four chilled plates, season with salt and pepper. Brush the beef slices generously with olive oil, and sprinkle the onions and basil on top. Using a vegetable peeler, cut shavings of the Parmesan directly on top of the beef. Serve immediately to preserve a nice red color.

Lobster Bisque with Dry Sherry

Yield: serves 6

2 whole lobsters, 1 1/2 pound each
1 medium onion, diced
1 celery rib, diced
6 cloves garlic, minced
2 tablespoons olive oil
1 tablespoon chopped tarragon
1 teaspoon thyme
5 cups fish stock or canned chicken stock
1/2 cup heavy cream
1/2 cup dry sherry
1 bay leaf
8 black pepper corns, crushed
2 tablespoons tomato paste
1 teaspoon Spanish paprika
2 tablespoons flour
1/4 stick butter

Fill 6-quart kettle three fourths full with salt water and bring to a boil. Plunge in the lobsters, head first. Cover the kettle and boil over high heat for 8 minutes. (The lobsters do not have to be cooked fully). Transfer the lobsters with tongs onto a cutting board, and reserve 4 cups of the lobster stock. Let the lobsters cool enough to handle, twist off the claws, and cut the carcass length wise in half. Remove the meat from the body and claws, reserving the shells. Cut the meat into small chunks and refrigerate.

Heat the oil in a 6 quart casserole over high heat, add the lobster shells, onions, celery, garlic, peppercorns, tarragon, thyme, and roast for 5 minutes. Add the tomato paste, paprika, bay leaf, and combine well. Pour the 5 cups fish stock over the mixture, and simmer for 1 hour uncovered, or until most of the liquid has evaporated to about 1 cup. Strain the mixture through a fine sieve into a 1-quart saucepan, and keep the reduced stock hot.

In a separate casserole, melt the butter, mix in the flour to make a roux, and cook over low heat for 3 minutes, but do not brown. Whisk in the 4 cups lobster stock, and reduced stock, a little at a time and bring to a boil. Simmer for 5 minutes until smooth, add the sherry, heavy cream, lobster meat, Tabasco sauce and heat, but do not boil. Season to your liking and serve in hot bowls with oyster crackers.

Manhattan Clam Chowder

Yield: serves 6

2 dozen cherrystone clams
(or 2 cans, 15 oz each)
4 large ripe tomatoes
1/4 cup olive oil
2 slices lean bacon, chopped very fine
1 cup onion, finely chopped
1/2 cup carrots, finely diced
1/2 cup celery, finely diced
1 tablespoon flour
1 tablespoon tomato paste
5 cups water or fish stock
2 bay leaves
1/4 teaspoon dried thyme
4 cloves garlic, crushed
1 tablespoon chopped parsley
1 large boiled potato, peeled and diced
1/2 teaspoon salt
A dash of black pepper
and 5 drops Tabasco sauce.

Bring 2 quarts of water to a boil. With a small paring knife cut a cross at the top of the tomatoes, and drop them into the boiling water for one minute. Chill under cold running water and remove the skin. Cut out the stems and cut the tomatoes in half. Squeeze the half to remove the juice and seeds, then dice the pulp.

Wash the clams, place them in a heavy-duty casserole, add 5 cups of water, and cover the pot and steam over high heat for 5 minutes. Remove the clams from the shell, and chop coarsely. Strain the broth through cheesecloth and set aside.

In a heavy saucepan, roast the bacon over high heat, then add the olive oil, onions, garlic, carrots and celery. Sauté for 5 minutes or until vegetables are soft but not brown. Dust with flour, then add the tomato paste, thyme, bay leaf, a dash of black pepper, 1/2 teaspoon salt, 5 drops Tabasco sauce, clam broth, and chopped clams. Stirring continuously, bring the clam chowder to a boil, simmer for 35 minutes. Add the diced potatoes and tomatoes, bring to a boil, add the chopped parsley and serve in individual soup plates.

Cream of Celery Soup with Crisp Bacon

Yield: serves 6

2 pounds knob celery, peeled
and diced
1 medium size onion, diced very fine
1/2 cup diced green celery stalks
4 slices thick bacon
1/8 cup olive oil
3 cups chicken stock
1 tablespoon flour
1 cup half and half cream
2 bay leaves
1 teaspoon salt
Fresh ground black pepper to taste
6 inner celery leaves for garnish
2 Granny Smith apples, peeled
and cut into juliennes for garnish
1/2 cup sour cream for garnish

Place the celery roots in a stock pot, add bay leaves, salt, cover with water and cook over low heat for half hour, or until the roots are soft. Most of the water should evaporate. Discard the bay leaves and purée the celery knobs in a blender. Cook the bacon in a frying pan, stirring constantly over moderate heat until light brown and crisp. Separate the bacon from the fat, and transfer on paper towels, set the bacon grease aside.

In a heavy-duty casserole heat the olive oil and two tablespoons bacon grease, add the diced onions and cook over low heat until the onions are glazed but not brown. Dust the mixture with flour, add the chicken stock, pureed celery and bring to a boil, simmer for 5 minutes. Add the half and half, black pepper and heat, but do not boil. If the soup is too thick add a little water, then season to your liking. Ladle the soup into heated individual soup plates. Place teaspoon of sour cream in the center, top with apple juliennes, crisp, crumbled bacon, garnish with a celery leaf, and serve at once.

Fresh Mussels in Garlic and Wine Sauce

Yield: serves 4

4 pounds mussels
1/4 cup minced shallots
5 cloves of garlic, minced
3 tablespoons olive oil
1 bay leaf
11/2 cups dry white wine
1/2 teaspoon dried thyme
1 1/2 cups very fine julienne strips of carrots
1 1/2 cups very fine julienne strips of leeks
1 1/2 cups very fine julienne strips of root celery
3 tablespoons soft butter
3 tablespoons flour
1/2 teaspoon salt
3 drops Tabasco sauce
2 tablespoons fresh lemon juice
1/4 cup freshly chopped parsley

Scrub the mussels well under cold running water. In a kettle heat the olive oil over moderately low heat, add the shallots, garlic, bay leaf, thyme, leeks, celery, and carrots. Cook the mixture for 5 minutes stirring the vegetable until crisp-tender. Add the wine, salt and 1/2 cup of water; bring the mixture to a boil. Add the cleaned mussels, cover the kettle and steam them in the vegetable-wine broth for 8 minutes, or until each mussel has opened. Discard any unopened mussels.

With a slotted spoon transfer the mussels and vegetables to a heated bowl, keep mussels covered. Strain the cooking liquid through a fine sieve into measuring cup, and if necessary add enough water to measure 4 cups of liquid. In a saucepan melt the butter, add the flour and cook over low heat for 1 minute to make a roux, do not brown the roux.

Whisk the broth, a little at a time into the roux, whisking and bringing the sauce to a boil. Simmer the sauce for two minute; add the lemon juice, Tabasco sauce, and season to your liking.

Divide the mussels and vegetables into 4 heated soup plates, pour the sauce over each serving, and top with fresh chopped parsley. Serve with crusty French bread.

Fresh Sautéed Soft Shell Crabs with Spring Vegetables

Yield: serves 4

2 large ripe tomatoes, peeled and diced
1 pounds snow peas, washed and snapped
16 stalks of fresh asparagus, peeled,
    top part only
1/2 stick butter
1 cup onions, finely chopped
3 cloves garlic, crushed
2 tablespoons fresh chopped basil
1 teaspoon salt
1/4 teaspoon black pepper
8 large soft shell crabs, cleaned
    (see note below)
1/2 cup vegetable oil
1/2 cup milk
1/2 cup flour
2 tablespoons butter
Lemon juice from one lemon
1/4 teaspoon Worcestershire sauce
2 tablespoons chopped parsley

Melt 1/2 stick butter in a skillet. Add onions, garlic and sauté for a few minutes over high heat. Add the tomatoes, asparagus, snow peas, salt, black pepper, basil, cover the skillet and steam for 5 minutes.

Heat the oil in a large frying pan. Dip the cleaned crabs first in milk, then in flour and sauté on both sides for 4 minutes (depending on the size), until cooked and golden brown. (You may have to fry them in two batches).

Discard the oil from the pan, and finish the crabs in brown butter, deglaze with Worcestershire sauce, and lemon juice, add the chopped parsley. To serve, divide the vegetables among four heated plates, place the crabs on top, and spoon the accumulated juices over the crabs.

Note: To clean the crabs, lift the top shell and remove the spongelike lungs on side, plus the eyes and antennae. Wash under cold running water.

Baked Whole Striped Bass
with Steamed Fennel

Yield: serves 4 to 6

1 whole striped bass (4-6 pounds)
1/4 cup butter (melted)
1 teaspoon salt
Juice of two lemons
2 cups dry white wine
1/2 cup chopped onion
1 medium size carrot, peeled and diced
1 stalk celery, washed and diced
1/4 teaspoon thyme
1 1/2 cups heavy cream
2 tablespoons Chinese oyster sauce
1 tablespoon chives, finely chopped
1 tablespoon parsley, finely chopped
1 tablespoon melted butter
1 tablespoon flour
2 knobs fresh fennel
1 tablespoon salt
1/4 cup olive oil

Cut off the stalks from the fennel, then cut the knobs in half, and slice very thin. In a 2 quart pot bring water to a boil; add the salt, olive oil and fennel. Cook for 5 minutes, drain the water and keep the fennel hot.

Clean the whole striped bass inside, leave the head on but trim off the fins and tail. Scale the fish and wash under running cold water. Score the skin with a sharp knife. Rub the salt inside and outside, and place the fish in a shallow baking pan and pour 1/4 cup of melted butter over the bass. Combine the lemon juice, wine, carrots, celery, onions, thyme, oyster sauce and pour over the fish.

Seal the dish tightly with cooking foil and bake at 375°F. for 35 minutes (depending on the size of the fish, you should be able to remove the meat from the bones easily). Place the steamed fennel on a heated serving platter. Carefully remove the whole fish from the baking dish, and place on top of the fennel and keep warm.

Strain the pan juices into a saucepan. Stir in the cream and over high heat bring to a boil to reduce to about 2 1/2 cups. Combine 1 tablespoon of melted butter with one tablespoon of flour to make a paste. Whisk the mixture into the boiling liquid and simmer for a few minutes until the sauce is smooth and thickens. Pour the sauce evenly over the fish and fennel, serve immediately. Serve with new boiled potatoes.

New York Roasted Sirloin of Beef

Yield: Serves 6

3 pounds boneless sirloin strip
(one piece, well trimmed of the fat)
1/2 cup shallots, finely chopped
1 cup dry red wine
1 cup beef broth, canned or fresh
1/2 tablespoon cornstarch dissolved
in 1 tablespoon water
1 tablespoon butter
Salt and black pepper to taste

Remove the meat from the refrigerator one hour before roasting. Sprinkle the sirloin with salt and pepper, and place in a shallow roasting pan. Roast at 500°F for 20 minutes, reduce the heat to 350°F and roast for another 10 minutes, and the beef will be medium – rare. Remove the sirloin to a heated serving platter and keep warm. Drain off all but one tablespoon fat from the roasting pan; add the shallots and brown lightly on top of the stove over low heat.

Add the beef broth, red wine, and boil for 10 minutes to reduce the liquid to about two cups. Reduce the heat, add dissolved cornstarch and stir for 1 minute until the sauce is thickened. Add the two tablespoons softened butter and mix well. Slice the sirloin with a sharp slicing knife and serve the sauce separately.

Sautéed Calf's Liver with Onions and Bacon

Yield: serves 4

1 1/2 pounds calf's liver, trimmed and
sliced thinly
3 tablespoons flour, for dredging
1/2 teaspoon salt
1/4 teaspoon black pepper
1 pound sweet onions, peeled and sliced thin
(Vidalias or Texas 1015s)
3 tablespoons vegetable oil
3 tablespoons butter
8 slices of bacon
2 Granny Smith apples, peeled,
cored and sliced

Place the bacon in a baking dish and bake at 400°F. in the middle of the oven until crisp. Drain on paper towels, and reserve the bacon grease. In a large skillet heat the butter. Add the onions and cook over moderate high heat, stirring occasionally until very soft and light brown. Remove from the pan and keep warm.

Heat the bacon fat in the same pan, add the sliced apples and sauté on both sides until cooked, transfer onto a platter and keep hot. Clean the skillet with paper towels, and heat the vegetable oil over high heat. Season the liver with salt and pepper, dredge in flour and sauté (4 slices at a time) in the hot oil 1 1/2 minute on each side until nicely browned, but still rosy inside. Place 2 apple slices on a heated serving plate, place two slices of liver on top. Spread a generous portion of the browned onions over the liver. Garnish with the crisp bacon and serve with your favorite potatoes and seasonal vegetables.

Poached Eggs in Red Wine Sauce

Yield: serves 4

Oeufs en Meurette

8 whole fresh eggs
2 tablespoons olive oil
3 tablespoons soft butter
5 slices slab bacon, coarsely chopped
1 1/2 cups sliced mushrooms
2 shallots, peeled and chopped
1 small carrot, peeled and chopped
1 bay leaf
1 dash dried thyme
2 cups dry red wine
1 1/2 cups brown sauce (demi-glace, canned or freshly made)
1 1/2 cups beef broth
2 tablespoons flour
Salt and freshly ground black pepper to taste
8 slices white bread, toasted and crusts removed
1/4 cup chopped chives
3 quarts of boiling water
3/4 cup cider vinegar

Heat the olive oil in a skillet over medium heat. Add bacon and cook until crisp. Transfer to a paper towel with a slotted spoon, and then add the mushrooms to skillet and cook, stirring occasionally, until golden brown. Transfer to a bowl. In the same skillet, melt 1 tablespoon butter; add the shallots and cook, stirring for one minute until fragrant. Stir in carrots, thyme, bay leaf and cook until carrots begin to brown. Add the red wine, brown sauce and increase the heat to medium, simmer for 10 minutes.

Combine the remaining butter and flour in a small bowl, forming a paste. Whisk the flour-butter paste into the sauce, and bring to a boil, stirring constantly, simmer for 5 minutes. Strain the sauce through a fine sieve into a small saucepan, add the mushrooms, crisp bacon, season to taste with salt, black pepper and keep hot.

In a 5-inch deep casserole bring the water to a boil, add the vinegar and reduce the heat. Poach eggs, by cracking each egg carefully into a coffee cup, then slipping them into the simmering water. Poach until whites are firm and the yolks are just set, but soft in the center. Using a slotted spoon, transfer the eggs to a kitchen towel to drain the water. Place two slices of toasted bread on serving plate, with a spatula lift the poached eggs on to the toast, then ladle a generous portion of the gravy over the eggs. Sprinkle to top with chopped chives and serve.

Steak au Poivre
Yield: serves 4

4 (12-ounce) sirloin steaks,
   1 inch thick
1 tablespoon kosher salt
2 tablespoons whole black peppercorns
1 tablespoon vegetable oil
2 tablespoons green peppercorns
1/4 cup shallots, finely chopped
1/2 stick butter, cut in 4 pieces
1/4 cup brandy
1/2 cup heavy cream
1/2 cup brown sauce

Pat steaks dry and season generously with salt. Coarsely crush peppercorns in a sealed plastic bag or cloth napkin with a meat mallet, and then press the peppercorns evenly onto both sides of the steaks. Heat a 12 inch cast iron skillet over high heat, then add the oil, swirling the skillet. Place 2 steaks, side by side into the hot oil and sauté 4 minutes on each side for medium rare. Place the steaks onto a serving platter and keep warm. Repeat the same with the remaining 2 steaks.

Pour off the fat from the skillet, and then add 2 pieces butter and melt over moderate heat. Add the shallots and simmer for 8 minuets, stirring and scrubbing up brown bits. Add the brandy (use caution; it most likely will ignite) brown sauce, and green peppercorns, bring the sauce to a boil and simmer for 3 minutes. Whisk in the remaining 2 pieces soft butter, add the cream and heat, but do not boil again. Serve the sauce with the steaks.

New York Style Cheesecake
Yield: 12 – 16 slices

Crust Ingredients:
   1 1/4 cups graham cracker crumbs
   1/4 cup melted butter
   2 tablespoons brown sugar

Filling Ingredients:
   3 packets cream cheese (8 oz. each) softened.
   3 whole eggs
   2 cups sour cream
   2 teaspoons vanilla extract
   Grated lemon rind from one lemon

Topping Ingredients:
   2 tablespoons sugar
   1 teaspoon vanilla

Heat the oven to 325°F. Combine all crust ingredients in a medium bowl, and press onto bottom of a 9-inch springform cake pan. Bake for 10 to 12 minutes until light brown. Let cool. Combine cream cheese and sugar in a large bowl. Beat with an electric mixer at medium speed (or use a wire whisk) until creamy. Gradually add eggs, one at a time, beat well until all lumps are gone. Reduce speed to low and add 1/2 cup sour cream, vanilla and lemon rinds.

Pour cream cheese mixture into baked crust, bake for about 1 hour and 30 minutes, until set. Meanwhile, combine remaining sour cream, 2 tablespoons sugar and 1 teaspoon vanilla extract in a bowl, and spread over the hot cheesecake. Continue baking for 10 minutes, remove from the oven and let cool. Remove sides from the pan and refrigerate the cake. Dust with powdered sugar, and serve each serving with a sprig of fresh mint and a ripe strawberry.

Tarte Tatin

Serves 8

Pastry Dough:

> 2/3 cup softened butter
> 1 3/4 cups cake flour
> 3 tablespoons sugar
> 1 egg yolk
> 3 pounds apples (I use Braeburn apples)
> 1/4 cup butter
> 3/4 cup sugar

Whipped Cream Chantilly:

> 3/4 cup heavy cream
> 1 teaspoon confectioners sugar
> 1/2 teaspoon vanilla extract

To make the pastry dough, rub the butter into flour until the mixture resembles fine bread crumbs. Stir in the sugar. Add the egg yolk and 2 –3 tablespoon chilled water; knead well with your hands to form the dough. Wrap in plastic wrap and refrigerate for one hour.

Peel, core and cut the apples into quarters. Melt the butter in a 10 inch frying pan with a fireproof handle (or use a copper tarte tatin pan), add the sugar, and cook over high heat until the butter and sugar have melted together. Arrange the apples one by one in the frying pan, making sure there are no gaps.

Cook the apples over low heat for about 35 minutes, or until the apples are soft, and the sugar has transformed into light brown caramel. Baste the apples with a pastry brush every so often, so that the top is caramelized as well. Preheat the oven to 375°.

Roll out the pastry dough on a floured surface into a circle slightly larger than the frying pan, about 1/8 inch thick. Lay the dough over the apples and press down around the edge to enclose it completely. With a small knife trim the excess dough to a neat finish. Bake the tarte tatin for 25 – 30 minutes until the dough is nice and golden brown. Remove from the oven and allow to rest for 5 minutes before turning it upside down on a serving platter. If any apple sticks to the pan, just stick it back into its place in the tart.

To make the crème Chantilly, pour the cream into a chilled bowl. Add the sugar, vanilla, and whisk until soft peaks form. Serve with the hot tarte tatin. Garnish with a sprig of fresh mint and a ripe strawberry.

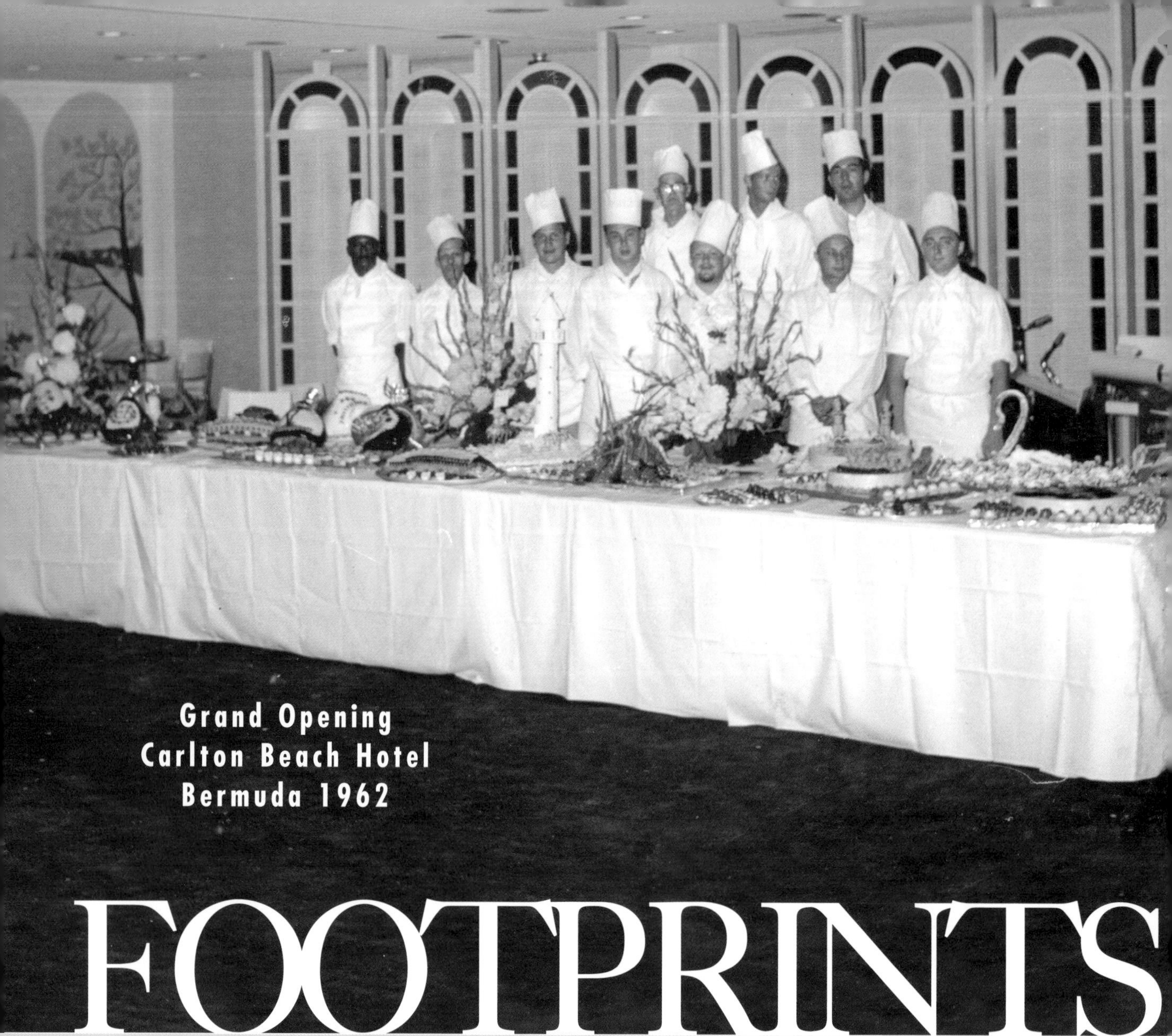

Grand Opening
Carlton Beach Hotel
Bermuda 1962

FOOTPRINTS
IN THE SAND

"Wait a moment, Joe," Sally said, looking up with a smile from all the papers, booklets and brochures that covered a travel agent's desk in those days, before computers and instant everything. "You know, the Carlton Beach Hotel in Bermuda is being developed by HCA – Hotel Corporation of America out of Boston (the name changed later to "Sonesta"). And they have a property right here in New York, it's the Roosevelt Hotel on Madison Avenue." She paused, as though planning the next few chapters of my life for me. "I'm sure if you go over there, they can give you more information on jobs. And they can probably tell you how to apply."

I went to that hotel in New York and asked for the general manager by name, insisting to his secretary that Mr. Baker was expecting me. Of course, his first question to me was "Do we know each other?" And I said, "No, not really, but I need your help." I told him I would like to get a job in Bermuda, preferably as an executive chef but perhaps as a sous chef. After insisting that the new Bermuda property was beyond his responsibilities, Mr. Baker let on that several of the corporate executives involved would be at the Roosevelt Hotel the very next day. He'd be happy, he said, to pass my resume on to them. Two weeks later, I received a very nice letter offering me a job at the Carlton Beach in Bermuda, as a sous chef. That sounded like music in my ears.

It was only another two weeks before I stood outside my apartment in Queens, flagging down a taxi with my two suitcases and making my way to LaGuardia Airport to catch my Eastern Airlines flight to Bermuda, all the while thinking about my 18 months in New York – which were, of course, my first 18 months in America I forever after would consider my home. I'd gained a lot of experience in New York, and even though I'd celebrated only my 22nd birthday there, I thought of myself as much more grown-up as I headed for the airport and the next chapter in my life. New York is a very exciting place, full of intriguing people, and you grow up very fast there.

I had no vision of what Bermuda would be like, and therefore I had no idea the place would change my life. Unlike the islands in the Caribbean farther south, Bermuda is really one single island sitting all by itself way out in the Atlantic – a place with a Caribbean look and feel, in some senses a Caribbean culture but all of that held firmly within a British approach to things, an extremely British attitude. Things tend to be much more proper in Bermuda than on other popular islands, especially back in the 1960s when many Englishmen still clung to centuries of colonialism. At first, though, all I knew about Bermuda was the most beautiful water I had ever seen in my life – a thousand shades of turquoise as the plane came down slowly over bright ridges of coral and sand. There was beauty everywhere – the water, of course, and flowers bursting from anyplace they could find, and lots and lots of smiling faces. In the terminal, I realized for the first but hardly the last time that the British love to dress up their officials rather nicely: here was a man in a clean, pressed white shirt, and then the same idea expressed in shorts worn atop long socks. I'd never seen this look before, but now we know the lower half of the man's uniform as Bermuda shorts.

As I walked out of the terminal after passing through customs and immigration, I was welcomed to Bermuda by a man with a great big smile who said his name was Billy Tucker. I'd learn later that all over Bermuda, almost all taxi drivers in those days would tell you their surname was Tucker. It was not a joke, or some island version of British slang. Almost all the taxi drivers were related to one another. As we drove along the harbor road, in fact, Billy Tucker recognized the driver of another taxi coming the opposite way and stopped to chat, window to window, for about 15 minutes. Once that was over, we drove a little ways more, and he stopped with another driver to do the same thing. Billy must have noticed I was growing impatient, maybe even a little angry. "Young man," he said, once we were under way yet again, "let me tell you something about Bermuda. Out here on the highway, the speed limit is 25 miles per hour. Once you get to Hamilton or some other town that becomes 15 miles per hour. If we go any faster than that, we get a speeding ticket." In Bermuda, he explained to me, there is no rush. The island, after all, is only 6 miles wide and 18 miles long. You're not, Billy said, going to miss anything anywhere.

Frankly, when we got to my hotel, the Carlton Beach, there wasn't much of a hotel. There was some kind of building, with some kind of roof on it – but there must have been about hundred huge containers (the kind pulled along highways in the States to become 18-wheelers), all just sitting there waiting for something to be done. I met the general manager, Bing Morris, and he welcomed me to Bermuda while also wearing Bermuda shorts. He noticed what must have been a very strange look on my face, and when he asked what was wrong, I said, "I came here to work at this hotel, and it isn't even built yet." He sat me down then and explained a few things to me – that nothing in this hotel was native to Bermuda, nothing was purchased here. HCA had figured out exactly what they'd need to finish this project: how many screws, how many beds, every stove or sink or tile in the kitchen was shipped here in these containers from New York and Boston. They brought the entire hotel in two big ships and set it out like this, on this plot of ground, until it could be assembled like a giant jigsaw puzzle. "The pieces of your restaurant," he said, "are still in the containers. We have to unpack them now."

Over the next few days, that's exactly what we did. Happily, one of the few things that had been finished first was the dormitory. They had a nice dormitory. It was on a little bay, and the first thing I did was take my goggles and flippers and jump right into the water. There, with the streaks of sunlight glinting down toward the bottom, there was complete beauty as I found myself surrounded by every color of tropical fish.

A lot of young people came from all over the world, and before long you could see the hotel start-ing to take shape. The goal was to have it open in about two months. It was fun, because we were all in our 20s. And of course, the biggest excitement was when the first planeload of waitresses arrived, one of them even from Germany, from my own hometown in Munich. All of us guys took to talking round the clock about how we were going to go out on a date with this one or that one. One morning I came to work for breakfast and the entire kitchen was crazy with excitement. I asked our garde-manger Werner Blum what the stir was all about and he told me a whole new planeload of waitresses had arrived that morning, this time from Quebec in French Canada. I got my own view of the excitement a few minutes later, as the waitresses came into the kitchen after serving breakfast to all the hotel executives gathered in Bermuda for our construction project. The service uniforms weren't finished yet, so all they were wear-ing was shorts and tanktops, and I must say it made for quite a beautiful picture.

Truth is, I had had in my life very little experi-ence with women. As long as I could remember, I'd had to work all the time. And even in South Africa, which had probably given me the greatest sense of freedom so far, there were few women actually available to a young man like me. Many of them were Indian or Chinese, and those were barriers you couldn't or wouldn't cross in those days. And the rest were Zulus or Bantus, or maybe the Afrikaners in charge with their own laws of "Apartheid". And you didn't mess with them if you didn't want to end up with at least two years in jail. I'd never stayed anywhere long enough to have a real relationship with a woman, and as a result I was a little shy in this whole situation.

We had to prepare for the grand opening, and it was an especially big deal since ours was the first hotel to be built in Bermuda since World War II. There were lovely hotels in Bermuda, of course, going back to the island's golden days when it host-ed a regular season each year for the wealthiest fam-ilies of New York and the rest of the Northeast. Even Mark Twain was part of all that, long after he had abandoned his "life on the Mississippi" for the pampering of a literary celebrity living in Connecticut. You'd still hear a few stories about this crusty old man, all of his suits as white as his hair, jabbing his trademark cigar in the air as he offered some comment about the joys and frustrations of island life. As the opening neared, we realized the whole world was watching how well we handled things, from our rooms to our food and beverage to our activities relating to the lovely beach. Our general manager drilled the idea home as well. "You know," he said, "we had hundreds and hundreds of applicants here, and we picked you and brought you from all over the world for a single reason – because we decided you were the best."

There was a problem, though. Back in New York, we were told that those of us imported would take the leadership positions and the local population would fill the positions beneath us, as was so commonly done all over the world. As it turned out, the Bermudians were such a different people, with all their "stiff upper lip" culture and class, that they refused to apply for positions cooking in a kitchen, washing dishes or making beds. They felt these kinds of labor were beneath them as British subjects, sounding like they'd be servants in the colonial empire, and they just didn't want to do that. The locals just wanted to be taxi drivers or bartenders, and there were only so many of those jobs available. As a result, so many young Bermudians, once they got an education in the British tradition, left the island to find what they considered more meaningful careers far away. Other parts of the British Commonwealth were attractive to them for many reasons, maybe Australia or New Zealand or South Africa. They could go to Canada, of course, and it was pretty easy for them to go to the United States.

When the whole thing was finished, it looked like a wonderland.

We had little to no help, meaning those of us who were there had to work 15, 17, 18-hour days. As the opening pressed upon us, we realized something else too. As much as we in the kitchen wanted to create huge food showpieces to welcome all the dignitaries and our first guests, there was no room for any such thing in the freezers. After all, on an island that grew virtually nothing anymore (not even Bermuda onions!) everything had to be flown in and stored not only for guests but as insurance during the hurricane season. At any moment, we learned, a hurricane could strand guests on the island for a week, maybe two weeks, and we had to be ready at all times to keep them fed. Still, those of us in charge of making our opening grand looked around at what we had – and one of the things we had most of, as a construction site, was Styrofoam. We ended up creating all of our "food" decorations out of this Styrofoam, and these we didn't have to refrigerate. When the whole thing was finished, it looked like a wonderland. We put a rope around all these beautiful creations, along with a sign that read FOR SHOW ONLY, and then we got busy passing hors d'oeuvres that people could actually eat.

Long after we all survived the grand opening, in fact long after our Bermuda hotel had begun to showcase Sonesta as a significant player in our industry, my education in the strange ways of the island continued. One day, for instance, I was visited in the kitchen by a pig farmer called Slim. Why we called him that was obvious enough – since he was very tall and slender – but what he was after wasn't so clear. He asked me, at the start, if I would be so kind as to gather up all the food scraps, cuttings and peels from our work and supply them to him for his pigs. I said, "You know, Slim, that's a lot of work for me, and we're too busy here to take on extra jobs.

"Oh, I'll make it worth your while. Every three months, I will give you one nice, fat pig."

"Slim," I said, "when I was younger I raised chickens and goats and rabbits, just about anything I could raise in fact. But I didn't come all the way to Bermuda to be a pig farmer."

"No, no, that's not what I meant at all." Slim paused for a moment, thinking. "Let me tell you how things work here. I'm going to give you a slaughtered pig. You can roast it on the beach and have a big party."

"Yes, I like parties."

"There are several hundred people just like you, from all over the world, and those young people are not supposed to mix with the guests from other hotels. So what the larger hotels do is have a staff club, with a bar and entertainment. And that's not just for their employees but for workers from all the other hotels as well. Each hotel puts some money toward its staff club, plus all the revenue from the vending machines, cigarette machines and all that. I think you need to open up a staff club right here."

"Well, that sounds fine."

"So every three months you can hold a big party on the beach and roast one of my pigs. And since there are all these hotels, that means that at least once or twice a month, somebody is having a party."

I immediately started saving all our swill for Slim's pigs.

One day I went into the town of Hamilton with the idea of visiting the island's newspaper, which had expressed an interest in writing a feature story about the grand opening. The man I met with at the paper was Donald Baxter, who described himself as a third-generation Bermudian whose family had lived there for about 150 years and had indeed started the newspaper. The more we talked about different things, the more we talked about things other than the hotel. Perhaps most importantly, Donald told me about this trio of residential properties his family owned right on the bright blue water – he described a main house, a former slave quarters and a former barn, all of which were intended for free human beings by the time I was living in Bermuda. And the more I listened, the more I thought about my own room at the hotel. In the beginning, I'd had a room to myself but as more and more employees arrived, I'd been forced to share, and that was a tight squeeze. When Donald said one of the houses had recently developed a vacancy, I jumped right up and asked to lease the place. He said, of course. From that moment on, I started virtually every day by going for a swim in that beautiful warm water.

By the time I'd been in Bermuda a little over a year, two story lines developed rather quickly side by side. One story line was the development of one of those French Canadian waitresses. Her name was Gigi, and our first date came about in a rather unusual way. For one of those beach parties that were so much a part of our life on the island, I asked a waitress named Andrea if she would go with me on my motor scooter. Andrea said yes, but by the time I drove up to the hotel to pick her up, she said she was feeling a little bit ill and perhaps I should simply take one of her roommates instead, the one named Gigi. Not really happy about the change, I said that would be fine. Two weeks later, Andrea became our group's first tragedy, as she died suddenly from her illness. We were in shock with the loss of our friend, a condition that over time made me feel even closer to Gigi. We went to many parties and other social events together, till one of my friends even introduced Gigi to Donald Baxter one day as "Mrs. Mannke." I felt I had to set my landlord straight on that little detail.

The second story line, not surprisingly, involved my career and my development as a chef. As a sous chef at the resort I had worked hard and learned a lot, and by this time was able to give the place the considerable benefit of my experience in Europe, South Africa and New York. I had become far more teacher than apprentice in the hard years since I had chosen my profession. One day the big boss Allen Hubsch came from Boston to the island and told me how pleased the entire Sonesta management was with the job I had done as sous chef in Bermuda – and asserted it was time for me to get a promotion to executive chef. Being the top chef must be every sous chef's dream, the thing that drives him forward every day and often late into the night. But the promotion they had decided to offer me required me to leave Bermuda, a place I consid-

ered paradise but, to be honest, had also begun to feel a little stagnant in. As so often in my life, I was sure there had to be something more. I didn't really want to go to another island but Puerto Rico sounded different enough from Bermuda to be interesting to me. I told them I would accept the job.

"There is one catch," then Mr. Hubsch said. His pause made me wonder where this was going. "What are you going to do with your French Canadian girlfriend?"

"Well," I said, "I think she needs to stay here or go back to Montreal."

"Why don't you take her along?"

I was caught off guard by what he suggested and told him I didn't know if that was a good idea. He insisted I should marry Gigi and take her to Puerto Rico as my wife, but I was fairly convinced that was moving things along too fast. Still, the idea of my marrying Gigi took hold all over the hotel. The property, I was told, will pick up all the expenses of the wedding, with waiters volunteering right and left to do the serving. The plan – pulled together, it seemed, by everybody but Gigi and me – was to get married in Bermuda, travel home for the Christmas holidays with my family in Germany, then back to corporate headquarters in Boston, then onward to the start of our life together in Puerto Rico.

One morning on the island I still think of as paradise, Gigi stood beside me wearing a white dress. I said, "Ja, ja" and she said "Oui, oui," and we were husband and wife.

One day Gigi came home and told me she'd been talking to a priest. I said, what was that all about? She said, Joe, you've got to understand, two of my sisters are nuns, one of them is a Mother Superior. And since you were born in Prussia, I presume you are a Protestant and I'm a Catholic. I don't want to hurt my Mom or my Dad by marrying someone outside my religion. But, she told me, the priest said we could get married, since we're both Christian. Maybe it was all these different people working so hard to get us to the altar, and maybe it was that several of my best friends at the hotel were all getting married around this same time. I thought maybe it really was my turn. One morning on the island I still think of as paradise, Gigi stood beside me wearing a white dress. I said, "Ja, ja" and she said "Oui, oui," and we were husband and wife.

It was 1963, you have to understand, and there was lots of talk about Puerto Rico. Of course, much of what I knew was about its next-door neighbor Cuba, since this was the time after the end of the Cuban dictatorship of Batista and the rise to power of Fidel Castro, first as a friend of the United States but quickly after that as a communist partner of the Soviet Union. By this point, history reminds us, Cuba and the entire Caribbean were on virtually all American minds, thanks to the tense showdown between President Kennedy and Premier Khrushchev known as the Cuban Missile Crisis. With the evils of communism right at America's back door, 90 miles from Florida, it was hard – especially amid the fears of that Cold War time – for Gigi and me to think of Puerto Rico as just a paradise for fun in the sun.

About 4 million people lived in Puerto Rico and the language was Spanish, but there had been an immense influence from the United States since this country purchased the island in 1898. It was suggested, by some Puerto Rican governors more than others, that English be made the national language. Still, it went back and forth, from governor to governor. Also at the time, there was a program called Operation Bootstrap that used tax breaks to encourage U.S. companies to do business in Puerto Rico. This was especially appealing to hotels, who had suffered the loss of Cuba as the ultimate Caribbean gambling and nightlife destination after Castro nationalized every business he could lay his hands on. Gambling was legalized in Puerto Rico, as a direct way of making the island, and the capital of San Juan in particular, into the new Havana.

As my wife and I arrived in San Juan, the place couldn't have been more different from the proper and British Bermuda. It seemed like everybody in the airport and quite possibly everybody on the whole island was talking loudly and at once. There were no lines to go anywhere or get anything, from immigration and customs to taxis, just a mob of people pushing and shouting as though that were simply how it's done. Nobody seemed especially mean; I remember thinking – just insane. And in the tradition of no place in my life as much as South Africa, the people came in a rainbow of colors from whitest white to blackest black. Music was playing everywhere. When I asked someone about the chaos swirling around us, I was told the planes were overbooked. You see, the phones in Puerto Rico didn't work very well, and the electricity wasn't dependable either, meaning that people did their best to confirm flights off the island but, when all else failed, they just showed up at the airport and tried to get on a plane. For an orderly German whose most recent work was in the British Commonwealth, this was all a bit overwhelming. Looking on the bright side, there was a lovely lady there who went around passing out colorful tropical cocktails made of Ronrico rum. And I had to admit, for all the confusion, almost everybody was smiling.

I got a taxi for us outside the terminal and told him we wanted to go to the El Miramar Hotel in Santurce. And being already a quite experienced traveler, I asked him what the fare would be. "Oh," the driver said, "for you, amigo, it will be only $50, a very good price." And I said, "Listen, amigo, for $50 I'd walk to the El Miramar. It's only about two or three miles away!" He laughed at me with a friendly smile, tapped me on the shoulder and said, "How about $25, amigo?" I said that was also too much and offered to pay him $15 for the trip or I'd walk. "Amigo, $15 would be just fine."

On the way to the Miramar in Santurce, we passed along the north coast of Puerto Rico, through the beautiful upscale section known as Dorado with its luxury resorts and the incredible beach. Beautiful hotels and condominiums, in every color, plus huge royal palms with graceful fronds swaying in the breeze and heavy coconuts hanging there. I liked Puerto Rico already. I smiled at my wife and said, "This is going to be just fine." At the hotel, we met the general manager, Albert Elovic, and he was just a neat guy. He was a very intelligent man, and it didn't take long for me to add him to my list of mentors. After explaining that the hotel was over-booked, Albert told us there was an apartment that belonged to the hotel and we were welcome to stay there as long as we wanted.

The next day, I dressed to start work, my first job as an executive chef. I had lots of confidence. After all, I'd already worked with Bantus, Zulus and Hottentots, the Chinese in New York, the Bermudians, so what the heck. From the very beginning in Puerto Rico, I was surprised by the quality of the employees – of the cooks as well as servers – which was so different from what I'd found in Bermuda. It didn't take me more than a few con-versations, though, to realize that almost every one of them had spent time doing the job in New York City, that they'd gotten some of the finest training available there and only then came back to their native island to make a living. The enormous boom in the tourism industry had lured them home, and that was wonderful for me.

In our Rooftop Restaurant, we had a very clever idea. We just had the smallest kitchen you can imagine up there, but there was this gorgeous view of the whole bay. Here we started a rib room, flying in hundreds and hundreds of prime ribs. We cooked 20 or more ribs a day. It was very, very easy. And it made good money for the hotel because we got a good price on the beef. Hotel Corporation of America had this big contract with beef growers in Iowa by way of packers in Chicago, so the quality was obviously very high. All we had to do was make a baked potato, some salads and a few pies for dessert. It was simple menu, but we had a packed house seven nights a week. On

Friday nights, we did a seafood buffet – and after my experiences in South Africa, I was right on top of it. We even did some wonderful South African dishes to expand diners horizons, things like pickled fish, and shrimp Piri-Piri. And of course we added quite a few Puerto Rican specialties, like escabeche, asopoa , bacaloa, and cocido de rinones. Everything we did was very successful.

After the season, I got to meet my colleagues at the other hotels in Puerto Rico. I got to have a social life, and I was quite impressed. Places like the Americana, which had a German head chef, and the El Convento, a beautiful property in Old San Juan where the chef was Swiss. And then there was the Caribe Hilton, which was actually the oldest hotel on the island, a flagship, a very large hotel with a Swiss chef and a very large crew work-ing. But the most fascinating hotel for me was the Dorado Beach, which was not just a hotel, but also a whole resort with golf courses right up against the beach with all those beautiful palm trees. The executive chef had his whole family there, living with him right in a bunga-low on the beach – and this was one of my dreams, to be the executive chef in a place like the Dorado Beach.

It was interesting: while all of us chefs spoke the same lan-guage, German, all of them were married to native ladies, either from Puerto Rico or maybe from the Havana Hilton once the exodus from Cuba had begun. All these chefs came as young men, and I can certainly understand. Back home in the old countries, all the girls looked the same, with a little blonde hair and pigtails, and most of us had never seen anybody with black hair and black eyes and olive skin. Opposites definitely attracted in the Caribbean. I, of course was married to my Huguenot from Quebec, and we were happy, and everything turned out fine – as I'd predicted to her that first day arriving at San Juan airport.

On weekends I rented a car and we visited other cities around the island, like Mayagüez and Ponce. I must say the island was just booming. One time we were guests at the Bacardi rum distillery, and we stayed a few days in their guesthouse. I knew the man from the hotel, where we of course poured plenty of their rum. He showed us the distillery, and they had a beautiful equestrian center there with those Andalusian horses, and there was a museum with rum and molasses barrels there from the 17th century. It was very interesting to me, picturing those lives lived here so long ago.

One day I was walking through the lobby of my hotel when I was stopped in my tracks by someone calling, "Hello, Ekkehard. Hello, Ekkehard." Since I'd always been known as Joe since I was given that name by Mr. B at the Stork Club, I had to turn and see who was calling me by my original German name. I looked and it was Hans Leber, a German fellow who'd always repaired my Audi in Port Elizabeth, South Africa. Seeing him here in Puerto Rico was unusual – I couldn't believe my eyes. But it was really Hans.

"Ekkehard," he said, shaking my hand enthusiastically, "what the heck are you doing in Puerto Rico?"

"Well, I'm doing cooking. But I could ask you the same."

"I've been transferred here from Port Elizabeth. I repair Audis, Mercedes and other European cars."

We renewed our friendship. And one day he came over to my house driving a beautiful white convertible Mercedes 500 SL, and I said, "Hans, you must do very well!"

"Not really," he says. "There was the guy who had me fix the car and there was plenty wrong with it. So when the work was done, he didn't want to pay that much – so he made me a deal on buying it from him. And you know, any time you need a car to drive around the island, you just let me know. I'd be happy to lend it to you."

This was a wonderful offer. Mr. Elovic the general manager suggested I take a week off during the hot season, so I called Hans and said I would take him up on it. I got to take my bride up to the El Yunque Rain Forest, and to the wonderful Luquillo Beach, plus we did some fishing and diving in Fajardo. Up in the mountains, there were all these tiny villages like Cabo Rojo, and Aquadilla. I didn't really speak any Spanish, but that didn't matter because the people were so friendly. And every little village had a marketplace in the center. Television had just come to Puerto Rico, so in the evenings someone brought a TV out and all the families brought out tables and chairs and something to eat and drink. Sometimes 30 families with children would gather around. And I thought: These people have so little when it comes to material things, but they really have so much when it comes to family life and tradition. One day we pulled into a small village near Arecibo on the east coast during a wedding celebration, with these big pigs roasting on sticks and everything so festive. The host invited us to join in the celebration. Of course, we couldn't speak Spanish but they passed this big bottle of rum around and, before midnight, everybody could speak Spanish – even a young man from Pomerania and a young woman from Quebec! We stayed in that village for two days.

These are only a few of the memories I have of our life in Puerto Rico. But I also have another memory, the day my wife told me I had some mail from New York. It took me only a moment to see it was an official letter, about as official as letters get: a draft notice from the United States Army, instructing me to report to the famous fort in Old San Juan called El Morro for a physical examination. I said to myself, it's the wrong time and the wrong place, I'm just married and there was a war getting worse by the minute in Vietnam; but after all, my father was a military man and I'm a descendant of the Vikings. So what the heck, let's join the Army.

I went down there. There were about 20 of us. I was the only Caucasian, and I was one and sometimes two feet taller than anybody else. With all our clothes off, I stood out like some kind of white giant. There were several doctors, each checking a different part of us. I finally got to the last doctor.

"You," he said, "have flat feet."

"Yes, I do. I may need special shoes, but I sure can run very, very fast."

He explained that's not good enough for the U.S. Army and he would have to declare me 4-F, unfit for service. In the meantime, naturally, I'd decided that I really wanted to join. I told him I was in the prime of my life and was an excellent swimmer. Could you, I asked the doctor, train me as a Navy Seal? That would be lots of fun. But that wasn't going to happen, he said, because not only was that a different branch of the service but I wasn't even an American citizen. By the time I did become an American citizen, I guess I had different interests, and I was a bit too old to become a Navy Seal!

Even without the U.S. military, though, there were big changes awaiting me that I couldn't even see. One day I walked into the hotel only to be called into the general manager's office. He spent a considerable amount of time telling me what a good job I'd done during my nine months in Puerto Rico, especially when it came to training the staff. He said HCA's vice president of food and beverage Allen Hubsch was coming to the island the very next day to talk about my future – and I said, "What's that future going to be?" He said he couldn't tell me, I'd have to wait another 24 hours, but there would be a change. Still, when I prodded him a bit more, when I played off the friendship he and I had always enjoyed, he let on slowly, "We're going to send you to Boston."

"Please," I said, "not Boston. Look, there's something you don't understand. I'm not Irish. I'm not Italian. I'm not even Catholic, and I don't think I'd fit in Boston at all. Plus, it's very cold in Boston, and I really can't stand the cold."

"You'll understand tomorrow. You have to go on a mission to Boston."

"Well," I said, "I'm not a missionary. What's my mission?"

"It's all about what a great job you've done here training people. You'll be right there in Boston with the home office, and there are a lot of plans for growth that you need to be a part of. We are building new hotels in Quito in Ecuador, in London and Brussels, even in Tel Aviv. It would be good for you. There's a great future for you in Boston, and you really need to go."

My wife, I think, was pleased with the news – Boston would be so much closer to her parents in Quebec. But I loved Puerto Rico, everything about its way of life and, of course, all the wonderful people we had met there in our first big adventure together as husband and wife. I felt like my whole life was going to pieces.

Asopa de Pollo

Yield: serves 4

1 roasting chicken (2 pounds),
   cut into 8 pieces
3 slices thick bacon, sliced
1 tablespoon flour
1/2 cup smoked ham coarsely chopped
2 medium size tomatoes, finely chopped
1 medium size onion, finely chopped
1 medium size green bell pepper,
   seeded and chopped
1 tablespoon drained capers
1/2 cup pimento stuffed olives, diced
2 cups medium grain white rice (12oz)
1 1/2 cups frozen green peas
4 whole pimentos, sliced
3/4 cup Parmesan cheese
1 teaspoon dried oregano
3 cloves garlic, minced
1 teaspoon seasoning salt
6 1/2 cups chicken stock or water

In a small bowl combine the oregano, salt and garlic. Rub the seasoning generously on the chicken pieces. In a heavy duty casserole cook the bacon over medium heat until the fat is rendered. Remove the bacon bits and set aside. Dust the chicken with flour, add to the bacon fat and cook over moderately high heat, turning until browned on all sides. Transfer to a plate, and brown the remaining chicken, add the ham, tomatoes, onions and green peppers. Cover the casserole and simmer over low heat until the chicken is totally cooked, about 25-30 minutes. Set aside and let cool.

Remove the chicken meat from the bones. Discard the bones and skin; return the meat to the casserole. Add 6 1/2 cups of water or chicken broth (use low sodium can broth), the capers, olives and simmer for 5 minutes. Stir in the rice, 1 teaspoon salt, bring to a boil, cover the casserole and simmer over low heat for about 20 minutes, or until the rice is tender. With a fork stir the "asopao" and season if necessary, garnish with the green peas, pimentos, and sprinkle with Parmesan. Serve at once; otherwise it will lose its characteristic soupiness. Sprinkle with fresh chopped parsley.

Salt Cod with Tomatoes and Bacon

Yield: serves 4

1 1/2 pounds skinless, boneless cod,
   1 inch thick
3/4 cup chopped and drained pimentos
1 can Italian plum tomatoes (28 oz can)
1/4 teaspoon cayenne pepper
1/4 stick butter
1/3 cup flour
4 slices bacon, cut into 1-inch pieces
1 tablespoon olive oil
1 large onion, cut in half and diced very fine
2 cloves garlic, minced
1/2 teaspoon oregano
1/2 teaspoon sugar
1/4 cup chopped fresh parsley
Black pepper and salt to taste

Cut the cod into 1 1/2 inch pieces, transfer to a large ceramic bowl cover with cold water and soak for 24 hours, changing the water several times. In a blender purée the pimentos with 1/4 cup juice from the tomatoes, and set aside. Drain the salt cod, transfer to a platter, and dust with flour. In a large skillet cook the bacon over moderate heat until crisp, stirring it with a wooden spoon. With a slotted spoon, remove the bacon from the skillet and drain on a paper towel.

Add 1 tablespoon oil to the skillet, and heat the oil-bacon fat mixture. Place half of the salt cod into the skillet and brown the fish pieces on all sides, repeat the same way with the other half. Transfer the browned fish to a serving platter. Using the same skillet, add the butter, onions, garlic, and sauté until golden brown. Add the pureed pimentos, plum tomatoes, oregano, cayenne, black pepper, salt, sugar, crisp bacon and bring the stew to a boil. Cover the skillet and simmer over low heat for one hour, stirring occasionally and breaking up the tomatoes. Sprinkle the top with chopped parsley, and serve with boiled rice.

Bacalao a la Miramar

Baked
Caribbean Lobster Thermidor
Yield 2 – 4

2 lobsters (1 1/2 pounds each)
3 tablespoons butter
2 tablespoons brandy
1/4 cup finely diced onions
1 bay leave
2 tablespoons flour
1 cup half and half, heated
1 tablespoon Dijon mustard
3/4 cup fresh mushrooms, sliced
1/2 cup grated Parmesan cheese for baking
Salt and white pepper to taste

Bring a large saucepan of salt water to a boil. Put the lobsters into the boiling water head first and cook for 10 minutes. Chill the lobsters under cold water, place on a cutting board and with a sharp knife cut the lobster lengthwise in half. Discard the dark sac behind the eyes, and then pull out the string like intestine from the tail. Remove the meat from the shells, then rinse the shells, and cut the meat into bite-size pieces.

Melt 2 tablespoons butter in a saucepan over medium heat, add the onions and cook for a few minutes. Stir in the flour and cook gently for 5 minutes, do not brown the roux. Pour in the heated cream, whisking vigorously until smooth, combine with salt, pepper, Dijon mustard and simmer for 5 minutes over low heat. Heat the remaining tablespoon of butter in a frying pan, add the lobster chunks and sliced mushrooms. Sauté for two minutes, remove the pan from the stove and deglaze the pan with the brandy, add the cream sauce and bring to a boil.

Preheat the broiler. Arrange the lobster shells on a cookie-baking pan, and divide the lobster mixture evenly among the shells. Sprinkle lightly with grated Parmesan cheese and bake until golden brown.

Garnish with sprigs of fresh dill.

Banana Rum Cake

Yield: 8 servings

2 medium size, very ripe bananas, mashed
1/2 cup dark rum
1/2 cup raisins
1 1/2 cups all-purpose flour
1/2 teaspoon salt
1/2 teaspoon baking powder
1/2 teaspoon baking soda
1/2 teaspoon ground ginger
1 teaspoon ground cinnamon
1/2 teaspoon vanilla extract
1 stick (4 ounces) soft butter
1 cup dark brown sugar
3 large whole eggs, separated
1/3 cup sour cream
1/2 cup ground walnuts
1 cup confectioner's sugar
1 tablespoon white rum
1 tablespoon lemon juice
1/2 cup sliced almonds, toasted

Preheat the oven to 350°. Generously grease and flour a 9-inch springform cake pan.
In a small saucepan, heat the dark rum over low heat until warm. Remove from the heat and add the raisins. Set aside to cool. Sift the flour, baking powder, soda, ginger and cinnamon together into a medium size-mixing bowl.
In a separate bowl cream the butter and brown sugar with an electric mixer until fluffy. Add the egg yolks, vanilla, and beat on medium speed for one minute. Add the banana puree and sour cream, combine well.
In a medium bowl, beat the egg whites until stiff, but not dry. Add the flour mixture to the banana mixture and beat at low speed, until just blended. Drain the raisins and stir into the batter. Gently fold 1/3 of the egg whites into the batter to lighten the mixture. Once the batter is smooth, fold in the remaining egg whites. Then fold in ground walnuts.
Pour the batter in the prepared pan and bake in the middle of the oven for 45 minutes, or until a cake tester inserted in the center comes out clean. Let the cake cool for 10 minutes, then remove the sides and let cool completely. In a saucepan heat the lemon juice, white rum, whisk in the confectioners sugar and whisk until all the lumps have been dissolved. Pour the glaze over the cooled cake, allowing it to drip down the sides. Garnish the top with the toasted almonds. Slice and serve with whipped cream

Bermuda Fish Chowder

Yield: serves 6

3 pounds whole grouper or snapper
1 teaspoon salt
1/4 cup fresh lime juice
1/2 cup olive oil
1 pound large shrimp, peeled and deveined
2 jalapeno chilies seeded and minced
2 medium onions, diced
4 strips thick bacon, thinly sliced
4 stalks celery, washed and diced
2 stalks leeks, washed and sliced thinly
5 cloves garlic, peeled and minced
2 sweet green peppers, seeded and diced
1 sweet red pepper, seeded and diced
2 medium potatoes, peeled and diced
1/2 teaspoon dried thyme
2 bay leaves
1/2 cup black rum
2 tablespoons flour
1/4 cup tomato paste
4 large tomatoes peeled and diced
1/4 cup fresh chopped parsley
Black pepper and salt to taste

Clean the fish under running cold water, cut into large pieces, place in a large stockpot, cover with water and simmer for one hour. Remove the fish, place on a platter and discard all the bones, reserve the fish and stock. Heat the olive oil in a heavy-duty soup pot, add the bacon and sauté until light brown. Add the onions, celery, peppers, garlic, jalapenos, potatoes, tomato paste and shrimp. Sauté until the vegetables are cooked, but not brown, then dust with 2 tablespoon flour, and combine well.

Cover with fish stock, add thyme, bay leaves and bring to a boil, simmer for 30 minutes over low heat. Add the black rum, chopped tomatoes, cooked fish pieces, chopped parsley, heat again, and serve in hot soup plates.

Grilled
Caribbean Grouper Fillets
Yield: serves 6

3 pounds grouper fillets, or red snapper (skin on)
4 ripe mangos, peeled and cut into strips
6 ripe pears, unpeeled, cored, and cut into 1/8
3 ripe avocados, peeled cut into quarters
1/2 pound cleaned baby spinach
1/2 cup walnut oil
1/4 cup Italian salad dressing
1 cup orange juice
1/2 cup lime juice

Prepare a wood or charcoal grill and let it burn to ember. Rub the fish fillets generously with the Caribbean seasoning on both sides, place in a dish and refrigerate for 20 minutes. Spray the fish with walnut oil and grill over low heat for about 8 minutes on one side and 6 minutes on the other side (depending on the thickness of the fish). Remove from grill and keep hot.

Lightly oil the pears and mangos and grill for about 3 minutes until light brown. Place in a stainless steel bowl, and toss with the Italian dressing, orange juice, and lime juice. Place the baby spinach on individual plates, garnish with the avocado, and spoon the fruit dressing over the spinach.

Caribbean Seasoning

1 teaspoon sea salt
6 teaspoons minced garlic
6 teaspoons dried onions
3 teaspoons allspice
2 teaspoons chopped chipolte
2 teaspoons Spanish paprika
3 teaspoons brown sugar
3 teaspoons dried thyme
2 teaspoons cinnamon
1/2 teaspoon ground nutmeg
2 lemon zest

This can be prepared in advance. Mix well and place in a tight container.

Kingfish
with Hot and Sour
Pineapple Relish
Yield: serves 4

4 fish fillets, with the skin on,
    6 ounces each
1/3 cup finely chopped shallots
1/4 cup vegetable oil
1/4 cup flour
1 fresh chili, seeded and chopped very fine
1 medium size pineapple, peeled,
    cored and cut into small cubes
    (3 1/2 cups)
2 teaspoons Asian fish sauce
1 tablespoon sugar
1/4 teaspoon salt
2 tablespoons fresh lime juice
1 small bunch of cilantro leaves for garnish

Heat 2 tablespoons of oil in a skillet; add the shallots, chilies and cook over moderate heat, stirring occasionally until light brown. Add the sugar, salt, fish sauce, pineapples and simmer until the pineapples are soft, and most of the liquid has evaporated. Remove from the heat and stir in the lime juice. Transfer the relish into a bowl.

Heat the remaining oil in a clean skillet. Pat the fish fillets dry, season with salt, dust with flour and place in the frying pan skin down. Cook first on one side, then on the other side until golden brown (10 - 12 minutes total, depending on the thickness). Serve the fish topped with the relish, and garnished with sprigs of fresh cilantro.

Puerto Rican
Pork and Beans
Yield: serves 6

6 pork loin spare ribs
    (2 1/2 to 3 pounds)
1 cup vegetable oil
6 cups water or chicken stock
2 carrots, medium size, peeled and
    cut into 1/4 inch cubes
2 onions, large size, peeled and
    cut into 1/2 inch cubes
9 cloves garlic, crushed
5 bay leaves
1 teaspoon dried oregano
6 whole tomatoes cut into quarters
1 small jalapeno, cut in half,
    seeded and chopped
3 tablespoons salt
1 1/2 pounds dried kidney beans
    sorted and soaked
    in cold water over night
1 cup chopped fresh cilantro leaves

Heat the oil in a fireproof casserole. Place the pork spare ribs in the oil, and brown on both sides. Add all the remaining ingredients (except the cilantro) and bring to a boil. Reduce the heat and simmer for two hours, or until the meat is tender and falls off the bones. Sprinkle with the chopped cilantro leaves, and serve with rice or potatoes.

British Roast
Prime Ribs of Beef
Yield: serves 10 to 12

5 rib standing rib roast, about 10 pounds
1 tablespoon coarse black pepper
2 bay leaves, chopped very fine
1/2 stick butter, softened
1/4 cup flour
2 teaspoons sea salt
1 pound whole shallots
2 heads of garlic, separated into cloves
6 sprigs of fresh rosemary
For the sauce:
1/2 cup dry red wine
2 cups canned beef broth
1/2 cup dry Madeira
1 tablespoon cornstarch

Preheat the oven to 500°F. In a small bowl combine the soft butter, salt, black pepper, chopped bay leaves, and flour to form a paste. Rub the meat with the paste, and place into a roasting pan, rib side down. Roast for 30 minutes to seal the meat, reduce the heat to 350°F. and roast for another 2 hours, or until a meat thermometer inserted in a fleshy section registers 130°F. 1/2 hour before the roast is done add the shallots and garlic around the meat, and brown lightly.

Transfer the roast to a serving platter, cover with foil and keep warm. The roast should be resting for 20 minutes before carving. With a slotted spoon remove the garlic and shallots from the beef rendering, and set aside. Make the sauce by skimming of the fat from the drippings, (reserve for the Yorkshire Pudding).

Deglaze the pan with the red wine, and simmer over low heat, scraping up the brown roasting bits. Transfer the juice to a small saucepan, add beef broth and bring to a boil.

In a small bowl dissolve the cornstarch with the Madeira, and whisk the mixture into the gravy. Season with salt and pepper, then strain into a heated sauceboat. Arrange the shallots, the garlic, and the fresh rosemary around the roast, slice the meat with a sharp knife and serve with the sauce.

Yorkshire Pudding
Yield: serves 10

1 cup milk
2 large eggs
3/4 teaspoon salt
1 cup flour
1 dash of nutmeg
1/4 cup rib roast
    pan drippings fat

Sift the flour into a mixing bowl, add the salt and nutmeg. In a blender blend the milk and eggs for a few seconds. With the motor running add the flour mixture, a little at a time, and combine the mixture at high speed for 2 minutes. Let the batter rest for half hour before baking. In a 10-inch cast iron skillet heat the reserved beef renderings in a preheated oven 450°F. oven for 10 minutes. Mix the batter with a wooden spoon and pour into the skillet. Bake the pudding in the middle of the oven for 20 minutes. Reduce the heat to 300°F. and bake another 10 minutes until golden brown. Transfer the pudding to a serving platter, cut into wedges and serve with the rib roast.

Caribbean Beef, Egg and Banana Casserole
Yield: serves 4 – 6

6 slices lean bacon, chopped coarse
1 pound lean ground beef
1 medium size onion, finely chopped
4 cloves garlic, minced
1 red bell pepper, cut in half, seeded and diced fine
2 whole hard boiled eggs, chopped
5 large pimento stuffed olives, chopped
1 cup canned tomato puree
1 1/2 teaspoons dried oregano
1 teaspoon salt
1 pound cooked green beans
2 teaspoons vegetable oil
6 large eggs, beaten with a dash of black pepper, and 1/2 teaspoon salt
8 firm-ripe bananas, peeled and cut in half lengthwise

Preheat the oven to 350°. Heat a large heavy duty skillet, add the bacon and cook over moderate heat, stirring occasionally until crisp. Transfer with a slotted spoon to paper towels to drain. Add the beef, onions, garlic, and bell peppers to the skillet; roast the meat mixture in the bacon fat, stirring and breaking up the beef until fully cooked. Add the hard boiled eggs, olives, green beans, tomato puree, oregano, and combine all ingredients well. Add salt and pepper to your taste.

Brush a 10-inch round baking dish (3 inches deep) with the oil. Pour half the beaten eggs into the dish, and arrange half the bananas in one layer on the bottom of the pan. Spread half of the meat-vegetable mixture over the bananas. Arrange the remaining bananas on the beef mixture, and add another layer of the remaining beef mixture. Pour the remaining beaten eggs over the meat, and bake the piñón in the middle of the oven for 35 minutes, or until the eggs are cooked and nicely browned. Serve with Chimichurri.

Chimichurri Sauce
To make two cups:

1 cup olive oil
1/2 cup red wine vinegar
1 cup chopped onions
2 teaspoons chopped garlic
1/2 cup finely chopped parsley
1 teaspoon oregano
1/4 teaspoon cayenne pepper
1 teaspoon black pepper

In a bowl combine the oil and vinegar, and beat them together with a whisk. Add all the ingredients and let rest in room temperature for two hours.

Bermuda Walnut Scones
for 5 o'clock tea
Yield: 12 scones

11/2 cups all-purpose flour
2/3 cup whole-wheat flour
1/3 cup bran flakes
1/4 cup light brown sugar
3/4 cup chopped walnuts
2/3 cup raisins
1 1/2 teaspoons freshly grated lemon rind
1 tablespoon baking powder
3/4 teaspoon baking soda
1/2 teaspoon salt
3/4 stick butter, cut into bits
1/2 cup buttermilk
1 whole egg
Egg wash, made from 1 egg yolk
    with 2 tablespoons milk

Preheat the oven to 375°. Into a bowl sift together the unbleached flour, the brown sugar, and the salt. Blend in the butter bits until the mixture resembles coarse meal, and stir in the whole wheat flour, bran flakes, chopped walnuts, and raisins, knead until the mixture is combined. In a small bowl whisk together the lemon rind, buttermilk, and combine with the flour mixture. Transfer the mixture to a well-floured working surface, and knead to form manageable dough. With a rolling pin roll the dough to a 3/4 inch thick round.

Cut out rounds with a 2-inch cookie cutter dipped in flour. Arrange each scone, 3/4 inch apart on a baking sheet. Form the scraps into a ball, pat the dough 3/4 inch thick, and also cut out 2-inch scones.

Brush the tops with the egg wash, and bake in the middle of the oven for 15 to 20 minutes until they are golden brown. Serve the scones with soft butter and marmalade.

Chocolate & Pistachio
Biscotti
Yield: 6 dozen

2 cups flour
3/4 cup unsweetened cocoa powder
1/2 teaspoon baking soda
3 large eggs
11/4 cups light brown sugar
4 tablespoons butter, softened
1 tablespoon pure vanilla extract
1 teaspoon instant coffee powder
1 teaspoon almond extract
8 ounces bittersweet chocolate, chopped
1 cup unsalted shelled pistachios
Pinch of salt

Preheat the oven to 350°F. Line 2 baking sheets with parchment paper. In a large bowl, sift together the flour, cocoa powder, baking soda and salt. Using an electric mixer beat in the eggs at low speed until crumbling dough forms. In another bowl, beat the brown sugar with the butter and vanilla, coffee powder and almond extract until combined. Scrape the mixture into the crumbling dough and beat at medium speed until soft, sticky dough forms. Add the chopped chocolate and shelled pistachios and beat at low speed until combined.

Divide the dough into 4 parts, and transfer to a floured surface. Roll each part of the dough into an 8-inch long rope, about 2 1/2 inches thick. Place on a cookie baking sheet, and bake for 20 minutes until the logs are puffed and golden brown. Let the logs cool for about one hour, and then carefully transfer to a cutting board.

Using a sharp bread knife cut the logs crosswise into 1/4-inch thick slices. Each log should yield about 20 biscotti. Set the oven to 250°. Return the slices, 1/2 inch apart from each other to the baking sheet, and bake for about 25 to 30 minutes. Serve with tea, coffee or cappuccino.

Caribbean Caramel Flan
Yield: serves 6

1 cup sugar
1 teaspoon cider vinegar
1/2 cup water
1 1/2 cups heavy cream
1 cup milk
1 tablespoon instant coffee granules
1/4 cup dark rum
7 egg yolks
4 egg whites

Preheat the oven to 325°F. In a medium size saucepan combine the water, vinegar and 1/2 cup of sugar. Stir over low heat until the sugar has dissolved and the liquid is clear. Increase the heat and bring to a boil. With a wet pastry brush, wash down the sides of the pan to prevent crystallization of the boiling sugar syrup. Boil without stirring until the syrup is golden brown. Quickly pour the caramel into a 9 inch metal pie pan. Working quickly, tilt the pan to spread the caramel evenly and as thin as possible on the bottom of the pan.

Without rinsing the saucepan, add the cream, milk, coffee granules, 1/4 cup sugar, and dark rum. Bring the mixture almost to a boil over moderate heat, stirring occasionally.

Meanwhile, in a large heatproof bowl, whisk together the egg yolks, egg whites, and the remaining 1/4 cup sugar until blended. Gradually, in a slow stream whisk in the hot cream mixture. Set the prepared pie pan in a larger pan (creating a bain marie). Pour the custard into the pie pan, then place both pans in the middle of the oven, and pour warm water into the larger pan. Bake for 40 minutes, or until the custard is set.

Remove the custard from the oven, let cool and refrigerate over night.

Loosen the custard from the sides of the pie pan with a small knife. Place a large round serving platter on top of the pan and invert to unmold the custard. Garnish with fresh berries of the season, fresh sprigs of mint and serve in chilled glass bowls.

Floating Island with Guava Sauce
Serves 4

5 egg yolks
1/4 cup sugar
1/2 teaspoon vanilla extract
2 cups light cream
1/2 cup guava jelly
2 egg whites
1/2 cup whipping cream
2 tablespoons confectioners' sugar
1/3 cup dark Puerto Rican rum
8 large ripe strawberries, cut into quarters
Fresh sprigs of mint for garnish.

In a heavy duty 1 1/2 quart saucepan bring the light cream and vanilla to a boil. In a small bowl combine the egg yolks and sugar. Whisking constantly, pour the hot cream into the egg-sugar mixture. Return the mixture to the saucepan and warm over moderate heat, stirring constantly with a wooden spoon until the custard thickens. Do not allow the mixture to come near the boiling point, or it may curdle. Pour the custard into a 2 inch deep, and 9 inch round serving dish, and refrigerate for 3 hours, until set and firm.

Just before serving, melt the guava jelly in a small skillet over low heat, and set aside.

With a rotary electric beater, whisk the egg whites until stiff. Beating constantly, pour the melted guava jelly in a small stream into the egg whites.

To make the "floating island" use a small ice cream scoop, and scoop the egg whites onto the chilled custard, spacing each island by 1/4 inch. In a separate chilled bowl, beat the heavy cream until it begins to thicken. Add the confectioners sugar and the dark rum; continue beating until the cream is stiff but not buttery. Ladle a heaping tablespoon of the whipped cream over the islands. Garnish with fresh sprigs of mint, and quartered strawberries.

Molten Chocolate Cakes with Black Rum-Ginger Ice Cream
Yield: serves 8

14 ounces bittersweet chocolate,
    coarsely chopped
2 1/2 sticks soft butter
1 teaspoon ground coriander
1 teaspoon cinnamon
1/2 teaspoon ground cloves
1/8 teaspoon ground white pepper
6 large eggs
6 large egg yolks
2 teaspoons vanilla extract
3 cups powdered sugar
1 cup cake flour
Additional powdered sugar for dusting

Generously butter eight soufflé cups. In a double boiler melt the chocolate over low heat. Add the cloves, cinnamon, coriander and white pepper, mix well and set aside to cool slightly. With an electric mixer whisk eggs, egg yolks, vanilla, and sugar until pale yellow. Combine with the melted chocolate, and then fold in the flour. Transfer the batter into the prepared soufflé dishes, dividing evenly.

Preheat oven to 400°F. Bake cakes for about 15 minutes, until batter has risen above the rim of the dishes. The top should be crispy, dark brown, but the center has to be soft and runny. Run a small knife around cakes to loosen, and allow the cakes to rest for 5 minutes. Using a kitchen towel, holding the hot soufflé cup firmly, remove the cakes and place on a serving dish. Repeat with remaining cakes. Dust with powdered sugar and serve with dark-rum ginger ice cream.

Rum-Ginger ice cream

Combine a quart of softened vanilla ice cream with 1/2 cup dark rum and 3/4 cup of chopped crystallized ginger.

Puerto Rican Banana Bread
Yield: 1 loaf, 9-by-5-by-3 inch

1 stick butter
3/4 cup coarsely chopped pecans nuts
1/4 cup seedless raisins
2 cups flour
1/2 cup sugar
1 teaspoon baking powder
1/4 teaspoon ground nutmeg
1/2 teaspoon salt
2 large ripe bananas (about one pound)
1 teaspoon vanilla extract
1 whole egg

Preheat the oven to 350°F. Sift the flour; salt and baking powder into a mixing bowl, add the pecans and raisins mix well. In another bowl cream the butter, egg, vanilla extract and sugar until light and fluffy. With the back of a table fork, mash the bananas to a purée. Gently, using a wooden spoon, fold the egg, butter and sugar mixture with the flour and raisins, add the bananas, and combine well. Ladle the batter into a well-buttered loaf pan, and bake in the middle of the oven for 50 to 60 minutes. Remove the bread from the oven and let cool in the pan for 5 minutes, and then turn it out on a wire rack. Slice and serve with softened cream cheese.

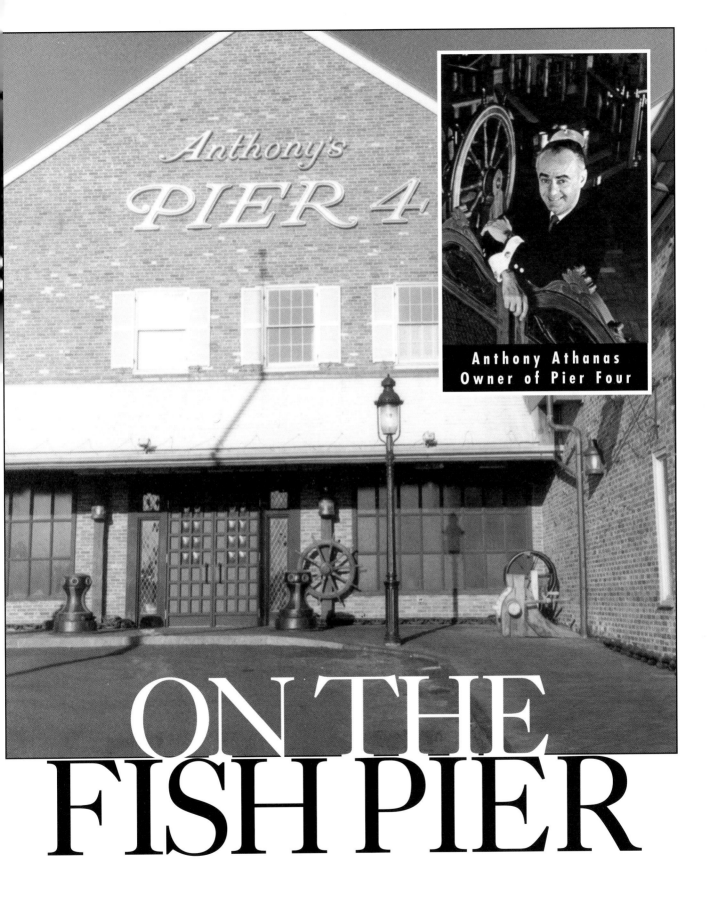

Anthony Athanas
Owner of Pier Four

ON THE FISH PIER

It was gray and drizzly the day our plane touched down at Boston's Logan Airport. There was nothing much to see, certainly none of the wild, rainbow colors that I'd become so accustomed to in the Caribbean – just gray, gray, and more gray. Boston, of course, is a very old city. But when it is raining, it seems even older. The people didn't look happy here. They were gray too, and they all had long faces. I was not a happy camper when I arrived in Boston, but maybe that was just me. I didn't want to go there. The only person in the whole airport who was smiling that day was my boss and my friend, Allen Hubsch, the vice president of Sonesta Hotels. "Welcome to Boston," he said.

On the way from the airport, Allen explained my mission. Sonesta had a string of hotels – more like motels, really – called Charter House. And while every Charter House had some kind of restaurant, none of the food and beverage operations seemed to be doing as well as they'd hoped. So the idea now, approved by Sonesta's board of directors, was to introduce a steakhouse that could then be a signature in all the Charter Houses.

We arrived at the old city of Lynn maybe 15 or 20 miles outside of Boston, a place that had certainly seen better days. Like a lot of smaller cities in Massachusetts, it had once drawn what wealth it had from textiles. When that industry dried up decades earlier, these cities pretty much dried up right along with it. Across from a GE plant turning out airplane engines for the Vietnam War was this crumby little motel. It was supposed to be my place of work for the next months. You can imagine how it felt to check into this old, beat-up, rundown Charter House after the Caribe Hilton, the El Conquistador or the El Convento in Puerto Rico.

I was given a few days to get settled, and we found a place the next day – an apartment up in the attic of an old Victorian house in nearby Swampscott. Right next door was the lovely coastal village of Marblehead, a port in the grand old days of textiles when captains sailed merchant ships from here as far away as China. Many of those captains had beautiful homes in Swampscott.

The basis of our idea for putting a steakhouse in each Charter House was a very successful operation in the suburb of Boston called Saugus, owned by a man named Frank Giuffrida. Allen suggested I go talk to this guy, whose place was serving an amazing 2,000 or more steaks everyday. I felt a bit like a spy, since I wasn't supposed to say anything about why I wanted to know. I was just a chef, curious about how this steakhouse had so many customers and made so much money. I drove up to Saugus, to the place called the Hilltop Steakhouse. The restaurant actually was on top of a hill, but after that nothing much fit together. It was a huge building with a parking lot just about as big as the one at Logan Airport, and almost every spot had a car in it.

I was just a chef, curious about how this steakhouse had so many customers and made so much money.

I asked for Frank Giuffrida, explaining that I was a chef who had just arrived in the Boston area from Puerto Rico and that I'd heard so many compliments about his place that I just had to learn more. After praising him extravagantly in this way, I finally got to meet this man – and he revealed what he saw as the reasons for his success.

Frank was the son of a Boston Italian immigrant family, and he grew up with a father who wanted him to be a butcher – a typical occupation for Boston Italians at that time. To that end, Frank learned his way thoroughly around cutting beef, pork, chicken and just about anything else he was likely to see in any butcher shop. One day, though, he decided to be an entrepreneur. A previous effort in show business didn't work out for him, so instead he traveled 20 miles or so out Route 1 from Boston, bought a little patch of land at the top of a hill and set about opening a restaurant. Well, it wasn't exactly a restaurant. It was a topless bar. Since this was only the 1960s, which around a conservative town like Saugus still felt a lot like the 1950s, it didn't take the city fathers long to figure out that a topless bar didn't fit their vision of things. They shut Frank down. So he had to figure out something to do with this building.

As Frank told me the story that day, he bought a few short loins of beef and used a bandsaw he'd picked up to make a nice 14-ounce, bone-in steak, and from the tenderloin he cut lovely filet mignons, and from the tenderloin tips he made sautéed beef with peppers and onions. Basically, he had only three dishes on the menu – plus an early version of a Greek salad with feta cheese and black olives, and some wonderful rolls he baked right there. Everybody got a big potato and a half stick of butter, and he sold this whole thing for $3.50. Even in those days, that was a very reasonable price to get such a beautiful steak. Frank started the Hilltop Steakhouse with about 100 seats, and every year he added another 100. By the time I talked to him, he had almost 850 seats.

There were no frills in all of this, of course - no tablecloths, and everything was just stainless steel. No credit cards or checks were accepted, only cash. And there were no reservations. People showed up, got a number, and sometimes the wait could get pretty long, but thousands of people decided every single day that the place was worth the wait. Talking with Frank helped me understand that if you only make a little bit of money on each steak, that's not so good if you only sell one or two. But if you sell 2,000 or even 3,000 steaks in a day, even making a little off each one, you have a lot of money at the end. And that didn't even count the wonderful pies he sold for dessert (a much higher profit item than steaks), hundreds and hundreds of bottles of beer, and upwards of 600 packs of cigarettes every day. In those days, of course, everybody smoked.

It didn't take an economist to show me what I needed to be doing at the Charter House. I may not be the smartest person in this world, but I've always made it a point to be around smart people. If you ask a lot of questions of these very smart people, I always figured that eventually I'd get very smart myself.

The story of the first Charter Steakhouse was a lesson for me in so many ways. My visit with Frank had taught me a lot – perhaps the most important lesson being that copying his approach wouldn't make us any money. After all, Frank Giuffrida was playing with 850 seats – and our restaurants had only 80, which we might use twice in an evening for a total of 160 steaks. I explained all this to the Sonesta corporate people (my first real experience in corporate America), only to be told that it wasn't my job to figure out if it would work – smarter people than I had already decided it would. It was my job to execute their plans, to apply my skills to making it work. So that's what I did. I started cutting up short loins just the way Frank had learned to do, baking potatoes and whipping up fresh rolls, creating great desserts. We had a terrific location right on the highway, and before long our place was packed every single night – just like Hilltop Steakhouse.

You can imagine how I felt when the accountants finally got around to sharpening their pencils and walked in to announce one day that – woops – our steakhouse wasn't making any money. I assured the bosses that I was all set to open steakhouses in Charter House after Charter House all over the Boston area. Funny how not making any money douses the corporate enthusiasm for an otherwise brilliant idea.

One day, though, as always in my life, something else came along. I picked up my wife from where she was working, at the General Glover House, and in the process met her boss – a very energetic man with shining eyes who called me "Son" from the moment we met. Gigi had told him all about me, and probably about my situation at Sonesta as well. "Son," he said, "why don't you come work for me?" I told him thanks but I really wasn't interested, since one of my big goals at the time was to get out of Boston. Still, a week later, he came out to greet me again and asked, "Can I show you the restaurant I'm building in downtown Boston?" I said of course. First, though, we sat down in front of the fireplace at the General Glover House and this man told me his life story.

He came from Albania with his father when he was about 6 years old. The family was very, very poor, living in the old whaling town of New Bedford. His father made something like a living peddling vegetables from a cart, and the young boy helped his father do this every day, pushing the cart through the streets and calling out what they had for sale. To supplement this meager income, as soon as he was old enough, the young man worked other jobs in hotels and restaurants. Basically, he never slept. When this young man's father passed away, he found himself the man of the house as the oldest of six children. It required more than he was making at all this work to keep bread on the family table, so he managed to open his own tiny restaurant in Lynn.

The young man couldn't afford a staff, so he himself greeted each guest who came through the door. He was a wonderful personality, very charismatic and outgoing. He connected very easily with people, made them feel both comfortably at home and mildly honored to be in his presence.

The man's restaurant operated like this: he would greet each group of customers and get them seated; then while chatting with them charmingly, he would take their order - for instance, two lobsters, one scrod and one fried fish. He'd then go back to the kitchen and holler to his chef, "Two lobsters… one scrod… one fried fish!" And then, because he didn't actually have a chef, he'd cook

And it wouldn't take much longer before Anthony's vision revitalized Boston's waterfront with the nation's highest-grossing restaurant.

the food himself very fast, thank the chef loudly for his fine work and rush the plates out to the table. That was the beginning. It didn't take long for Anthony's Hawthorne in Lynn – and its multitasking, visionary owner, Anthony Athanas - to become a huge success. And it wouldn't take much longer before Anthony's vision revitalized Boston's waterfront with the nation's highest-grossing restaurant.

All the time Anthony was speaking in front of that fire, I kept thinking back to my old boss Sherman Billingsley at the Stork Club in New York. Mr. B started as a bootlegger and became a millionaire, and Anthony started peddling vegetables and certainly seemed to be a millionaire by now. I had a lot of faith in the system, since becoming a millionaire was why I came to America in the first place. If those two can do it, I can too.

The next day Anthony took me to the fish pier in Boston and we looked out through the gray drizzle at this enormous building, with him telling me tirelessly "We're going to do this" and "We're going to do that." At one point he looked me straight in the eyes and said, "Are you sure you don't want to work for me?" All I was thinking of was the sunshine in Puerto Rico, Bermuda and South Africa, but strangely, what came out was that I didn't think I was qualified to run the kitchen for a restaurant with 800 seats. Anthony look shocked by my response, and then he seemed to get a little angry. "Look, son, you are underestimating my intelligence." I remember his exact words to this day. He said, "If I didn't believe for one second that you could do this job, I wouldn't ask you. Let me tell you something: Anything you want to do, you can do. But first, you have to want to."

Before the next chapter in my Boston story

could begin, it was time to take my wife Gigi home for a visit with her French-speaking family. This winter journey through the fields and woods and deep snows of New England and Canada was one of our happiest times together. We visited her parents and dozens of her relatives in a tiny farming community of St. Honore, (including a trip into the woods where the family kept a still turning out white lightning.) Believe me, after a few hours of drinking with them, I'm guessing I spoke French fluently. I also learned something fascinating about the family I'd married into. Though most French people I'd met in my life were short, most of Gigi's relatives were very tall. It turned out the family had come to Canada hundreds of years earlier from the exotic French coast of Brittany – and that there they considered themselves descendants of the Vikings. Just like me! It was a strange revelation, a bizarre discovery – but it made my sense of our shared destiny seem all the more real, all the more right. After our time in the lovely countryside, Gigi and I toured the grand old French Canadian cities of Quebec and Montreal.

Back in Boston, I returned to the Charter House to cut some more steaks. But I seriously wasn't in the mood. I was confident, in fact, that in a few more days or weeks we would pack our belongings once again and move from the gray of the Northeast to the sunshine of southern California – to San Diego, in fact, which is about as far south in California as you can go. A whole new life awaited. But like so many other times in my life, things changed from one moment to the next.

I remember that morning so well: eating breakfast, reading the paper, then seeing my wife step out of the bathroom. I realized immediately that she was sick.

"Gigi," I asked, "are you feeling all right?"

"No," she said. "And let me tell you another thing. I think you're going to be a daddy."

I had been afraid of something like this, in fact I had been for some time. My concern had only grown after hearing my Catholic wife explain all about the calendar, about what they called the "rhythm method," and then seeing that every relative of hers in Quebec came from a family of 12, 14 or, in her case, 16 children. It was clear to me in Boston, as it had been among her family in Canada, that this whole calendar family planning thing left a lot to be desired.

My wife was happy when I got home from work that evening. In fact, she had a bottle of champagne waiting for me with two glasses. I, on the other hand, was a tangle of conflicting emotions. I certainly wanted to start a family with Gigi sooner or later; it was what we both looked forward to. But now? On the verge of leaving my job in the Boston area and moving across the entire continent with just my usual certainty that if I poked around long enough something would turn up? It was a risky business, our little escape to the sunshine. And what had seemed a lovely adventure one day earlier now seemed frightening, possibly even stupid. I told Gigi that I thought we should remain in Boston, at least where I had my job cutting steaks and making tenderloin tips over the grill. It wasn't a great job, I knew, but I felt confident that with Sonesta opening hotels elsewhere, including sunnier places like Key Biscayne, Florida, and the French Quarter of New Orleans, surely something better would appear if I – if we – would just be patient. The next morning, after forcing myself to sleep through one big change in my life plan, my life plan changed once again.

My wife was talking on the phone, apparently to someone she knew rather well. And it slowly dawned on me she was talking to her boss at the General Clover House, Anthony Athanas. "Oui, oui," she kept saying. "I will tell him." Gigi said Mr. Athanas wanted me to join him for lunch the next day at Anthony's Pier 4. It was, she said, very important, that I go see him. Anthony's Pier 4 was packed for lunch when I arrived. Mr. Athanas was the host, as always, personable and gracious to everyone. But he sat me down and said something very simply and direct.

"Son," he said, "I want to make you an offer.

We've been open here three months and the place is quite successful. We had a chef here but he didn't work out. He had a temper, you know. I think we need somebody like you."

I was still reluctant, thinking about my work with Sonesta. They paid pretty well, though by no means enough to support a family. But it was a good situation and, I was sure, would

get better. Mr. Athanas clearly saw all these thoughts racing through my mind, and he could see I wasn't doing very well making sense of them all.

"Son," he said, "how much are you making right now?"

I told him.

"So what would you think if I doubled that?"

"Sir," I said calmly, "You just got yourself a chef."

Believe me, I started at Anthony's Pier 4 the very next week, and rather quickly the place became not only the highest volume restaurant in America (serving as many as 3,000 meals per day) but the favored dining haunt in Boston for celebrity after celebrity. It seemed like Edward G. Robinson was in our dining room every time I turned around, along with Bob Hope, Red Skelton, Danny Kaye, Burl Ives. Steve McQueen made a movie there with Fay Dunaway. We also celebrated Shakespeare with Elizabeth Taylor and one of her many husbands, Michael Todd. Of course, anyone with the name

Kennedy came there to eat all the time, as did just about everybody who was anybody in the underworld. Anthony's was one of those magical places – because Anthony himself was one of those magical men – whose appeal was wide and vast and deep. It was a universal gathering place, where opposing lawyers, contending political candidates, even mobsters and the FBI agents trying to put them behind bars, could all nod and smile at each other over their dinners at different tables. It was as though everybody left their grudges at the door when it was time to eat at Anthony Athanas' place.

Looking back after all these years – especially after owning and operating my own restaurant – I can see so clearly that Anthony was a man ahead of his time. Truth is, it wasn't until fairly recently that our business came to be about marketing and public relations. Word of mouth was all we had (or at least all most of us thought of) for the longest time, not press, not radio or TV, not hosting our own cooking show on the Food Network. All the same, it's obvious with 20/20 hindsight that most of the industry's biggest success stories understood marketing and PR before many of us even knew the words. Anthony always knew how to get his name and his picture in the Boston Globe, with one bit of delicious silliness or another. In the beginning, for instance, our lobsters came into the kitchen just like everything else in a typical restaurant – through a very unromantic delivery door in the back. Then Anthony had a better idea. One night, as guests were settling in over their cocktails and appetizers, the lobsters started being delivered, live and squirming, right through the dining room. The message, of course: look how fresh our lobsters are! This little stroke of genius earned Anthony and his restaurant a ton of free advertising, and kept the people of Boston babbling about the place for months.

A much more drawn-out publicity coup was Anthony's search for a cocktail lounge. There was always a wait for a table at the restaurant, so we needed someplace to park these people – preferably someplace where they could be spending money. Anthony had the idea of pulling some kind of boat up to the restaurant and letting that be our cocktail lounge. Well, that sounded simple but turned out to be a project and a half. The boss' first effort was to hire Japanese designers to create and construct the perfect boat, but he lost interest fast after learning how long that would take. "Two years?" he shouted. "I don't have two years! I want that thing here tomorrow!" Then he settled on buying the oldest American schooner still under sail – the Alice S. Wentworth and having it towed into Boston Harbor. One of the first things it did was sink, but that wasn't until after Mr. Athanas had enjoyed publicity in newspapers all over the world. Finally he located a boat, a large paddle wheeler called the Peter Styvesant," and had it refurbished and delivered dockside - only to be told that what he had in mind was forbidden by the Harbor Master. The problem had to do with the rising and falling tides, upwards of 6 feet up or down, more than that in a storm.

Anthony and young chef Joe

As it turned out, what was forbidden for a vessel floating on the tides in Boston Harbor was allowed for one permanently attached to the land at Anthony's restaurant. And that's the way it worked out. More than $2 million after starting this boat conversation, we had our cocktail lounge at last. In fact, in time, the smokestack of the boat was removed to make room for an elevator to deliver food. That way we could take in even more money for private parties.

I have to say, in addition to my admiration for the visionary side of Anthony Athanas, I truly enjoyed working at the restaurant with his four sons – the four young guys who took over Anthony's Pier 4 when their father passed away. It might have been the opposite: Anthony might have worked hard all his life so his sons wouldn't have to, and they'd have played around like so many sons and daughters of successful restaurateurs and let the goose that lays golden eggs die of natural or unnatural causes. Anthony's sons, to his credit, were all raised to be hard workers like their Dad – with no job too lowly or disgusting, and believe me, in a restaurant there's never a shortage of those! I've kept up with sons Anthony, Michael, Robert and Paul through the years – and I especially remember a time when Paul was only 14. I found him in the pantry cutting 400 baked Alaskas and topping them with strawberry sauce. At the end of his 10-hour shift, Paul looked like a strawberry himself. As a result of such hard work, Anthony's Pier 4 remains the destination it was for Bostonians and visitors alike all those years ago when I was the chef.

It was one night shortly after my first Thanksgiving as chef at Anthony's Pier 4 that my wife got up in the middle of the night and I found her fixing her hair in the bathroom.

"Are you going somewhere?" I asked.

"Yes, I am. And so are you. You need to take me to the hospital. I'm going to have a baby."

We went to Salem Hospital, and with her big coat and her hair done and all the makeup, I think Gigi looked more like a model than a pregnant woman. As it turned out, this time we spent only about an hour at the hospital before everyone agreed the baby wasn't quite ready yet. A week later, though, Gigi woke me up again with the assurance that this was it. And it was.

I remember the moment the nurse led me in to take my first look at my daughter, whom we named Monique Chantal. She was this tiny little creature, maybe no more than a half hour old. And I looked at her and I said, "Sweetheart, you and me, we're going to be best friends for the rest of my life. And if you ever climb up a tree and fall down, I'll be there to catch you." That's the way it has been, for the past 40 years.

Boston became much friendlier, especially for me, once springtime had rolled around. We took day trips to beautiful seaside towns like Rockport and Gloucester, and when it was finally warm enough, went to beaches with names like Crane's and Ipswich where the great clams come from. It wasn't long before my second daughter came along – and since our first child was named Monique for the French side of the family, we decided to name our second Erika for the German side. With my work at Anthony's Pier 4 going well and two beautiful daughters, we went ahead and bought our first home, in the suburb of West Peabody.

Life was good for me and my family, but what had started out to be only six months ended up lasting more than seven years. Even with all the fine things in our life, I knew that each year when fall came around I would get depressed. I knew it would happen, as surely as the movement on a Swiss clock. And some falls my wife responded to the coming of cold, miserable weather even worse than I did. One day the phone rang and I recognized the voice immediately. It was my longtime boss from Sonesta days, Allen Hubsch.

"Well, my friend," he said, "how's Boston?"

"Well, my friend, it's cold."

Allen told me about all the things he'd been doing since I'd last seen him, first at the Sonesta resort down in Key Biscayne and then with a hotel in Disneyland in Anaheim, California. It felt so good to catch up with him, to swap war stories about people we had known and worked with over the years. Allen and I had always worked well together, and he wondered if I'd be the least bit interested in hearing about a project he was starting.

As I listened to him speak for the next few minutes, I got excited. And yes, in a sense, my life really did flash before my eyes. You see, I'd always wanted to be part of something big, something like Dorado Beach in Puerto Rico, something like Anthony's Pier 4 on the harbor in Boston. I'd always thought the places I'd worked and the things I'd done in my career were big; but the place and thing Allen was telling me about made everything else seem miniscule.

"I'll send you a plane ticket," he said finally. "And I'll pick you up at the airport in Orlando."

Anthony's
Baked Finnan Haddie
Yield: serves 4

3 pounds smoked haddock
(possibly with bone in)
2 cups whole milk
1/2 stick melted butter (4 ounces)
1/2 teaspoon white pepper
1/4 cup freshly chopped chives
2 large russet potatoes, peeled
and sliced thin

Set the oven to 400°F. Cut the haddock into four individual servings. Place skin down in a shallow buttered baking dish, arrange the potatoes around the fish and add enough milk to partially cover the fish and potatoes. Sprinkle with pepper and butter, cover the baking dish, and bake in the oven for 15 minutes, remove the cover and bake for another 10 minutes basting the fish with the liquid. Place on a serving platter, remove the bones, baste again with the hot milk, sprinkle with chopped chives and serve with green vegetables.

Anthony's
Fish Chowder
Yield: 12 servings

2 pounds cod or pollock,
cut into large pieces
2 cups clam juice or fish stock
2 teaspoons celery salt
1 teaspoon white pepper
4 teaspoons Worcestershire sauce
4 drops Tabasco sauce
4 bay leaves
1 cup diced celery
1 cup diced potatoes
1 cup diced onions
1/4 cup melted butter
1/4 cup finely ground salt pork
1 tablespoon flour
1 quart half and half cream

Heat the butter and salt pork in a heavy-duty casserole, add the onions, celery and potatoes, sauté for a few minutes. Dust with flour and cover with the fish stock and cream, bring to a boil. Add the cod, white pepper, celery salt, Worcestershire sauce, and Tabasco. Simmer for 25 minutes, and serve with a loaf of bread and plenty of oyster crackers.

New England Oyster Stew

Yield: serves 4

4 dozen fresh oysters, shucked,
  with their liquid reserved
  (or 2 pints shucked oyster)
2 tablespoons butter
1 medium Spanish onion,
  finely chopped
1/4 teaspoon salt
2 cups milk
2 cups heavy cream
2 tablespoons fresh chopped parsley
1/8 teaspoon black pepper or taste
2 drops Tabasco sauce
2 cups oyster crackers

Melt the butter in a sauté pan, add the onions and cook the onions over low heat for about 10 minutes until soft but not brown. Add the oyster and their liquid, heat to a simmer until the oysters begin to curl, do not overcook. With a slotted spoon remove the oysters from the liquid and transfer into a bowl. Add the milk, cream, salt, and black pepper to the oyster liquid, bring to a boil, reduce the heat and simmer for 5 minutes.

Return the oysters to the pan, bring to a boil, just to heat the stew, and ladle into 4 individual bowls. Sprinkle the fresh chopped parsley on top, and serve with oyster crackers.

Winter Beef and Vegetable Soup

Yield: makes 2 1/2 quart

4 pounds beef shin bones
10 cups water
1/2 cup diced onions
1/2 cup diced celery
1/2 cup diced carrots
1/2 cup diced green peppers
1 cup, seeded and
  diced ripe tomatoes
3 cloves garlic, crushed
1/2 head green cabbage,
  cut into small pieces
2 teaspoons salt
2 bay leaves
1/4 teaspoon dried thyme
1/4 cup vegetable oil
1 tablespoon tomato paste
2 tablespoons flour

In a large stockpot bring the water and beef bones to a boil, skim the foam and simmer for two hours (or until the meat falls from the bone). Remove the meat from the bone, cut into small cubes, set aside.

Heat the oil in a casserole, add the vegetables and garlic. Sauté for a few minutes, but do not brown. Add the tomato paste, thyme, salt, bay leaves and dust with flour, combine well. Pour the beef stock over the vegetables and simmer for 40 minutes, add the diced beef and tomatoes. Bring to a boil, season to your liking and serve with crusty brown bread

Butternut Squash and Apple Bisque
Yield: serves 6

1 butternut squash, about 1 1/2 pounds
    (peeled, cut in half, seeded,
    and cut into chunks)
2 tart apples, peeled, cored and chopped
1 medium size onion chopped
1 quart chicken stock (fresh or canned)
3 slices white bread, trimmed and cubed
3 egg yolks
1/2 cup heavy cream
1 tablespoon sugar
1 tablespoon chopped parsley
Pinch of rosemary, nutmeg and marjoram
Salt and pepper to taste

Combine the squash, chopped apples, onions, herbs, bread cubes, and chicken stock in a large stockpot or saucepan and bring to a boil. Simmer for 45 minutes, or until the vegetables are soft. With a slotted spoon remove the vegetables, and puree in a blender. Return the vegetables to the stock and bring to a boil.

In a small bowl, beat the egg yolks and cream together. Beat in a little of the hot soup, then stir back into the pot. Heat but do not boil, add the sugar, salt and pepper to your liking, and serve in hot bowls. Sprinkle a little freshly chopped parsley on top.

Baked Stuffed Lobster a la Hawthorne
Yield: 2

2 fresh whole lobsters
    1 1/4 pounds each
4 ounces lobster meat
    or fresh crabmeat
2 cups course breadcrumbs
1/2 cup melted butter

Place the live lobsters on its back on a cutting board, and split the lobster down in the middle. Remove the claws and discard the membranes and vein from the tail. Preheat the oven to 450°F. Remove the green liver and coral roe. Combine the breadcrumbs and butter, and place half of the mixture in the body cavity, add half of the lobster meat, and cover with the rest of the breadcrumbs.

Place the lobsters and claws on a baking sheet, add 1/2 cup of water into the pan and bake the lobster for 20 to 25 minutes until the stuffing is golden brown and the lobsters a bright red. Use a cleaver or heavy-duty knife to spit the claws. Serve with additional melted butter.

Baked Lobster Savannah

Yield: serves 4 to 8

2 New England lobsters (3 pounds each)
2 tablespoons salt to boil the lobster
1/2 cup clarified butter
5 shallots, chopped very fine
1 glove garlic, minced
2 teaspoons freshly chopped parsley
1 cup sliced fresh mushrooms
1/2 cup pimentos
1/4 cup thinly sliced green bell peppers
1/2 cup breadcrumbs
1/4 cup brandy
1/2 teaspoon French Dijon mustard
2 teaspoons Worcestershire sauce
2 drops Tabasco sauce
1/8 teaspoon white pepper

Bechamel Sauce:
1/2 cup butter
1/2 cup flour
1 cup hot lobster stock
2 cups hot light cream

In a large stockpot bring the water to a boil, add the salt, and boil the lobster for about 10 minutes. With a sharp knife cut off 1/3 from the top of the back, remove the meat from the shell and claws. Cut the tail in half and remove string like intestine, cut the lobster meat into large chunks. Wash the shell and retain. In a saucepan heat the butter, add onions and garlic, and sauté until onions are cooked, but not brown. Add the lobster meat, mushrooms, pimentos, green bell peppers and simmer for a few minutes, add the brandy and flambé. Remove from the fire, add the béchamel sauce, mustard, Worcestershire sauce, Tabasco sauce, chopped parsley, a dash of white pepper, fill the shells with the mixture, sprinkle with breadcrumbs and place under the broiler for a few minutes to brown.

In a saucepan, melt the butter, add the flour and make a roux. Whisk together and cook over low heat (do not let the mixture get brown). Let it get cool for a few minutes, then gradually add the hot lobster stock, whisk vigorously to prevent lumps. Add the hot cream, whisk continuously, and simmer for 15 minutes. The sauce should have a thick consistency.

Pan Roasted Block Island Swordfish "Alice"
Yield: serves 4

4 swordfish steaks, (6 to 8 ounces each)
1/2 stick butter
1/2 teaspoon salt
1/8 teaspoon black pepper
1/4 cup cake flour
1/2 cup almonds, blanched and
    chopped very fine
1 tablespoon each of the following, chopped:
    basil, garlic, rosemary, thyme,
    and cilantro

Sauce:
1/4 cup Worcestershire sauce
1/4 cup honey
1/4 cup beef stock
1/4 cup cold water
1 tablespoon cornstarch

To make the sauce, dissolve the cornstarch in the cold water. Place the remaining ingredients in a sauce pot and bring to a slow boil. Remove from the stove, and whisk in the cornstarch, return to the stove and simmer over low heat until the sauce thickens.

Place the chopped almond, flour, and all the herbs, plus salt and pepper in a mixing bowl and mix well thoroughly. Press both sides of the steaks into the herb mixture. Heat the butter in a sauté pan. Sauté the herbed steaks on one side until golden brown, turn the steaks with a spatula, and repeat. Cook to desired doneness. Do not overcook. Place the steaks on mashed potatoes, ladle the sauce over it and serve with seasonal vegetables.

Broiled Boston Scrod
Yield: serves 4

2 pounds scrod
    (fresh small cod fillets,
    skin on)
1/2 cup melted butter
1/2 cup bread crumbs
2 tablespoons lemon juice
1/2 teaspoon celery salt
White pepper to taste

Wash the fish under running cold water, and pat dry with a paper towel. Season lightly with salt and pepper, and then sprinkle generously with melted butter. Dip in fresh bread crumbs, place skin down on a baking pan, sprinkle again with a little more melted butter, and broil for 15-20 minutes (depending on the thickness of the fish fillets) until the fish has a light brown crust. Serve with extra melted butter with lemon juice stirred in, plus new boiled potatoes with fresh dill and seasonal vegetables.

Baked Salmon Fillet
with Egg Sauce

Yield: serves 6

A New England specialty on the Fourth of July

6 fillets of fresh salmon, 6 to 8 ounces each
1/4 cup melted butter
1/2 cup chopped shallots
1 cup dry white wine
1 cup milk
Salt and white pepper to taste

Egg sauce:
1/4 cup butter
1/2 cup flour
1 cup milk
1/2 cup heavy cream
1/2 teaspoon salt
1/8 teaspoon white pepper
1 bay leaf
6 hard cooked eggs
2 drops of Tabasco sauce
Fresh dill sprigs for garnish

Set the oven to 375°F. Generously butter a fireproof baking dish. Sprinkle the shallots on the bottom and place the salmon fillets on top. Pour the white wine and milk over it and season with salt and pepper to your liking. Close the baking dish tightly with aluminum foil, and bake in the oven for 25 minutes. Drain, and reserve the fish stock, keep the fish warm.

In a heavy-duty 2 quart saucepan heat the butter over moderate heat. Stir in the flour and mix together with a wire whisk. In a separate pot combine the fish stock, milk, cream, and bring to a boil. Stir the liquid in to the roux stirring constantly with a whisk. Add the bay leaf, salt, Tabasco sauce, and white pepper. Cook over high heat until the sauce boils and thickens. Reduce the heat to low, and simmer for 20 minutes, stirring from time to time.

Remove the bay leaf. Remove the saucepan from the stove, and gently stir in the hard-boiled eggs. Place the salmon fillets on a hot serving platter, ladle the sauce over it, garnish with dill sprigs, and serve with new boiled potatoes.

Rockport
Baked Seafood Casserole
Yield: serves 6

1/2 pound small bay scallops
1/2 pound raw shrimp
2 tablespoons butter
1/2 medium size onion, chopped
1 stalk leeks (white part only, cut in half, washed and sliced)
1/4 cup dry sherry
1/4 cup clam juice
1/4 cup dry white wine
1/2 cup heavy cream
1 teaspoon salt
Pinch white pepper, and two drops Tabasco sauce
Juice of 1/2 lemon
1 teaspoon Spanish paprika
1 teaspoon English mustard
1 teaspoon salt
1 pound crabmeat
2 teaspoons cornstarch dissolved in about 2 tablespoons cold water.
3 egg yolks
5 tablespoons mayonnaise
1/2 cup grated Parmesan cheese

Peel, devein, and wash shrimp and scallops under running cold water. Melt the butter in a frying pan, add the onions, scallions, shrimp and scallops and sauté over medium heat for a few minutes. Add the paprika, English mustard and combine well. Add the white wine, sherry, clam juice, crabmeat, and heat. Remove the scallops, shrimps, and crab-meat with a slotted spoon to a shallow ovenproof dish. Retain the juices over medium heat and bind with the dissolved cornstarch. Remove from the heat. In a bowl beat the egg yolks, stir in the cream and mayonnaise and fold into the warm sauce. Season the sauce to your liking and pour over the seafood, sprinkle with Parmesan cheese. Bake at 400°F for about 10 minutes until golden brown.

Yankee Chicken Pot Pie

Yield: serves 6

2 whole chicken, 2-3 pounds each
1 large carrot, peeled and cut into large pieces
1 onion, peeled and cut into large pieces
2.bay leaves
3 teaspoon salt

Place the chicken, vegetables, salt and bay leaves into a large stockpot, cover with cold water and bring to a boil. Skim off the foam and simmer for one hour. Remove the chicken from the broth and place in cold water to chill. Separate the meat from the bones, set the meat aside and the return the bones to the stockpot. Over low heat simmer the stock for 30 minutes to reduce the liquid to half.

To make the sauce:

1/2 stick butter
5 tablespoons flour
1/2 cup heavy cream
5 cups chicken stock
1 cup mushrooms, sliced
Salt and pepper to taste
1 package (10 ounces) frozen peas
   and carrot mix.

Melt the butter in a heavy-duty casserole, add the flour and cook for two minutes over low heat, stirring constantly. Gradually whisk in the hot chicken stock in a steady stream, whisking constantly to prevent lumps from forming. Simmer over low heat until the sauce has a thick creamy consistency, then add the heavy cream, and bring to a boil again. Cut the chicken into large chunks, and place into a buttered 8 X 12 inch baking dish, top with the mushrooms and vegetables. Strain the sauce over the chicken, vegetable- mixture and cover with pastry.

To make the pastry:

2 1/2 cups all-purpose flour
1/4 teaspoon baking powder
1/2 teaspoon salt
1/2 stick butter, cut into large pieces
1 (3 ounce) package cream cheese,
   cut into pieces
3 eggs
1/4 cup ice water.
4 tablespoons whole milk or cream
   for brushing

Sift the flour, baking powder and salt into a mixing bowl, add the eggs, butter, cream cheese and knead with your hands to make a firm dough, add ice water as needed. Wrap with plastic wrap and refrigerate for one hour. On a lightly floured counter, roll the dough slightly larger then the dish. Lift the dough onto the rolling pin and ease it onto the chicken and vegetables.

With a fork press the edges of the pastry into the rim all around the dish, and brush the dough with milk or cream. Prick the dough in a few places to let the steam escape during the baking process. Preheat oven to 375°F. and bake the chicken pot pie for 45-60 minutes until the pastry is golden brown and the filling is bubbling, Spoon with crust onto hot plates.

New England Boiled Dinner
with Horseradish Sauce
Yield: serves 8-10

1 brisket of beef, 5-6 pounds
6 new potatoes, peeled and cut into quarters
6 medium size carrots, peeled and cut into large slices
5 turnips, peeled and cut coarsely
3 rutabagas, peeled and cut coarsely
2 medium size onions cut into quarters
1 large head cabbage cut into wedges
3 teaspoons salt
4 bay leaves

Horseradish Sauce:
1/2 stick butter
2 tablespoons flour
2 cups beef stock
1 cup light cream
4 tablespoons horseradish
Salt and white pepper to taste

Place the brisket in a large stockpot, cover with water, add the salt, bay leaves, and bring to a boil. Skim off the foam, and simmer approximately for 3 hours. Add the potatoes, carrots, turnips, onions, and rutabagas during the last hour. Add the cabbage during the last 20 minutes.

To make the sauce, melt the butter in a small pot, add the flour and make a roux. Slowly whisk in the beef stock, and then add the cream. Bring to a boil stirring constantly; add the horseradish, salt and pepper. Remove the brisket from the pot and slice the beef across the grain. Place the cabbage wedges on a serving platter, place the sliced brisket over the cabbage and arrange the rest of the vegetables around the meat. Serve the sauce on the side.

Boston Baked Beans
Yield: serves 6

1 cups navy beans
1/2 cup sugar
1/2 cup dark molasses
1/2 pound salt pork, sliced
1 teaspoon dry mustard
1 teaspoon white pepper
1 teaspoon salt

Soak the beans over night in cold water. Drain. Place the beans in a heavy duty stock pot, fill with water half inch above the beans, and boil for 30 minutes or until the beans are tender, but not overcooked. Drain and rinse, saving the stock. Preheat the oven to 375°F. Place half the salt pork in the bottom of a large ovenproof dish. In a mixing bowl combine the stock, beans, mustard, white pepper, salt, molasses and sugar. Pour the mixture into the baking dish, top with the remaining salt pork. Cover the dish with a lid or foil and bake for two hours, remove the cover and bake for another hour until most of the moisture has evaporated and the top is nice and brown. Served as a side dish on Saturday for lunch or dinner.

Boston Brown Bread
Yield: Makes one loaf

1/3 cup yellow corn meal
1/3 cup rye flour
1/3 cup all purpose flour
1/3 cup dry breadcrumbs
1 teaspoon baking powder
1/2 teaspoon salt
1 cup buttermilk
1/2 cup dark molasses
1/3 cup dark raisins

In a medium size bowl whisk together the cornmeal, flours, breadcrumbs, baking soda, and salt. Stir in the buttermilk and molasses, and mix with a wooden spoon, add the raisins. (do not overmix) Coat a 1 1/2 quart, metal steaming or any other tin with vegetable oil cooking spray. Pour the batter into the tin, and cover tightly with the lid or foil. Using a deep stock pot with a rack, (or lay a canning jar ring on the bottom) place the mold on the rack, add enough water to reach two thirds up the sides of the mold, and cover the pot.

Bring the water to a simmer and steam the bread for 2 1/2 hours on low heat. Check the pot from time to time to make sure the water is not boiling away. Remove the mold from the water and let sit for 25 minutes; turn the bread out onto a wire rack and let cool. To serve, cut in slices and serve with soft cream cheese.

Parker House Rolls

Yield: 3 dozen

6 cups flour
1/4 cup lukewarm water
1 package dry yeast
1/2 cup sugar
2 cups lukewarm milk
1 egg, lightly beaten
1/2 stick butter
1/4 cup melted butter for brushing
1 teaspoon salt

Pour the warm water in a small bowl and sprinkle the yeast and 1 teaspoon sugar, plus one-teaspoon flour over it. Whisk together and let the yeast mixture rest in a warm place for 10 minutes, until the yeast bubbles up. Place the flour on a working surface, and make a well in the center. Pour the yeast mixture into the well; add the egg, salt, soft butter and milk. With your hands knead the dough for 20 minutes until the dough is smooth, shiny and elastic.

With a pastry brush, spread 2 tablespoons melted butter evenly over the inside of a large bowl (this prevents the dough from sticking to the bowl). Cover the bowl with a kitchen towel and let the dough raise double in volume, in a warm and draft free place. Return the dough to the flour dusted work surface, punch it down and roll it out to 1/4 inch thick. With a cookie cutter or the rim of a glass, cut the dough into 3 inch rounds. Gather the scraps into a ball, and roll the dough out again, and cut rounds. Place the rolls on a buttered baking pan, brush with butter, let rise again for 15 minutes and bake in a pre-heated oven at 375°F for 12 to 15 minutes until light brown.

New England Corn Bread

Yield: make 15 servings

1 cup yellow corn meal
1/4 cup sugar
2 cups cake flour
1/2 cup milk powder
1 1/2 cups milk
1/4 cup vegetable oil
2 whole eggs, beaten
3 teaspoons baking powder
2 tablespoons soft butter
    (to butter the baking pan)

Preheat the oven to 400°F. In a bowl mix the sugar and beaten eggs. In a separate bowl sift the flour, milk powder, baking powder and salt. Add the flour mixture to the egg mixture. Add the cornmeal, vegetable oil, and milk. Beat just enough to mix. Generously butter an 8x12-inch baking pan, pour the mixture into the pan and bake for 30 minutes until golden brown. Cut into squares and serve.

This recipe is from the late John Cases at Hugo's Lighthouse in Cohasset.

Boston Cream Pie

Yield: makes one 9 inch pie

Cake:

1 1/2 sticks unsalted, soft butter
1 1/4 cups sugar
1 teaspoon vanilla
2 large eggs
1 1/2 tablespoons corn syrup
2 1/2 teaspoons baking powder
1/2 teaspoon salt
1/4 cup milk

Custard:

3 tablespoons cornstarch
1/4 cup sugar
1 cup milk
3 large eggs
1/2 cup heavy cream
1/4 teaspoon salt
1 teaspoon vanilla extract
3 tablespoons sugar

Glaze:

6 ounces bittersweet chocolate
3 tablespoons water
2 tablespoons unsalted butter
1 1/2 tablespoons corn syrup
1/4 teaspoon salt

Preheat the oven to 350 °F. Butter generously a 9 1/2 inch springform cake pan. In a medium size mixing bowl cream together the butter, sugar and vanilla until light and fluffy, beat in the eggs one at a time, beating well after each addition. In a separate bowl sift together the flour, salt, baking powder, and beat into the butter-eggs mixture in batches alternately with the milk, beginning and ending with the flour. Pour the batter into the springform pan and bake in the middle of the oven for 45 to 55 minutes or until a tester (or toothpick) comes out clean. Let the cake cool in the pan on a cake rack.

To make the custard:

Bring the milk to a boil. In a mixing bowl whisk together the cornstarch, vanilla, sugar, eggs and cream. Whisking vigorously pour the boiling milk into the eggs and cream mixture. Return to the pot and heat over moderate heat, but do not boil. Remove the pot from the heat, and whisk in the butter. Let the custard cool completely, stirring occasionally.

To make the glaze:

In a double boiler melt the chocolate with the water, butter, corn syrup, and salt, stirring until the glaze is smooth. Remove from the heat, and set aside. Cut the cooled cake in half horizontally and place the bottom half on a serving platter. Top the bottom half evenly with the custard, spreading it to the edge. Place the remaining cake half on top of the custard, and pour the chocolate glaze on top, spread it to the edge and let it drip down the side. Cut into 8 wedges, garnish with a fresh strawberry and a sprig of fresh mint.

New England Apple Pie
Yield: 12 servings

5 large, firm, tart apples (about 3 1/2 pounds)
1 tablespoon fresh squeezed lemon juice
1 1/2 tablespoons flour
1/2 cup sugar
1/4 teaspoon ground cinnamon
1/8 teaspoon ground cloves
1/2 stick butter, cut into 8 pieces
1/4 cup milk, and one egg for egg-wash
1 pie crust (see recipe below)

Preheat the oven to 375°. Divide the pie dough in half; keep half refrigerated. On a lightly floured surface, roll the dough into a 12 inch circle. Fold the dough in half and place it over a 9 inch pie pan. Unfold the dough to cover the pie dish completely. Lift the edges of the dough, and fit into the pan, gently press against the bottom and sides without stretching. Refrigerate until needed.

Peel, core and cut each apple in half. Cut them into wedges and put them into a bowl. Add the lemon juice, flour, sugar, cinnamon, and cloves. Toss gently and spoon the apple mixture into the refrigerated pie shell. Dot the butter pieces over the apples, and set aside. On a lightly floured surface, roll out the remaining pastry dough into a 12 inch circle. Whisk the egg and milk together; use part of it to brush the exposed rim.

Fold the second circle dough in half, and place on top of the pie to cover the apples completely.

Press the dough around the rim together, and cut the excess overlapping dough. Brush the top with egg-milk wash, and crimp decoratively. Place the pie into the center of the preheated oven and bake for 1 hour, until the apples are bubbling in their juice, and the top crust is golden brown. Let cool and serve with whipped cream or vanilla ice cream.

Pie Crust:

2 cups all-purpose flour
1/2 pound vegetable shortening
1 tablespoon cider vinegar
1/4 teaspoon salt
2 tablespoons sugar

Sift the flour into a mixing bowl, and place in the freezer for 1 hour. In a small bowl dissolve the salt and vinegar in 6 tablespoon ice water, set aside. Remove the flour from the freezer and pile onto a working surface. Make a well in the center and put the shortening in it. With your hands, mix the shortening into the flour intil it becomes a granulated texture. Add the sugar, then make another well in this mixture. Add ice water and vinegar and mix in with your fingers only until the water is absorbed. Do not overmix. Form the dough into a ball, flatten out slightly with a rolling pin, wrap in plastic wrap and refrigerate for 1 hour.

Apple Brown Betty

Yield: serves 6 to 8

6 cups peeled, cored
　　and sliced apples
1/2 cup raisins
1/2 cup regular sugar
2 teaspoons cornstarch
1/2 cup melted butter
2 1/2 cups bread crumbs
1/2 cup light brown sugar
1 teaspoon lemon juice
1 teaspoon cinnamon
1/4 teaspoon ground cloves

Preheat the oven to 350°F. In a mixing bowl combine the apples, raisins, cornstarch, lemon juice, white sugar, cinnamon, and cloves. In another bowl mix the breadcrumbs, brown sugar and melted butter. Generously butter a 2 quart baking dish. Sprinkle a few bread crumbs on the bottom and place the apples on top, cover evenly with the rest of the crumbs and bake in the middle in the oven for one hour, or until nice and brown. Scoop into individual bowls and serve hot with vanilla ice cream.

Baked Indian Pudding

Yield: serves 6

2 cups milk
1/2 cup yellow corn meal
1/4 cup dark molasses
1/4 teaspoon cinnamon
3 eggs
2 tablespoons sugar
2 tablespoons butter
1/4 teaspoon salt
1/2 teaspoon
　　baking powder

Set the oven to 325°F. Bring the milk, sugar, molasses, cinnamon, salt and butter to a boil. Whisking constantly, add the cornmeal to the boiling milk. Simmer for 15 minutes. Crack the eggs into a mixing bowl and beat, then whisk the cornmeal mixture into the eggs. Pour the mixture into a well-buttered stone crock and bake for 1 1/2 hour, or until set and golden brown on the top. Serve warm with whipped cream or ice cream.

Strawberry Shortcake

Yield: makes 6 cakes

2 cups flour
3 tablespoons baking powder
1/2 teaspoon salt
2 tablespoons plus 1 cup sugar
1/2 cup vegetable shortening
3/4 cup milk
2 quarts ripe strawberries,
　　sliced
1 cup whipping cream,
　　whipped with
　　2 tablespoons sugar

To make the shortcakes, preheat the oven to 400°F. In a mixing bowl sift together the flour, salt, 2 tablespoons sugar and baking powder. With your hands knead in the shorting and milk until there is smooth soft dough. Place on a floured board and form 6 individual balls, place on a cookie sheet, push each ball down to form a little cake and bake for 15 minutes until light brown. Add the remaining cup sugar to the sliced strawberries and let soak for 20 minutes. When the biscuits are done, remove from the oven cut in half, spread the first half with the strawberries, top with the second layer, and top generously with the whipped cream.

Disney's Contemporary Hotel

THE MAGIC OF DISNEY

A Thousand Recipes to Feed Millions

During the Christmas season of 1970, we were very, very busy at Anthony's Pier 4. We were serving about 600 lobsters a night, 200 pounds of shrimp and tons of fish. Our fish came in by the hundreds of pounds, and that was whole fish, which we then had to cut into serving sizes for our guests. It's freshest that way, of course. And even though we were world famous as a seafood restaurant on the water in a seafood-loving town, we also served 20-25 prime ribs every night. Whole prime ribs, I mean, not just orders. It was a big undertaking, and Gigi and I, and our two daughters were happy enough in Boston with our house in the suburb of Peabody. But somehow I always felt something was missing.

There were second thoughts, as I got ready to head down to Florida to meet my old boss and learn all about his new project, the Contemporary Resort Hotel at the not-yet-built Walt Disney World. Part of me hated to even think about leaving Anthony Athanas. It was a good job, and I was making good money and getting a lot of encouragement every day from Anthony and his four sons. But it was still Boston, it was still cold a great deal of the time, and there were so many days when the snow meant not knowing exactly how I'd get in to work. Allen Hubsch knew this about me, he knew of my love for sunshine and warm climates, and I guess he figured out that if he could show me the right challenge and package it with the right weather, I would probably become his executive chef. That's what he wanted, of course – that's what any general manager would want, a familiar and capable commodity to lift the burdens of food and beverage off his already too-busy shoulders. I was being courted for the Disney World job, and over the long weekend of my visit to the farming community called Orlando, I didn't mind being courted one bit.

The Eastern Airlines jet had little more than an airstrip to set down on in those days, surrounded by miles and miles of orange groves. "Welcome to the Sunshine State," Allen said as he met me coming off the plane. Between the bright blue of the sky and the bright green of the land, my old friend had me

practically ready to sign a contract already.

Allen and I agreed to have dinner together that evening and tour whatever there was to see of the property the following day. Honestly, I wasn't sure what Allen would tell me about Disney – and I'd already told him I knew almost nothing about the company. I'd never been to California to see the original Disneyland, so whatever would be the same at Disney World would still be new to me. When it came to Disney, I'd seen a couple of movies. That was it.

"This whole area," Allen said, gazing out the window after we'd had a bite, "this whole landscape of central Florida is going to be changed within a very few years."

Walt Disney himself, I was told, has chosen the very center of Florida for his second U.S. theme park, inspired not only by the beauty of the land but by the coming together of one north-south turnpike with an east-west interstate highway. Access was key, he understood. But he'd also learned quite a few hard lessons from his experiences around Anaheim in Orange County, Calif., where at times it seemed he had built an entire tourist industry with his theme park so all the surrounding hotels and restaurants could make most of the money. This time, things would be different, he vowed. A process began involving high levels of secrecy, dummy corporations with addresses far from the Sunshine State, and real estate shenanigans galore – all aimed at acquiring farmland at farmland prices, without anyone realizing this would soon become some of the most valuable property in America. Disney bought piece by piece by piece, this orange grove or that grapefruit orchard followed by this small cattle ranch. Before long, they'd pulled together an enormous piece of land – at an average price of $182 per acre.

As Allen explained to me, by the time the Mouse was out of the bag, the land was already purchased and it was time to start building. And that's exactly what was going on when I got my tour the next morning. Allen showed me models and maps to get a sense of the various "lands" that would make up Walt Disney World – you know, Fantasyland, Adventureland, Tomorrowland and the rest – along with the hotels and golf courses and lakes that would turn central Florida into one big resort. The more I saw of this future, the more excited I got to come to work here.

To that end, Allen took me not to some luxury resort but to a trailer park, which was the scene of all the offices at that early stage. I made my way through the three trailers marked FOOD & BEVERAGE, then let Allen lead me through a series of meetings with the bosses of the resort – all of which left me with the confidence that I had the job. Finally, he directed my gaze to a piece of land right on a lake with a really strange building taking shape, very long and skinny.

"And what," Allen asked me, "do you think that's going to be?"

"I think it's going to be a garage for a blimp."

"No," he said. "That's going to be your hotel. The Contemporary Resort Hotel."

I was smiling, but I was also a little over-whelmed. It was such a huge place.

My career intuitions proved correct. I was over at a neighbor's house back in snowy Peabody when the long-distance call came through a couple days after my return from sunny Florida. My daughter came running over to get me, in those long-ago days when you went to the phone rather than the phone coming to you. It was one of the big bosses at Disney World, Tom Eastman, telling me they'd decided to give me the job. Still, if that phone conversation was happy, the one I had in person with Anthony Athanas was as bittersweet as can be.

"I have some bad news," I told the man who had singlehandedly turned Boston Harbor into a dining destination. "I have to resign. I'm moving to Florida for Disney World."

"Well, my son," he said. "I've known you for a long time and there's nothing I can do to stop you. Your mind is made up. The only thing I can do is offer that my best wishes go with you."

Actually, being Anthony Athanas, he went the extra mile even in saying goodbye. He was generous enough to offer to buy our house if it didn't sell quickly and, when I left, he handed me a big envelope full of traveling money. He was that generous a man, and we were friends for many, many years after I stopped working at Anthony's Pier 4. We kept in touch, warmly, until the day he died in 2004 at the age of 92.

A whole new world was opening for me, a new job and a new life. I bought a new car, a Grand Prix with air conditioning, so we could drive south from Boston and arrive in style. Right after we crossed beneath the huge arch proclaiming "Welcome to the Sunshine State," I pulled to the side of the road. You see, I still had my ski pants, ski jacket and ski boots on.

"What are you doing?" my wife asked as I practically undressed then and there.

"I'm taking these things off," I said. "And I hope I never have to put them on again."

As though to stack my life's deck as much as possible, I tossed those dark, cold-weather clothes into the bushes. We crawled back into our Grand Prix and headed south for the sun.

The Disney people were very well organized. They had real estate people call us. And since just about nothing was built yet, we looked at sheets of paper to choose where we would live and other sheets of paper to choose the style of our house. We chose a subdivision called Pine Hills – even though when the real estate agent took us on a tour, there was nothing there but orange groves. Still, just like everything else about the Disney World project, within 90 days the place had been changed completely. They cut down the orange trees, planted the pine trees, built the houses along with all the water and electricity and everything else people would need to live, and Pine Hills was a reality. My daughters started at their new school – and I went to work. I had my own office in one of the trailers, with my own desk. I had my name on the door and my own business cards with a golden Mickey Mouse on them. I was very impressed.

Allen showed me the blueprints for the Contemporary Resort Hotel and it had eight kitchens. What's more, it was a convention hotel. I didn't let on, but I actually knew nothing about being a chef in a convention hotel. I told myself that if I could handle the volume at Anthony's Pier 4, I could probably handle anything. Still, working with a corporation this huge was a new thing for me – a lot more manuals to write and organizational struc-

tures to create. I had done all the parts of this job before, hiring and firing employees, writing new menus, managing costs of everything from napkins to potatoes – but I'd never had to do it in such an official way. I was glad they were promising me my own secretary. I'd never had one of those, but it was beginning to look like I was going to need one.

I wasn't a chef anymore. I was a manager. I was on the same level as the person who was building the monorail or Space Mountain. Every Thursday we all gathered in a parking lot on the Disney property and took a bus to what would soon be the Hall of Presidents. Of course, there were no presidents there yet – just us – and the place wasn't the least bit finished. But we had a meeting there, and one or two managers got up to make a presentation about how their area of the operation was going to work. It was fascinating for me to listen to all these people, whether it was about getting electricity to all the pieces of the park or getting the tons of garbage gathered and carted off at the end of each day or to make beautiful costumes for 28,000 new employees. So finally, it was my turn to stand up and tell everyone how I was going to serve food and drink to 6,000 or 8,000 people every day.

For me, it was very difficult. I'd never stood up in front of 200 intelligent people before, speaking into a microphone and using a flip chart to show them how I was going to do it. I was still very shy, but I realized that here were all these smart people listening to what I had to say. That gave me a lot of confidence.

One day as all this was progressing, Allen came to me and asked if I'd ever been to California. When I admitted I hadn't, he said I was about to go there for two weeks, to a Disney seminar about how all things were supposed to work within this company. I remember one of the things he said: "We're going to put some pixie dust on you, there's a fairy godmother waiting to help you!" I protested that with all the work I had ahead of me, there was no way I could run off to Anaheim for two weeks. But he seemed to lose some of his joking. "Listen, my friend, every single manager of every single department goes to California. There is a Disney way to do all things, and every manager has to learn it."

There were 12 of us flying out. We all had first-class tickets from Orlando to Los Angeles, and when

129

we got to the airport in LA, there was a brand-new Ford Mustang awaiting each two of us. Every person had his own condominium. We knew we were going to have some fun, and we were going to learn a whole lot.

It didn't take me long to figure out some things about the Disney organization. All these years later, I have to say these were some of the most important business lessons I ever learned. As a European trained chef, I came from  a different world. You are encouraged when you're becoming a traditional chef to build the whole world around yourself – around your ideas, your talent, your control of everything and everybody. As a chef, as we say in America, it's all about you. At Disney, it is never about you. It's about the team. From the very beginning in this wonderful organization, they work on you to stop saying "I" and stop saying "me." It's always "we," except when it's "us." You might think it's silly, people telling you how you should and shouldn't express yourself. But believe me, how you express yourself before long becomes how you see yourself. And when you're part of Disney, you see yourself always as part of a big, talented team. I never looked at my life, my family or my work in the restaurant business the same after spending two weeks in California learning the Disney Way.

I couldn't have started my training better – selling tickets at the entrance to Disneyland. At first, as you'd expect, I thought there had to be some mistake. "Excuse me," I told anybody who would listen, "I'm in food and beverage, not in ticket sales." But no, I was told, I had to do this to understand the most basic, most foundational lesson in what we were all about. All it took was a change into my costume – at Disney, everyone is an actor, not just an employee wearing a uniform – and a few minutes greeting our guests as they approached the window to buy an admission ticket to the park. All it took was that simple experience to see the anticipation and expectation in all those wide eyes.

I'd greeted guests before, in Europe, in Africa, in New York and Boston – and everybody I'd ever greeted was looking forward to a good meal. But this was different, this was more. Walt Disney had it right when he wove the idea of "magic" into everything he touched, because I understood absolutely that we weren't just here to sell food and beverage. We weren't just here to sell hotel rooms. We weren't just here to sell rides and exhibits and dozens of other attractions. I had been called here, by Walt and the entire organization he had formed around him, to sell people little pieces of magic.

On my second day at Disneyland, I figured they'd made another "mistake." I was told I'd spend that day as the captain of the submarine, the one that tools around that blue lagoon as passengers look out their portholes at mermaids and sponge divers and all kinds of colorful sealife. The thing is, I'd always kind of wanted to be the captain of a submarine, but I never envisioned it as part of a ride in an amusement park. I had a lot of fun as the captain, seeing all the excitement in my passengers. And I have to say, for once in my life, I had the right accent. "Achtung! Achtung!" I'd shout at the start of each little trip, as the bubbles came up to shroud the submarine for its journey beneath the waves.

I was sent to the Entertainment Division at the start of my third day, and this really had me baffled. I explained to people making the assignments that I couldn't sing or dance, so surely this was a mistake. Or at least a very bad idea. But… as always before at Disney, where you're sent is where you go. The guy at the Entertainment Division took one look at me and said, "Hey, great, you're tall. You can be Balloo the Bear in our parade." All children know Balloo, naturally, from the animated version of The Jungle Book. I was helped into this huge costume – I think it weighed 85 pounds – and even as tall as I was, I looked out at the world from a little window in Balloo's neck. It was pretty awkward, but I was assured there'd be somebody with me at all times to guide me and protect me from any trouble.

"If somebody kicks you during the parade," I was told, "remember, you are a Disney character and you're not allowed to kick back!" After the parade there were hundreds of people who wanted to have their picture taken with Balloo the Bear, and I felt very, very important.

At dinner that night, our teacher talked with me about what I'd learned from my first three days at Disneyland, initially at the ticket window, then in the submarine and finally in the parade.

"When you were selling tickets," he said, "couldn't you feel the expectation?"

"Yes, absolutely"

"And then in that submarine, didn't you fulfill that expectation?"

"Yes," I said, feeling a swell of pride, "everybody had a great time on my submarine."

"And in the parade this afternoon, in that costume, didn't you feel some of the magic?"

"Of course."

"That's what it's all about, Joe. That's what we're all about. That's what we have to do. For every single guest. Every single time."

It's been more than 30 years since I learned this lesson, courtesy of the Disney organization. I sure didn't leave it behind at a theme park in southern California, or at its newer sibling in central Florida. It was a lesson I've carried with me until now, all about how people feel when they walk into a restaurant, about what they want and expect and deserve, and about each day finding the very best ways of serving it to them. In my restaurants, as at a Disney theme park, things are often not magical behind the scenes, for the cooks and waiters who have to do these difficult jobs. But things, as I've passed on to hundreds and hundreds of young people, always have to be magical in the dining room for our guests.

Everybody who works for Disney has a storyboard. I learned about storyboards during that life-changing visit to southern California, when we went to tour the entertainment operation after completing our little apprenticeships at Disneyland. The idea for the storyboard is simple enough – and it comes from the world of animation in which, of course, Disney artists set the pace for so many decades. Some people don't use them, I'm told – they just draw a character or a backdrop the way they think it should be, and that's about it. But the Disney Way was to draw something and hang it up on your storyboard. This lets you glance at it over and over, here and there, throughout the day and night, getting better ideas and making changes as often as you like. I think it's a good way for an animator to work, but Disney convinced me that every profession could benefit from its own version of the storyboard. As soon as I got back to our massive project in central Florida, I put together a storyboard as a way of organizing and constantly improving my ideas. To this day, if I'm working on a big project, I have a storyboard.

Oct. 1, 1971, was chosen as the grand opening of Walt Disney World, with Bob Hope as the master of ceremonies, Julie Andrews (Disney's own Mary Poppins) singing, and a 1,000-piece marching band on Main Street USA. I kept listening to the talk about 2,000 dignitaries from around the world, sampling food and drink representing places all over America and all over the world, all staged in and around the Contemporary Resort Hotel. I kept getting more and more excited hearing the scope and scale of this great and glorious event – until all of a sudden I realized: Geez, he's talking about me! The entire Magic Kingdom was a construction site, and we were running out of time.

Staffing Disney World was an overwhelming task, with management figuring we needed to hire... oh, about 28,000 people – including about 400 chefs spread across all different levels of training, from culinary helper on up to culinary managers like me. One problem was that just about anybody who could handle our jobs lived nowhere near Orlando. Remember, the place originally had citrus orchards and horse or cattle ranches, not exactly the best place to go shopping for hospitality employees. Miami had quite a few nice hotels, but the industry there was so seasonal that either people had gone away or were too busy to give us the time of day.

Instead of looking south, we looked a bit north, traveling up to Hyde Park, N.Y., on a recruiting trip built around the president of the Culinary Institute of America. That school was smaller and much less of a household word then than it is now, when almost everybody knows someone who's going to the CIA in hopes of becoming a chef. What we asked the president was to point us toward graduates and even the more promising attendees, so we could assess their skills in light of the positions we needed to fill rather quickly.

We took all those hundreds and hundreds of names back to Orlando, had a huge staff of secretaries sort through them according to experience level and then sent applications to every one that looked appropriate. We ended up conducting hundreds of interviews in nearly 10 cities and hired people right on the spot. Some chefs and kitchen employees were so excited to get an offer from Disney they forgot to ask how much we paid. We had to say, "Hold on, here's what we're talking about…" Many of them said Yes to the idea before money was even mentioned.

Opening day came closer and closer until – as we knew it would – it became the very next day. Thousands and thousands of people started arriving from all over the world, and we were so aware that even though they were excited and positive about the experience, we were also under intense pressure. At the same time all these people were busy laughing and celebrating, most of them were on the lookout for any little thing that went wrong. In the restaurant business, I made my peace with that quirk of human nature years ago. All you can do is plan, prepare and execute – everything and every time. That's all there is to it!

Allen Hubsch
Director of Foods and Hotels

There was still the challenge of numbers. Since it was the grand opening, there was of course no "history" (the term hotels and restaurants use to estimate how many people will check in on such and such a day or call for dinner reservations on such and such an evening). We had nothing, but we had to be ready with plenty enough food for anyone who showed up. To help us with this, Disney management devised an elaborate system to count the visitors coming to Orlando, combining the numbers flying in via Eastern Airlines (a major partner in the Florida park's beginnings) along with the numbers committing to Orlando at key points on the interstate and turnpike system. We actually put crews working four-hour shifts at all the major junctures, counting cars along with the number of people inside. At the end of the day, we had our number. And it turned out to be pretty close. On that first day, we served no fewer than 125,000 meals.

It took all of Day One to hand us Problem One as well. You see, the Contemporary Resort Hotel was built as a convention hotel, and the very first convention scheduled to check in was the Shriners – on that same Oct. 1. The rooms were ready for them, the main kitchen was ready for them – but not the various ballrooms where they had planned to have all their meetings and meals. We tried to explain the situation before our opening day, to which the Shriners' response basically was: We don't care, we're coming, it's your problem. The big bosses called a meeting for all our managers to brainstorm, and one of our guys who lived in Sarasota reminded us that was the winter home of Ringling Bros., Barnum and Bailey Circus. The circus, he told us, was still on the road but the museum in Sarasota just might have a big circus tent we could borrow. They'd probably love the free advertising to all the folks gathering at Walt Disney World, the manager said. That's exactly the way it worked out. The executives from Disney didn't like it very much – a circus is a circus, you know, and that wasn't exactly their image of Mickey Mouse. But I was happy because I finally had a place to serve our first convention the breakfast, lunch and dinner that were in their contract.

Looking back, I'm sure I learned more from opening Disney World and from the four years I worked there than most people learn from four years in college – and that includes the wonderful hotel-restaurant programs that started at Cornell and slowly spread to other universities around the country. It was an enormous, enormous job, and it was often very difficult. Every day was a show, every day was a parade, and every night there were fireworks. We never really slowed down, day or night, rain or shine.

At the same time, my life was wonderful and my life was hard. Work was going well, for all the challenges. After the initial hoopla of the opening, we began to lose kitchen staff to other hotels being built all over the central Florida area, so in response (after a research trip to a similar program at the Greenbriar Resort in West Virginia) we opened a Disney culinary school right at the theme park. After all, if we trained people, they might (up to a point!) be a bit more loyal, and at least we'd know they were properly trained. In my personal life too, there were pluses and minuses. I liked where I worked, I liked where we lived in the suburbs, and I liked having my own boat to go out on the beautiful lakes and rivers the area had in abundance. But our life continued to be less than my wife Gigi felt she wanted. More and more, she wanted to be an actress – not just somebody's mom living in the suburbs. My daughters themselves presented frustrations, as they were coming into serious school age long before the Orlando area had the good systems I'm sure they have now. That meant private schools, and that meant finding them and visiting them and choosing them, not to mention of course affording them. Gigi and I had many a late-night conversation about all these things, and very few of these conversations had happy endings.

It seemed silly to start looking for another job when I already had a job with one of the best companies on earth. So I really wasn't looking at all when I picked up the phone and it was my old friend Kurt Stielhack, now working with Hyatt on a massive expansion of first-class hotels all over America. He seemed genuinely excited about the company's plans for growth, building large properties in important cities for business and tourism, and arranging to put several restaurants in each one. You might say each Hyatt was a small-scale theme park, which besides our long friendship was probably why Kurt thought of me.

"Well, Joe," he said, "what would it take to get you away from Disney?"

I wasn't sure what to say, since I wasn't planning to leave Disney. But naturally I created an answer, the same answer anyone who knows me has heard me give about a hundred times. I'd want someplace good and big and professional, with a lot of commitment to quality and a lot of room to grow my own destiny. I'd want something that felt entrepreneurial, even though it was framed within a large and successful corporation. It would have to be in the south, where I could be warm. It would have to be near the water so I could enjoy my boat. And it would have to have excellent schools for my daughters.

"That's all it would take, Kurt," I said with a smile. "Go find me that and then we can talk."

When we hung up our phones that day, I wasn't sure when or if I'd ever hear from my old friend again. It took him five days to call me back.

He told me about this property as though it were floating somewhere out in the cosmos: it was the flagship of Hyatt, a beautiful hotel with 1,200 rooms and six restaurants, in a great city with a terrific management team, and it was only three months old. It's a perfect opportunity, he said, and all you have to do is say Yes.

I waited one long beat. And then another. He was going to make me ask.

"Okay, Kurt. So where is this incredible hotel?"

"It's the Hyatt Regency. In Houston, Texas."

Smoked Salmon Spread with Cocktail Biscuits

Yield: 12 servings

1 small red onion, chopped very fine
1/4 cup white distilled vinegar
1/2 teaspoon sugar
2 cups flour
2 teaspoons baking powder
1 1/4 teaspoons salt
1/4 teaspoon dry mustard
1/8 teaspoon freshly ground black pepper
1/3 cup vegetable shortening
1 tablespoon chopped parley
3/4 cup, plus 3 tablespoons chilled milk
1 cucumber, unpeeled and sliced crosswise
24 small sprigs of fresh dill, for garnish

Preheat the oven to 400°F. In a medium bowl, toss the chopped onions, sugar and vinegar. Cover and set aside to marinate at room temperature for 30 minutes. On a flat working surface, sift together the flour, salt, pepper, mustard and baking powder. Stir in the parsley, and with your hands knead in the shortening and milk, forming a moist dough. With floured hands pat the dough into a 3/4 inch thick, 8 X 10 inch rectangle. Sprinkle a little more flour on top. Using a 11/2 inch round cookie cutter cut out 24 rounds of dough. Place the rounds of dough on a greased baking sheet, and bake for 20 minutes until light brown.

With a spatula, transfer the biscuits on to a baking rack and let cool. Split each biscuit in half horizontally. Spread 1/2 teaspoon of the salmon spread on the bottom half. Layer a slice of cucumber, and then another teaspoon of the salmon spread on top. Garnish each biscuit with the pickled onions and a dill sprig.

Arrange the biscuits on a serving platter replace the top half of the biscuits slightly askew and serve with chilled sauvignon blanc or champagne.

Salmon Spread:
6 ounces cream cheese, softened at room temperature
2 ounces butter softened
1/2 teaspoon salt
3 drops Tabasco sauce
6 ounces ground smoked salmon tartar
1 teaspoon prepared horseradish
1 teaspoon lemon juice
2 tablespoons dry sherry
2 scallions, white part only, chopped finely

Place all ingredients into a food processor, and process until smooth. The spread can be made ahead of time and refrigerated.

Shrimp in Basil Tomato Sauce
With Fried Green Florida Tomatoes

Yield: serves 4

2 pounds shelled and deveined large shrimp
1/4 cup olive oil
1 medium size onion, diced very fine
6 cloves garlic, minced
2 serrano chilies, seeded and chopped fine
1 teaspoon cumin powder
1/2 teaspoon oregano
1/2 teaspoon ground coriander
2 tablespoons tomato paste
3 large ripe tomatoes, peeled and chopped
1 1/2 teaspoons brown sugar
1 cup coarsely chopped fresh basil
1 1/2 teaspoons salt, plus a dash of black pepper
1/2 cup dry white wine
1/2 cup grated Parmesan cheese

With a small kitchen knife remove the stem from the tomatoes and cut a little cross on the opposite side. Dip the tomatoes for 30 seconds in boiling water, remove the skin, and chop coarsely. Set aside.

Heat the vegetable oil in a large skillet. Add the onions, garlic, chilies and cook over moderately high heat. Stirring frequently.

Stir in the cumin, oregano, coriander, and cook the spices for two minutes over low heat. Add the chopped tomatoes, tomato paste, brown sugar, salt, black pepper, Parmesan cheese and white wine. Cook slowly until the sauce thickens slightly, about 10 minutes. Add the shrimp, fresh basil and simmer over moderate low heat, stirring frequently until the shrimp are pink and curled, about 5 minutes. Transfer the shrimp to shallow bowl and serve with green fried tomatoes.

Fried Green Florida Tomatoes:

3 large green tomatoes, sliced 1/2 inch thick
1/2 cup flour
1 cup dry bread crumbs
2 large eggs, beaten
1/4 teaspoon salt
1/3 cup grated Parmesan cheese
1 cup vegetable oil

In a medium size bowl, season the flour with salt and pepper. Whisk the eggs in another bowl, and toss the bread crumbs with the Parmesan in another bowl. Dredge the tomatoes first in the flour, and then coat them with the eggs. Press each tomato slice on both sides into the breadcrumb-Parmesan mixture and fry in the vegetable oil until golden brown, turning once. Transfer the tomato slices on to paper towel, season with a little salt and serve at once.

Baked Fillets of Bass with Hearts of Palm and Stone Crabs

Yield: serves 4

4 fillets of black sea bass,
   (skinned, 6 to 8 ounces each)
1 medium size onion, cut in half and sliced
2 cloves of garlic, peeled and sliced
2 scallions, sliced (lower part only)
6 tablespoons extra-virgin olive oil
1/2 cup dry white wine
1/8 teaspoon oregano
1 can (15 ounces) hearts of palm, or fresh
   (cut into 1 inch long logs)
1 can (15 ounces) stewed tomatoes
1/3 cup Kalamata black olives, chopped coarsely
1/2 cup clam juice
1/2 teaspoon salt
1/8 teaspoon sugar
1/8 teaspoon black pepper
1/4 stick butter cut into bits
2 tablespoons Chinese oyster sauce
1 teaspoon grated orange zest
4 to 8 stone crab claws, (depending on size)
   cracked with a cleaver or knife

Heat half of the oil in a heavy duty saucepan, add the onions, scallions, garlic and cook over moderate heat, stirring occasionally for 5 minutes until cooked but not brown. Add the wine and clam broth, simmer for 2 minutes, add the tomatoes (including the juice) chopped black olives, salt, sugar, pepper, and oregano. Simmer the sauce for 5 minutes over low heat.

Transfer the sauce to 13-by 9-inch low rim, ceramic baking dish, and place the bass fillets over the sauce, then arrange the hearts of palm and stone crabs around the fish. Brush each fillet with oyster sauce, dot with butter, seal the dish tightly with foil and bake for 15 minutes, or until the fish is just opaque and cooked though. In the meantime whisk together the remaining 3 tablespoons of olive oil with the orange zest. Transfer the fish with vegetables and broth to shallow, heated soup plates, and serve drizzled with orange zest oil.

Baked Florida Grouper with Scallions and Lime

Yield: serves 4

4 grouper fillets, 6 ounces each
1/2 cup all-purpose flour, for dredging
1/2 teaspoon Spanish paprika
1/2 stick butter
2/3 cup thinly sliced scallions
2 cloves garlic, minced
1 medium size red bell pepper, cut in half,
   seeded and diced
1/4 teaspoon salt
1/8 teaspoon black pepper
1 tablespoon lime juice
2 teaspoons minced lime zest
1 tablespoon chopped parsley
1 tablespoon fine, dry bread crumbs
1/2 cup white wine

Preheat the oven to 400°. Wash the fish fillets under cold running water and pat dry with paper towels. In a mixing bowl combine the flour, salt, paprika, and black pepper. Dredge the fish, one at a time in the flour mixture; shake off any excess. In a large skillet, melt the butter over moderately high heat. Add the fish fillets and sauté, turning once until light brown, about 2 minutes on each side. Transfer to a fireproof baking dish in a single layer.

Reduce the heat to low and add the scallions, garlic, and red bell peppers. Cook until soft, about 5 minutes; deglaze the pan with the wine. Increase the heat and boil for 4 minutes, scraping up any brown bits. Ladle the scallions-pepper sauce over the fish; drizzle with lime juice. Sprinkle on the lime zest, parsley and bread crumbs. Bake on the top shelf of the oven for 15 minutes, or until the fish fillets are firm and cooked.

Garnish with fresh dill sprigs and serve with new boiled potatoes and seasonal vegetables.

Red Snapper Fillets Meuniere with Citrus Vinaigrette

Yield: serves 6

6 red snapper fillets, (6 oz each, skin on)
3/4 cup vegetable oil
1/2 cup flour
Dash of salt and pepper
3 pounds butternut squash, peeled, seeded and cut into 2 inch chunks
1/4 stick butter
1 teaspoon brown sugar
1/4 teaspoon salt
1/8 teaspoon ground cloves

Citrus Vinaigrette:
1/2 cup fresh raspberries, pureed in a blender
1/4 cup fresh orange juice
2 tablespoons fresh lemon juice
2 tablespoons fresh lime juice
1 tablespoon sherry vinegar
1 teaspoon sugar
1/2 cup finely diced bell peppers, (green, yellow and red)
1 scallion, minced (lower part only)
1 tablespoon finely chopped cilantro
1 tablespoon chopped capers
1/3 cup extra-virgin olive oil
Salt and black pepper to taste

Whisk together the raspberry puree, sugar, citrus juices, and vinegar. Add olive oil in a slow stream, whisking until emulsified. Stir in remaining vinaigrette ingredients, season with salt and pepper, cover and set aside.

Place the squash into a 3-quart casserole, cover with water, add the salt and boil over moderate heat until tender. With a slotted spoon transfer the squash to a blender, add sugar, cloves, butter and puree. Return to the casserole and keep hot. Wash the fish under cold running water, pat dry with paper towels, and make 3 diagonal slashes through the skin of each fillet. Season with salt and pepper, dust with flour.

Heat the vegetable oil in a 12-inch non-stick frying pan over high heat until hot but not smoking. Fry 3 fillets at a time skin down until golden brown, about 3 minutes. Turn and fry another 2 minutes, or until just cooked through. Transfer to a heated platter and fry the remaining 3 fillets in the same manner.

Serve the red snapper fillets, skin sides up, on a bed of squash purée and drizzle generously with vinaigrette.

Whole Baked Red Snapper with Balsamic Vinegar
Yield: serves 4

1 whole red snapper, cleaned, 3-4 pounds
2 tablespoons flour
1/4 cup olive oil
4 tablespoons genuine balsamic vinegar
1/2 onion, chopped
1/2 cup dry white wine
2 cloves garlic, minced
1 tablespoon fresh rosemary, plus 4 sprigs for garnish
1 1/2 teaspoons fresh thyme, plus a few sprigs for garnish
1 teaspoon salt
1/2 teaspoon freshly ground black pepper
3 bay leaves
1 bottle clam juice (8 ounces)
2 tablespoons fresh lemon juice
8 lemon slices for garnish

Fish Velouté:
1/2 cup light cream
1 tablespoon flour
1 tablespoon melted butter
2 drops Tabasco sauce

Preheat the oven to 350°. Wash the fish inside and outside under running cold water.

Using a sharp knife, make 3 diagonal slashes, about 1/2 inch deep, on both sides of the fish. Season the fish with salt, pepper and dust with flour, dust off any excess. In a large, heavy duty roasting pan heat the olive oil over moderate heat. Add the fish and cook for two minutes on each side. Transfer the fish to a large platter and set aside.

Reduce the heat to low, add the onions, vinegar, white wine, rosemary, thyme, lemon juice and clam juice. Return the fish to the pan, place the bay leaves on top, seal the pan tightly with foil and bake for 35 minutes, basting the snapper from time to time. The fish should be firm, and flakes when removed from the bone. Transfer the fish gently with a spatula onto a heated serving platter.

Strain the liquid into a saucepan and bring to a boil over high heat. Combine the flour and melted butter, and whisk into the fish stock. Simmer over low heat for 5 minutes, and then add the cream. Heat but do not boil, add the Tabasco sauce, season to your liking, and serve with the baked red snapper. Recommended side dishes are new fingerling potatoes and sugar peas.

Grilled Whole Florida Pompano

Yield: serves 4

4 whole fresh pompano, 1 pound each
1/2 cup olive oil, plus 3 tablespoons olive oil for basting
5 large garlic clove, peeled
2 tablespoons rosemary
2 tablespoons oriental oyster sauce
1 tablespoon coarse salt
1 teaspoon freshly ground black pepper
Juice from one lemon
Lemon wedges and fresh dill sprigs for garnish

Light a grill and let the coals burn until they reach a white color.

In a food processor or blender, combine the 1/2 cup olive oil, garlic, rosemary, salt, oyster sauce, lemon juice and black pepper. Process to make a paste. Clean and wash the fish under cold running water, pat dry with paper towels and place on a cutting board. With a sharp knife cut two shallow slashes in each side of each pompano. Rub 3/4 quarter of the garlic-rosemary paste generously inside and outside of the fish.

Stir the remaining 3 tablespoons olive oil into the remaining garlic-rosemary paste and use the mixture for basting. Place the pompanos over medium hot coals on the grill, and baste occasionally with the reserved garlic-rosemary mixture. Grill each fish for about 8 minutes on each side until nicely browned and fully cooked. Transfer to a hot serving platter, garnish with lemon wedges and fresh dill sprigs.

Grilled Cornish Game Hens
With Pecan-Arugula Pesto
Yield: serves 4

4 Cornish game hens
4 cloves garlic, minced
4 shallots, chopped
4 thyme sprigs
2 tablespoons chopped parsley
1/2 cup olive oil
1/2 cup dry white wine
2 tablespoons Chinese oyster sauce
Zest from one lemon
Salt and freshly ground black pepper

Wash the hens under running cold water, and pat dry with paper towels. Place each hen firmly on a cutting board, and with a sharp butcher knife remove the backbone to butterfly the hen. In a large bowl toss all the ingredients, and brush generously in and outside of the Cornish hens. Place in a ceramic dish, cover with plastic wrap and refrigerate over night.

Light a grill using half charcoal briquettes and pieces of hardwood. When the flames have died down and the coals are white on the outside, brush the grill with vegetable oil and place the hens in the center, skin up. Close the grill and cook the hens for about 25 minute without turning, basting with olive oil from time to time. Turn the hens, and cook for another 20 minutes until cooked and nicely browned. An inserted thermometer should register 160 °. Transfer the hens to a carving board, cut into half and serves with the pesto (recipe below), and fresh vegetables of the season

Pecan – Arugula Pesto

1/2 cup pecan nuts
2 bunches fresh arugula, stems removed
5 cloves garlic, chopped
1/2 cup grated Parmesan cheese
1/8 teaspoon ground black pepper
1/2 teaspoon salt
Zest and lemon juice from one lemon
3/4 cup extra-virgin olive oil

Preheat the oven to 350°. Put the pecan nuts in a pie plate and toast for about 7 minutes, or until lightly browned and crisp. Remove and let cool. In a food processor, pulse the arugula with the pecan nuts and garlic until finely chopped. Add the Parmesan cheese, lemon juice and zest, plus salt and pepper. Pulse until combined, then add the olive oil slowly in a steady stream.

Lemon Chicken Stew with Pimentos and Toasted Almonds

Yield: serves 4

1 chicken 2 1/2 to 3 pounds
1/2 cup fresh lemon juice
1/2 cup flour
1 teaspoon Spanish paprika
1/2 cup vegetable oil
1 1/2 cups chicken stock
1/2 cup half and half
2 egg yolks
1/2 cup toasted almonds
1/4 cup diced pimentos
1 tablespoon brown sugar

Wash the chicken under cold running water, cut into 8 serving pieces and pat dry with paper towels.

Preheat the oven to 375°F. Combine the flour and paprika in a mixing bowl and roll the chicken one piece at a time in the flour and paprika mixture to cover all sides. Shake off the excess flour and set aside. In a heavy 12 inch frying pan heat the oil and brown 3 to 4 pieces at a time, starting the chicken skin down and turning them frequently. As they brown, arrange the pieces of chicken in one layer in a shallow fireproof baking dish. Pour off the remaining fat from the skillet and deglaze the pan with 1 1/2 cup chicken stock. Bring to a boil over high heat, scraping the browned particles that cling to the bottom and sides of the pan.

Add the brown sugar, lemon juice, whisk together and pour over the chicken. Seal the baking dish tightly with foil and bake in the middle of the oven for 35 minutes, or until the chicken is tender and the meat is easily removed from the bones. Transfer the chicken to a heated serving dish and keep hot. With a spoon, skim as much fat as possible from the surface; bring the rest of the gravy to a boil. Whisk the egg yolks and cream together, then strain the chicken gravy into egg yolk mixture, and mix well. Add the diced pimentos and ladle over the chicken. Top with toasted almonds and serve.

Veal Stew with Fresh Mushrooms

Yield: serves 6

2 1/2 pounds cubed boneless veal shoulder
2 cups sliced mushrooms
1 cup baby carrots
1 cup flour
1 teaspoon salt
1 teaspoon Spanish paprika
4 tablespoons butter
3 tablespoons olive oil
1 medium onion, diced finely
4 cloves garlic, minced
1 1/2 cups dry white wine
4 plum tomatoes, fresh or canned, peeled and diced
1/2 teaspoon oregano
1/4 teaspoon freshly ground black pepper
1 strip of lemon zest
1/2 cup heavy cream
2 tablespoons freshly chopped parsley

Combine the flour and paprika in a large bowl. Dredge the cubed veal in the flour-paprika mixture and shake off the excess. In a large heavy skillet, melt 1 tablespoon butter and 1 tablespoon of the olive oil over moderately high heat. Add one third of the veal and cook, stirring occasionally, until browned, about 10 minutes. With a slotted spoon, transfer the meat to a large flameproof casserole. Repeat twice with the remaining veal, using one more tablespoon of the oil for each batch.

Reduce the heat to moderate and add 1 tablespoon of the butter to the skillet. Add the onions and garlic and sauté until the onions are soft but not browned. Transfer the onions and garlic to the casserole with the veal.

Set the skillet over high heat, add the wine and bring to a boil, scraping up the brown bits from the bottom of the pan. Add the tomatoes, baby carrots, and bring to a boil for 2 minutes; pour the liquid over the veal. Season with the salt, pepper, oregano and add the lemon zest. Cover the casserole and simmer over low heat until the meat is tender, about 1 1/2 hour.

In a medium skillet, melt the remaining butter. Add the sliced mushrooms and sauté over high heat for 1 minute. Stir in the heavy cream and chopped parsley. Add to the veal stew and combine well.

Serve with any kind of your favorite pasta and fresh vegetables.

Cherry Orange Sour Cream Muffins

Yield: makes 12 muffins

1 cup sour cream
1 1/2 teaspoons freshly grated
    orange rind
1/4 cup fresh orange juice
1 large egg
1/3 cup light brown sugar
1/4 cup granulated sugar
1/2 stick butter
1 1/2 cups flour
2 teaspoon baking powder
1 teaspoon baking soda
1/2 teaspoon salt
1 teaspoon cinnamon
1 1/2 cups tart, dried cherries

Preheat the oven to 375°F. In a small bowl whisk together the sour cream, orange juice, egg, sugar and butter until the mixture is well blended. Sift the flour, baking soda, baking powder, cinnamon, and salt into the mixture. Add the orange juice, grated orange rinds, and dried cherries and combine well to make a firm batter. Divide the batter into 12 well-greased muffin tins, and bake in the middle of the oven for 15 to 20 minutes, or until golden brown and a tester comes out clean. Let the muffins cool in the tins for 10 minutes, and then turn them out onto a cake rack to cool completely.

Blueberry Sour Cream Crumb Cake

Yield: makes one 10-inch cake

1 pint fresh blueberries (2 1/2 cups)
1/2 teaspoon grated lemon zest
2 1/4 cups flour
1 cup sugar
1 1/2 sticks butter (6 ounces), room temperature
    and cut into small pieces
1 teaspoon baking soda
1 teaspoon fresh lemon juice
1/2 teaspoon grated lemon zest
1 large whole egg
1/2 cup sour cream

Preheat the oven to 400°. Butter a round 10-by-1-1/2 inch baking springform. In a medium bowl, toss the blueberries with the lemon zest. In a large bowl, combine 2 cups of flour with the sugar. Using your fingertips combine the butter with the flour-sugar until the mixture resembles coarse meal. Set 1-1/2 cups of the mixture aside for the crumb topping. In a small bowl combine the remaining 1/4 cup flour with the baking soda and mix well. Add the mealy mixture in the large bowl and knead until incorporated.

In a small bowl, lightly beat the egg. Stir in the sour cream and lemon juice. Add the dry ingredients in the large bowl and combine with a wooden spoon until well blended, then fold 1-1/2 cups of the blueberries. (Reserve 1 cup of the blueberries) Spread the batter in the prepared spring form and scatter the remaining cup blueberries on top.

Sprinkle the remaining crumb mixture evenly over the blueberries. Place the baking pan on a cookie sheet and bake in the middle of the oven for about 30 minutes. Reduce the heat to 350° and bake for another 20 minutes until the crumbs are golden brown and taster or toothpick inserted in the center of the cake comes out clean. Serve at room temperature with whipped cream.

Bread Pudding with Whiskey Sauce

Yield: 6 to 8

24 slices French bread, cut into 1/2 inch
1 stick melted butter, (4 ounces)
1 cup sugar
5 whole eggs, beaten
1 pint heavy cream
1 tablespoon vanilla extract
1/4 cup raisins
1/2 cup apricot preserves, heated with 1 tablespoon water

Preheat the oven to 350°. In a large bowl, using a hand-held electric mixer, beat together the sugar, eggs, cream, and vanilla extract. Stir in the raisins. Place the sliced French bread on a cookie sheet pan, and brush generously with the melted butter. Toast lightly in the over on both sides. Place the bread in a standing angle into a 9-inch square-baking pan. Ladle the egg-cream-raisin mixture over the bread, and let stand for 5 minutes to soak up some of the liquid. Push down the bread until covered with liquid.

Set the pan in a larger pan and pour in enough water to reach within 1/2 inch of the top of the inner pan. Cover with aluminum foil and bake for 35 minutes. Uncover the pudding and bake another 10 minutes longer until the top is browned and the pudding is still soft in the center. Glaze the top with the melted apricot preserves and spoon the pudding onto serving plates. Pass the Whiskey sauce separately.

Whiskey Sauce:

1 cup heavy cream
1 cup sugar
1/2 teaspoon cornstarch dissolved in 1/4 cup cold water
1/4 cup bourbon
1/2 teaspoon vanilla extract
1 tablespoon butter
Pinch of cinnamon

In a medium saucepan, combine the cream, butter, sugar, and cinnamon. Bring the mixture to a boil over high heat and cook, stirring frequently to dissolve the sugar, about 3 minutes. Whisk in the cornstarch and simmer for 2 minutes until the sauce thickens. Remove from the heat and stir in the bourbon.

Chardonnay Zabaglione with Tropical Fruits
Yield: serves 6

1 cup Chardonnay
1 cup sugar
6 egg yolks
1 tablespoon corn syrup
1/2 cup whipping cream
3 large oranges
1/2 pineapple, peeled and cored
2 kiwis, peeled and sliced
2 bananas
1 basket fresh strawberries
1 pomegranate for garnish

With a sharp knife remove the peel from the oranges. Then cut out the segments between the membranes. Dice the pineapple, peel and slice the bananas and kiwis. Wash and quarter the strawberries (leaving 6 strawberries whole for garnish). Arrange the fruits equally in 6 stem glasses and refrigerate, then prepare the Zabaglione.

Whisk chardonnay, sugar, yolks and corn syrup in a large stainless steel bowl. Set the bowl over a saucepan of simmering water (do not boil the water). Whisk constantly until mixture has tripled in volume. Remove from the heat, set the bowls in a larger bowl filled with crushed ice. Whisk Zabaglione until completely cooled and firm. Beat heavy cream to soft peaks in a medium bowl, then fold in the Zabaglione and ladle over the fresh fruit, garnish with a sprig of mint and a ripe strawberry and a spoon full pomegranate seeds.

Florida Key Lime Pie
Yield: makes one 9-inch pie

1 fully baked pie shell
6 egg yolks
1 can sweetened condensed milk
    (14 ounces)
3/4 cup fresh lime juice
3 egg whites
1 drop of green food coloring
Grated zest from 1 lime
1 tablespoon sugar
1 cup heavy cream, whipped with
    a dash of vanilla and
    1 tablespoon sugar

Preheat the oven to 350°F. Separate the eggs, place the 6 egg yolks in one bowl, and 3 egg whites in another bowl. With an electric wire whisk, beat the egg yolks until thick and creamy. Slowly beat in the condensed milk and lime juice. Add the sugar to the egg whites and beat with a clean wire whisk until they form soft peaks and are stiff.

With a rubber spatula, fold them gently into the egg yolk mixture, add the lime zest, green coloring and combine well. Spoon the mixture into the cooled pie shell, and bake in the middle of the oven for 20 minutes or until the filling is firm. Refrigerate the pie for several hours, cut in wedges, top with whipped cream and garnish with sprigs of fresh mint.

Florida Lemon Curd Tart with Citrus Compote

Yield: serves 10

10 large egg yolks
1 cup sugar
3/4 cup lemon juice
1 tablespoon grated lemon zest
1 stick butter, cut into cubes, softened
1 9 inch cookie pie crust

Dissolve the sugar with 2 tablespoons hot water and the lemon juice in a small pot over low heat.

In a medium heatproof bowl, whisk the egg yolks, add the dissolved sugar-lemon mixture and combine well. Fill a medium saucepan with 1 inch of water and bring to a boil. Set the bowl over the boiling water; reduce the heat to moderate and cook, whisking the lemon mixture constantly until pale yellow and thick.

Remove the bowl from the heat and whisk in the cubed butter and lemon zest. Fill the crust with the warm lemon curd and refrigerate until the curd is firm enough to cut. Remove the tart from the tart pan, cut into wedges and top with citrus fruit compote.

Pie Crust:

1 stick butter, softened	1 1/4 cups flour
1/2 stick butter, melted	3/4 cup pecans, finely ground
1/4 cup sugar	1/4 teaspoon baking powder
1/2 teaspoon lemon zest	1/8 teaspoon ground cinnamon
2 egg yolks	1/8 teaspoon ground cloves
1/2 teaspoon vanilla extract	Pinch of salt

In a medium size bowl cream the butter and sugar until light and fluffy. Add the egg yolks, lemon zest, vanilla and beat until combined. Sift the flour and baking powder into a large bowl, add the cloves, cinnamon, pecans and salt, combine well. Add the wet ingredients and beat just until combined. Flatten the dough, into the shape of a disk, wrap in plastic and refrigerate until firm (30 minutes).

Preheat the oven to 350°F. On a lightly floured working surface, roll out the dough 1/4 inch thick, cut into 4 pieces and transfer to 2 cookie baking sheets. Place in the oven and bake for 15 minutes until golden brown and crisp. Let cool on a rack. Crumble the cookies with a rolling pin, transfer to a food processor, add the 1/2 stick melted butter and process until moistened. Press the crumbs into a 9-1/2 inch fluted tart pan with a removable bottom, forming an even layer all around. Refrigerate the cookie pie shell for about 15 minutes before filling.

Citrus Fruit Compote:

2 large oranges	1 cup sugar
2 ripe grapefruits	1/4 cup water
2 limes	3/4 cup chopped pecans
1 stick butter	1/2 cup heavy cream
1/2 cup orange juice	1/4 cup Grand Marnier

Using a sharp knife, peel the oranges, grapefruits and limes, removing the bitter white pith. Cut between the membranes to release the citrus sections and set aside. In a medium skillet dissolve the water and sugar over medium heat; bring to a boil until the sugar caramelized to a golden brown. (do not burn the sugar). Add first the pecans, then the orange juice; simmer until the sugar is thickened to syrup.

Remove the skillet from the heat and add the Grand Marnier. Return the skillet to the heat and carefully ignite the liquid with a long match. When the flames subside, add the cream, and combine well. Just before serving, stir the fruit sections into the sauce, and ladle over the lemon curt tart.

Fresh Oranges de Menthe

Yield: serves 6 to 8

6 large navel oranges
1 quart vanilla ice cream
1/2 cup sugar
1/2 cup water
1 1/2 cups dry white wine
1/4 cup lemon juice
1 cinnamon stick
4 cloves
2 tablespoons white crème de menthe
2 tablespoons cognac
1/4 cup heavy cream
Fresh mint and ripe strawberries
    for garnish.

Peel and cut oranges into slices, and divide on individual plates. In a saucepan, boil sugar and water for 5 minutes over low heat. Add cinnamon stick, cloves, white wine and lemon juice. Simmer for 15 minutes until slightly thick. Remove the cinnamon, cloves, then chill the simple syrup for several hours. Add the cream, cognac, white crème de menthe, and mix well together. Ladle the sauce over the sliced oranges, garnish with a sprig of fresh mint and serve.

Lemon Charlotte

Yield: serves 8 to 10

1 envelope unflavored gelatin
1/2 cup freshly squeezed lemon juice
4 eggs separated
1 cup granulated sugar
1/8 teaspoon salt
1 1/2 cup heavy cream, whipped
16 to 20 ladyfingers
Grated rind from one large lemon

Sprinkle gelatin over lemon juice in a small bowl, let soften for 5 minutes. Beat together with an electric mixer, egg yolks, 1/2 cup sugar and the salt in a double boiler. Gradually beat in the gelatin mixture, stirring constantly until mixture starts to thicken and the gelatin is dissolved. The water in the double boiler should be simmering. Pour into a large bowl, add the lemon rind and chill until the mixture begins to mound, 15 to 20 minutes, stirring occasionally.

In the meantime, line bottom and sides of an 8x3-inch spring form pan with ladyfingers, curved side out.

Beat the egg whites with an electric mixer in a large bowl until soft and foamy. Gradually add remaining 1/2 cup sugar and beat until soft peaks form. Fold the beaten egg whites and whipped cream into the lemon-gelatin mixture. Spoon into ladyfinger-lined pan and chill for four hours or overnight. Remove the charlotte from the form, cut into wedges and serve with fresh raspberry sauce, whipped cream and garnish with fresh sprig of mint.

Panna Cotta
with Fresh Strawberries

Yield: serves 6

4 cups fresh strawberries,
   washed, hulled and cut into halves
   (2 one-pint baskets)
1 1/2 cups milk
1/2 cup whipping cream
1/3 cup sugar
1 envelope unflavored gelatin
1/2 teaspoon vanilla extract
1/4 cup honey
Fresh mint for garnish

Puree 2 cups fresh strawberries in a processor until smooth. Strain through a fine sieve, pressing with a rubber spatula to extract as much puree as possible; reserve the strained puree, and discard the seeds.

Whisk the milk, cream and sugar together in a medium size saucepan. Sprinkle gelatin over it, and let stand for 10 minutes to soften the gelatin. Heat the mixture over low heat, whisking constantly until the gelatin is dissolved. (about 3 minutes, but do not boil) remove from the heat.

Whisk the pureed strawberries and vanilla extract into the milk/cream mixture, and divide among six ramekins or custard cups. Refrigerate the panna cotta, and remaining 2 cups strawberries overnight.

Gently toss strawberry halves with honey in a medium size bowl to blend. Run a small sharp knife between panna cotta and ramekins to loosen. Dip the bottom of the ramekins for a few seconds in hot water, and invert each panna cotta onto a chilled serving plate, shaking gently to unmold. Spoon strawberry-honey mixture over it, garnishes with a fresh sprig of mint, and serve with any crisp cookies.

Pineapple Crêpes with Galliano

Yield: serves 4

For crêpes:
- 1/2 cup whole milk
- 1 large egg
- 1/2 cup flour
- 2 tablespoons melted butter
- 1 tablespoon confectioners sugar
- 1/4 teaspoon vanilla extract
- Pinch of salt
- 1/4 cup vegetable oil for frying the crêpes
- Confectioners sugar for dusting
- 6 ripe strawberries and sprigs of mint for garnish

For pineapple filling:
- 1 tablespoon butter
- 1 can shredded pineapple, 20 ounces
- 1/4 cup Galliano liqueur
- 1/4 cup orange blossom honey
- 1/3 cup fresh orange juice
- 1 1/2 teaspoon peeled, minced fresh ginger

Blend crêpe ingredients in a blender; chill the batter while preparing the pineapple filling. Heat butter in a 12 inch non-stick skillet over moderately high heat, add the pineapples, honey, ginger, and orange juice. Simmer until most of the liquid has evaporated and the mixture is syrupy, 3 to 5 minutes. Remove from the heat, add the Galliano, return to the heat and ignite the liquor. Set the pineapple filling aside and keep hot.

Make the crêpes: Brush a 9-inch nonstick skillet with oil and heat over moderately high heat until hot but not smoking. Holding the skillet off heat, pour in 1/4 cup batter, immediately swirling and tilting skillet, create a thin, even layer. Return the skillet to heat and cook until the crêpe is golden brown around the edges, and firm in the center, about 45 seconds. Using a spatula flip the crêpe carefully and cook another 30 seconds. Transfer to a heated platter and keep warm. Continue to make more crêpes in the same manner.

Spoon about 1/4 cup pineapple mixture over half of each crêpe, and then fold over the other half.

Repeat with the remaining crêpes pour the rest of the pineapple mixture over the folded crepes.

Dust with confectioners sugar, garnish with fresh mint, a ripe strawberry and serve with vanilla ice cream.

LIFE AS A TEXAN

The job offer from Hyatt presented me with a very difficult decision. I liked living in Florida and I liked my job at Disney World, where I had worked very hard for 4 1/2 years to get the massive amount of foodservice on a stable footing. In particular, I had struggled so long to put together a great team in Orlando that the thought of doing that all over again somewhere else was not appealing. An executive chef in a large hotel, after all, is more a coach than a player: If you don't put together the right team, you can't produce results. We had seven restaurants at the Contemporary Hotel, plus a busy banquet department, and they all required great people in order to make me look like a great chef. After a certain point in your career, if you rise to the challenges of the chef's profession, it simply isn't about how well you cook. At Disney, at the Contemporary Hotel and the Polynesian Village, it was all finally working like a clock.

By the way, I didn't know too much about Texas except for seeing a couple of movies with John Wayne. I saw Red River, which was very exciting with big cattle drives and plenty of dust, and I saw The Alamo. That's about all I knew about Texas. What I did know in Florida is that I liked my life. I loved living out in the country, which Orlando still was in those days, driving through miles and miles of orange trees to get to work. And I loved having my 20-foot boat that was so perfect for enjoying the water the way you're supposed to when you live in Florida.

On the surface, comparing job to job, the answer to my friends at Hyatt was absolutely No. But a man also has to think of his own personal happiness – and that means his wife's personal happiness too. Gigi was not happy in Florida. It was too backward, too "country" for someone who came from Montreal and wanted to get back to a big city. Plus, there were our children. I'm sure by now the schools are fine in Orlando, which has grown so explosively since we made our home there. But at that time, they were not very nice. The place had been a farming community so recently, and with the arrival of thousands and thousands of employees for Disney World, there were teacher shortages and decisions to combine schools and all kinds of other things that weren't the best. I was told all this would be fine in Texas, but it was very difficult to make this decision. Still, as had happened so many times in my life, something came up that would change my way of thinking.

One day a friend of mine called me from Houston to ask me to take care of a friend and her daughter who were going to visit the theme park. So I met this lady, Bertha Schepps whose family owned a whole string of dairies in different parts of Texas. I showed her and her daughter around the park, and she was all bubbly and fun and told me a lot I didn't know about Texas – which since I'd seen only two movies, wasn't very hard. She told me that in Houston just about everybody had lots and lots of money. Those people who don't have money, she said, always pretend they do – so you have this wonderful environment of success. She told me about the beautiful homes, about the Rodeo and the Barbecue Cook-Off.

Just as Texas was starting to sound better to me, Disney World suddenly started to sound worse. At the time, in 1974, there were embargoes on oil that were seriously cutting into how much Americans could travel by car, and even how much they could travel by plane. The whole travel industry runs on fuel, after all. Numbers were down at Disney World, and that didn't please the big bosses out in California or the shareholders, so they all felt something needed to be done. What that something was came in a memo to all of us executives – cut our staff by 25 percent. At the theme park level, I could see where this might be done, trimming the hours here and the personnel there, hopefully with no guests noticing a difference. But in a big hotel like ours, whether you have 5,000 guests or 3,000 guests, you need pretty much the same number of staff to get the job done. We all saw big changes coming, and we didn't see them as changes for the good.

The basic plan passed down from on high was that, as we cut more and more jobs from our individual, classically organized kitchens at the Contemporary Hotel and Polynesian Village, we would receive more and more of the food we'd serve pre-cooked from a central kitchen that, the executives assured me, was not working to full capacity. It was a typical "bean counter" response to a challenge. You want to cut somebody who knows what he's doing? Simply declare that anyone can actually do it and go find anyone who isn't too busy. Anyone familiar with the restaurant business can see its evolution over the past 20 or 30 years in this talk from Disney's home office. Once the province of highly trained chefs organized in time-honored brigades, foodservice became a world of kitchen managers supervising low-paid and mostly not-trained workers given tasks already mostly completed elsewhere. "Commissary cuisine," it has been called, and it's what most restaurants in America serve these days. But I was that old-fashioned, highly trained kind of chef, the sort of guy who knew the right way to do things and who would demand of his staff nothing less. I was not a happy camper.

One morning, when I was reading the paper and having a cup of coffee, I saw a fullpage ad. Considering what I was debating inside myself, the ad made me laugh out loud. It was for Southwest Airlines, which of course was based in Texas and flew into Houston, and it had this man wearing a business suit and carrying a briefcase – and wearing this big cowboy hat. The headline was: Go West, Young Man. This was all the sign I needed. I told my wife I'd be taking a couple days off from Disney World, catching a Southwest flight and going to see what this place called Texas was all about.

The airport in Houston was brand new and I was very impressed – it was the sort of thing modern Houston always does so well. Waiting for me at the airport was the Hyatt's food and beverage director, Wolf Baere. The name really suited him, because sometimes he could be a wolf and sometimes he could be a bear, but mostly he was this big, neat guy with a fancy smile.

Let me tell you: we drove from the airport

down I-45, and by the time we reached the Hyatt my mind was made up. There was no way I'd ever move to this city. In Orlando, everything had been pretty and manicured and green, everything seemed designed and managed by some unseen and artistic hand. Along I-45, there was nothing but one billboard after another, each trying to be uglier than the buildings that surrounded it, with no order, no rhyme, no reason. The air was muggy and hot, and as best I could tell it was polluted. There was so much traffic on the road that all I could think was: Who needs it? Not me!

The Hyatt Regency at that time was only about four months old, and it was a beautiful hotel. It's still a beautiful hotel, with silent elevators going up and down through that soaring atrium that Hyatt made its signature. There was a big bar in the center of the atrium, and it was a busy lunchtime in a city obsessed with doing business. At the bar, it seemed, every man was wearing an expensive suit and tie, and every woman was wearing designer clothes and beautiful makeup. Everything looked

Wolf Baere and me

very, very professional, with nobody in tank tops or bathing suits the way I was used to in Orlando.

In some ways, the Hyatt Regency was like most things I came to know in Houston, an act of financial showmanship. The place looked like no fortune had been spared on every detail – yes, as though money were no object, with the implied, very Houston message that the place would end up making so much money that, hey, it didn't matter how much it cost to get it up and running. Later, I learned the also very Houston truth: by the end of its construction, virtually all the money had run out and many cuts had to be made. Most of these, of course, were where they couldn't be seen, in the back of the house that would eventually be my world. What matters is all on the outside – that seemed to be the idea behind this city I was starting to love and hate at the same time.

That very day I met the big boss at the Hyatt, Dick Nelson, and you could tell right away he was not a Mickey Mouse man. He was a real hotelier, a Cornell graduate back before that great school had inspired hotel management programs at so many other universities. He spoke well – meaning he always knew the right thing to say. So when Dick met me, he said simply, "Welcome to the Hyatt Regency in Houston, Joe. We've heard some wonderful things about you. Hopefully you can join our team." As you can see, Dick Nelson knew exactly the right words to say to me. I knew we connected right away, even though I wasn't at all sure Houston was the place for me.

In the afternoon, Wolf had me attend the staff meeting – clearly working with the notion that if I could meet the people who would be "my team" here, I might be more likely to take the job. The staff meeting started and, looking around me, I couldn't believe it. It was a rainbow of different colors and different sizes. You have to understand what I was coming from. At Disney, to hire our initial 32,000 employees we had many times that number of applicants. Generally, Disney hired people not on the basis of what they knew but how they looked – and of course, how much personality they could turn on just like actors. As a result, most of the women working at Disney World looked like they could win a beauty pageant, and most of the men looked like they'd just stepped out of Esquire magazine. It was a whole different thing at the Hyatt. There were all kinds of different looks and nationalities, and each person at that staff meeting had a different accent. It was obvious that Hyatt hired people based on their knowledge to run their department, not on their looks. When you work for Disney, every day you're told what to do – it was like a school that never let out. At the Hyatt, you were expected to already know.

By 4 o'clock in the afternoon that day, I still was pretty sure I had no interest in leaving Orlando for Houston. Perhaps that was part of the reason I told Wolf Baere I wanted to go see my two friends in Houston – might as well, you know, since who knew if I'd ever visit this place again. So Wolf took me to see Horst Manhard at the Warwick Hotel, whom I hadn't seen since that day on the shores of Lake Geneva during a two-hour break in my flight from South Africa. Horst was the GM of one of the finest hotels in Houston, living with his family in a beautiful suite in the hotel, with cars and room service and anything else he could ever want as part of his package. Then later we went to visit Willi Rometsch, who owned several restaurants in town and also was partners in one of the hottest Houston discothèques, Bocaccio 2000. It was pretty slow at the disco when we arrived, since it was still early, but before long there was Dom Perignon flowing and caviar at every turn. Let me tell you, that place was hopping.

It was obvious that my friend Willi was a millionaire. That night, in fact, I met several people with ties to my past and I had to face an incredible truth

I met the big boss at the Hyatt, Dick Nelson, and you could tell right away he was not a Mickey Mouse man.

153

about them. Back when we were all 15 or 16 years old, one had been a butcher, one had been a hairdresser, one had been a cook, and another I'd just been to school with. As best I could tell, all had come to Houston on the way to someplace else – and they were all still here. In fact, every one of them was clearly a millionaire, which as you know was exactly what I'd dreamed of being back in Pomerania and working my way around the wreckage of Europe in the dark days after the war. Slowly that night at Bocaccio 2000, it began to dawn on me that Texas might be what I'd been looking for all along.

There was one more hurdle to The Great Texas Migration, and it wasn't one erected by my employers at Disney World. For the most part, they were sorry to lose my services but they understood that I was going to a much larger hotel company, with more opportunity for career growth and a core product that was actually what I did. At a theme park, after all, the main attraction is the attractions - Pirates of the Caribbean, for example, or Captain Nemo's submarine ride that I had "piloted" with my German accent what seemed a lifetime ago. When companies go through financial crunches, you realize all too well what their core products are – they're where suddenly everybody is putting focus and money. At Hyatt, the core product was the hotel and its food and beverage, placing me in a position of high desirability when it comes to having an impact on profitability. So everyone at Disney wished me the best in my new position. It was arriving in Texas itself that almost made me reverse my decision. There I was, with my wife and two daughters in the car, somewhere around Beaumont after the long drive up from Orlando then across Alabama, Mississippi and Louisiana, staring at nothing but oil wells and oil refineries. The air was thick with smoke and a million other things I didn't want to think about. And it all smelled like gasoline to me.

"I can't do this," I said to my wife after pulling to the side of the road. "I can't leave Florida for this! Look at this place!" Happily, in retrospect, my wife talked some calm and good sense into me. I finally crawled back behind the wheel of the car. Before long, there was the beautiful skyline of Houston. And not too long after that, we were pulling into the driveway of the Hyatt Regency, with everything fresh and new and full of money. I figured everything would be OK. It would have to be.

For the first couple of weeks, we lived at the hotel, but you can imagine how quickly that gets old when you have a family. So we figured out where we wanted to be in the suburbs, mostly on the basis of schools; and since we couldn't find something to buy right away, we rented an apartment in the area and took out a couple pieces of furniture to live on. Honestly, I think Gigi was happier about the move than I was. This is it, she kept telling me, I always wanted to live in a big city and that's Houston. I also knew that one of her dreams was to be an actress, and she felt that was feasible here in a way it never would be at Disney World, with nothing but Mickey Mouse and Zippidee-

With Hyatt boss Dick Nelson and Peter Graves

Doo-Dah! For my part, I made it through my first days and then weeks in the new job seeing what needed to be done. I met all the people and visited all our restaurants and bars, and I'm not going to say that anything was bad but I saw a lot of possibilities. The big layoff came at Disney World just about the time business took off in Houston, with all kinds of highrise office buildings going up and money flowing around everywhere you turned. I immediately brought over six of my best guys from Disney, including two sous chefs, a pastry chef and a garde manger. I wasn't alone here anymore, and I knew I could operate.

One day the boss called me in to say I was on the right track, but… the Hyatt had this little restaurant called The Window Box. It didn't have to make any money, he said, because the hotel was making lots of money. What it needed to be was a showcase, a place where our sales staff could sell the hotel by entertaining clients in an extravagant and impressive way. To that end, they flew me around to the best hotels in Texas, seeing what they were doing in their fine dining operations. We can spend some money, I was told, as long as the result is the finest food, wine and service to be found in any hotel in the state. And so we did. I became good friends with the food editors of Houston's two daily newspapers, the Chronicle and the Post, and The Window Box was always in the paper for something wonderful. Recipes from the restaurant were running with some picture of me every time I turned around. The Window Box at the Hyatt became quite famous in its day, and as these things happen, its chef became pretty famous right along with it.

A lot of the lessons I learned at Disney proved very useful in Houston. For one thing, we staged one of the city's first-ever crawfish festivals, shipping in truckload after truckload of live crawfish from Louisiana. It wasn't like it is here today, with so many restaurants serving crawfish this or that – and crawfish even being farmed right here in Texas, just off I-10 on the way to the Sabine River. No, it was all pretty much a big discovery back then – so I tore another page from Disney's book and made our festival a theatrical event. In addition to costuming our service staff, I pulled various people from the hotel offices and costumed them too. Obviously, the daily vision of thousands having their photos taken with Mickey and Goofy was not wasted on this chef. I wanted the same excitement that kids felt at Disney World to be felt by my grown-up customers at the Hyatt Regency, and crawfish were only the beginning. We did one party with a Polynesian theme – now there's something I knew how to do, with outriggers and torches everywhere – and another one themed around Gone With the Wind. Actually, this wasn't just a party – it was a whole "Disney production," complete with our hotel engineer building a replica of Tara in the ballroom with windows and a great big elegant veranda. Everybody was dressed in outfits from the Civil War, even the hotel's general manager and I. We, of course, were done up as Confederate generals, with the great hats and coats and boots. Nobody in Houston had ever done this at that time.

Nothing in a hotel ever stays the same, however, even when it's going great. One day my food and beverage director Wolf came to see me and tell me he was leaving – accepting a promotion to the Hyatt in Atlanta – and that was a cause for concern. When you're the head chef, getting along well with your F&B director is essential, since you have to move through each day and each night like one machine. When that relationship isn't right, all sorts of disasters can occur, which was exactly what I was afraid of. Later that day, our big boss Dick Nelson told me the news as well, but focused on my future with Hyatt. We both knew that I wanted to be the next F&B in Houston, but Dick assured me that was coming – just not yet. Another year or two with somebody else, then it would be my turn. He knew that now I'd begun to like Houston, I wouldn't want

to move my family all over again. Besides, he said, the new guy was terrific. His name was Rudi Lechner and he came from Austria, and Dick assured me Rudi was a total professional he had worked with in other cities.

Rudi turned out to be a real nice guy. We hit it off right away, and had a lot of things in common. We were both married to French ladies. We both had two daughters. And as it turned out, he bought a new house in the suburbs practically right next to the one I had just bought, so instead of driving two cars downtown each day we drove one. Instead of having long, stuffy meetings at the hotel, each day we discussed what we had to do on the way to the hotel – and then discussed everything that had gone right or not so right on the way home in the evenings. It was very productive, to say the least.

The first year in Houston went by pretty quickly. When my first Rodeo and Barbecue Cook-Off (a Houston tradition) rolled around, I made sure I bought a pair of cowboy boots. I was turning into a

1977 as director of food and beverage at the Hyatt Regency

real Western kind of guy, the kind I'd seen in movies like Red River and The Alamo in what now seemed a different universe. I slowly came to realize that Houston was perfect for me, growing on me a little more every day. While at first I imagined I'd be an "outsider" here among so many "Texans," it dawned on me that Houston is filled with people from all over the world, drawn here by work, by the chance to make progress, by the opportunity to do something good for themselves and their families. Far from finding myself surrounded by cowboys acting like John Wayne in the movies, I found myself surrounded by Vietnamese and Japanese, by people from all over the Middle East attracted by our oil industry, by people from India and Pakistan drawn by jobs in our amazing Medical Center. Houston, I suppose, could have made us all feel like outsiders. Instead, it made none of us feel like that. We were here, we were welcome, and most of us who thought we were in transit would choose to stay.

As Rudi and I commuted to the Hyatt from the suburbs each day, we had plenty of time to talk about our futures. As it turns out, we both wanted to become millionaires, and we both spent a good deal of time looking for some way to do that. Our conversations became more intense once Hyatt started sending us both to the food shows in New York and the mammoth annual restaurant show in Chicago. We saw lots of things, and of course met hundreds and hundreds of entrepreneurs trying to do exactly what we wanted to. But no brilliant idea ever came from this, until…

At one of these shows, we found ourselves stopped at an exhibit of food sold pre-chopped and pre-cooked and pretty much ready to heat and serve. We both understood the value of this instantly, especially for busy hotels that never have the staff they really need. In a memory that still makes me smile, Rudi turned to me and asked, "Joe, do you know how to make lots and lots of food." I had to laugh out loud. "Don't you remember where I came from?" I asked. "At Disney, we served 120,000 meals a day. I have thousands of recipes to feed millions. I can

make lots and lots of food!" Rudi and I were happy. We were already millionaires just talking about this.

Sadly, as happens so often, reality set in even before we made it back to Houston the next day. There were already, we realized, many big companies doing what we wanted to do – and doing it, if not better, then at least bigger. We decided we'd better not toss the Hyatt Regency aside anytime soon, but the scale of the idea definitely got our big dreams rolling along.

For instance, for all the different restaurants and bars we did operate at the hotel, there was one we didn't – The Crystal Forest. It was a nightclub really, which meant it only opened at 8 in the evening, and therefore sat there dead wasting time and money the rest of the day. We took that space, opened up a buffet for people to grab a quick bite before racing back to the office and took the downtown area by storm. People loved our carved meats, for instance, but they loved nothing as much as the traditional quiche Lorraine we served each day. Our quiche went over so big that Rudi and I got to talking about opening up a whole chain of restaurants devoted to different types, in the same spirit that was driving Wolfgang Puck to create all kinds of weird pizzas and inspiring all the creperies that were popping up every where. It worked for pizza and crepes – so why not for quiche?

Rudi and I talked and talked, eventually having a go at this quiche idea within the Hyatt itself. We even convinced the hotel to rent a lot of billboards all around Houston and advertise with the headline "Have a Quiche at the Hyatt." Unfortunately, we didn't realize that most Americans still didn't know what quiche was. Our GM kept getting complaints about our signs inviting people to "Have a Quickie at the Hyatt!" Suffice it to say, the billboards came down; but the idea was enough of a success that Rudi gathered some investors to do the concept on his own and leave his hotel job. I was pretty happy to stay where I was. Well, I was even happier than that, since my only goal for a good while had been to get Rudi's job!

Texas Gulf Coast Ceviche

Yield: serves 6

8 ounces fresh flounder fillets, cut into 1/4 in cubes
4 ounces tiny bay shrimp
4 ounces small bay scallops
4 ounces fresh crabmeat
1 1/2 cups fresh lime juice
1 red bell pepper, cut in half, seeded and diced
1 green bell pepper, cut in half, seeded and diced
1/2 half red onion, chopped
1 chayote, peeled and diced
3 cloves garlic, minced
1 teaspoon salt
1 jalapeño chili pepper, cut in half, seeded and chopped very fine
5 drops Tabasco Sauce
12 bibb lettuce leaves
1/2 cup olive oil
3 ripe avocado pears cut into slices
1/2 cup coarsely chopped fresh cilantro

Combine the seafood with the peppers, onions, chayote and garlic in a ceramic or stainless steel bowl. Toss with the lime juice, salt and 1/4 cup olive oil. Cover the bowl with plastic wrap and refrigerate for 12 hours turning the seafood periodically. To serve, arrange two bibb lettuce leaves on a chilled plate. With a slotted spoon divide the ceviche evenly in the center on each plate. Drizzle with the remaining 1/4 cup olive oil, garnish with sliced avocado, and sprinkle with chopped cilantro.

Grilled Lump Crab Cakes with Avocado Salsa

Yield: serves 4

1 pound fresh crabmeat
1/4 teaspoon ground black pepper
2 tablespoons chopped fresh parsley
2 scallions, chopped
1/4 cup finely chopped onions
1 stalk celery, diced very fine
3 dashes Tabasco sauce
1/2 teaspoon salt
1 teaspoon mustard
1/2 cup mayonnaise
1 whole egg
1/2 cup dried breadcrumbs
1 cup vegetable oil

Avocado Salsa:
2 large ripe tomatoes
2 ripe avocados
2 tablespoons red wine vinegar
1/4 teaspoon sugar
1/4 teaspoon black pepper
1/4 cup chopped mild onions
1/4 cup chopped black olives
1 tablespoon chopped cilantro
3 tablespoons olive oil
4 sprigs fresh dill

Place the crabmeat into a stainless steel or ceramic bowl; make sure there are no shells among the crabmeat. Add the black pepper, chopped parsley, scallions, celery, onions, salt, Tabasco sauce, mustard, mayonnaise, and one whole egg, 1/2 cup breadcrumbs, combine well. (If the mixture is too soft, add a little more breadcrumbs) Cover with plastic wrap and place in the refrigerator.

In the meantime make the Avocado Salsa. Place the tomatoes for one minute into boiling water, then chill and peel under cold running water. Seed and chop tomatoes. Peel, pit and dice avocados, place in a bowl, add the rest of the ingredients, and let marinate a few minutes. In a large skillet heat the vegetable oil, divide the crab mixture into eight patties, and place carefully into the skillet. Sauté gently on both sides for 4 minutes or until golden brown. Spoon the salsa on four individual plates, place patties on top, garnish with fresh dill and serve.

Guacamole
(Texas Avocado Dip)
Yield: serves 4-6

4 ripe avocados
1/4 cup fresh lemon juice
1/2 cup mayonnaise
1 tablespoon vegetable oil
2 cloves garlic, mashed very fine
2 tablespoons grated onions
1/4 teaspoon seasoning salt
1/4 teaspoon garlic salt
1/4 teaspoon Tabasco sauce
Salt, chili powder, cayenne and
    freshly ground black pepper
    to your taste.

Cut the avocado pears in half. Remove the large pit, and scoop out the soft avocado flesh using a large soupspoon. Place the avocado in a ceramic bowl and mash with a fork; add all the ingredients, except the lemon juice. Combine the mixture well with a wooden spoon, level the top and cover with the lemon juice. When ready, stir in the lemon juice. Serve with toasted tortilla chips.

Hill Country
Jalapeño Quiche
Yield: Serves 6

1 10-inch pie crust, unbaked
1/4 cup chopped scallions (white part only)
2 tablespoons butter
1 medium, ripe tomato, sliced
5 large whole eggs
1 cup whipping cream
1/2 teaspoon salt
1/8 teaspoon freshly ground black pepper
1 1/2 cups grated Monterey Jack
    cheddar cheese
1/8 cup seeded and chopped
    jalapeño peppers
1/4 cup chopped cilantro

Preheat oven to 350°F. Line the pie shell with foil, fill with beans or pie weights and bake for 15 minutes. Cool; remove the foil and beans. Sauté the scallions in butter until light brown. Spread tomato slices and scallions in the bottom of the shell. Beat together eggs, cream, salt, black pepper, cheddar cheese, and cilantro. Pour the mixture over the tomatoes and scallions. Sprinkle the chopped jalapeños peppers on top and bake for 40 to 50 minutes or until the quiche is firm in the center. Let the quiche set for 10 minutes, cut into individual portions, and serve with a crisp salad.

Chicken Quesadillas

Yield: serves 6 as an appetizer

2 large boneless chicken breasts
2 tablespoons butter
1 small red onion, finely diced
2 jalapeños, seeded and chopped very fine
2 chipotles chilies, seeded and chopped very fine
3 tablespoons cilantro, chopped
1 small zucchini, finely diced
1 small yellow squash, finely diced
1 large ripe tomato, cut in half, seeded and diced
2 tablespoons lime juice
1 tablespoon fresh lemon juice
4 tablespoons olive oil, to cook the quesadillas, plus 2 tablespoons olive oil for salsa
1/2 cup mayonnaise
1 tablespoon honey
1 cup Monterey Jack cheese, shredded
1/2 cup scallions, white and tender green parts, thinly sliced
6 flour tortillas, 8 inches each in diameter
Cilantro leaves for garnish.

Heat the butter in a skillet over moderate heat. Season the chicken breasts with salt, pepper and sauté on both sides until browned and fully cooked. Place on a cutting board and cut into thin strips. In a bowl, combine the chicken with half of the diced onion, jalapenos and one tablespoon cilantro. Let marinate for half hour.

In another bowl, mix the remaining onions with 1 tablespoon chopped cilantro, the zucchini, yellow squash, tomatoes, lime juice and 2 tablespoons of the olive oil. Season with a little salt and pepper. In a small bowl, whisk the mayonnaise with the honey, lemon juice, chipotles, and the remaining tablespoon cilantro.

Arrange the tortillas on a work surface. Spoon the chicken mixture over half of each tortilla and top generously with the shredded cheese. Fold the top half of each tortilla over the chicken filling. In a large skillet, heat 2 tablespoons of the olive oil. Add 3 of the quesadillas and cook over moderate heat, turning once, until crisp on the outside, and the cheese has melted, about 5 minutes.

Transfer the quesadillas to a baking pan and keep hot. Cook the remaining 3 quesadillas in the remaining olive oil. Cut each quesadilla in 3 triangles, and top a dot of chipotle mayonnaise, and a tablespoon full of the salsa. Garnish with scallions and fresh cilantro leaves.

Chilled Gazpacho with Crabmeat

Yield: serves 4-6

1 medium size green pepper
1 medium size red pepper
1 medium size cucumber
1 small onion
2 stalks celery
2 gloves garlic, peeled and
    chopped very fine
12 ounce can tomato juice
6 ounce can beef stock
1/2 cup tomato puree
1/4 teaspoon thyme, black pepper, and salt
2 tablespoons vinegar
2 tablespoons olive oil
1/4 teaspoon Tabasco sauce
1/4 cup freshly chopped parsley
1/2 pound fresh or canned crabmeat

Wash all the vegetables under cold water. Cut the peppers in half, remove the seeds and dice very fine. Peel the cucumber, cut in half, remove the seed with a soupspoon, and dice very fine. Also dice the onion and celery. Place the vegetables into a stainless steel or ceramic bowl, and cover with tomato juice, and beef consommé. Add the garlic, pepper, salt, thyme, tomato puree, vinegar, olive oil, and Tabasco sauce. Combine the mixture very well and chill for several hours.

To serve, divide the crabmeat into 6 chilled bowls, ladle the Gazpacho over it, and sprinkle with chopped parsley. Serve with crusty brown bread.

Texas Seafood Gumbo

Yield: serves 10

6 hard-shell crabs
3/4 cup vegetable oil
3/4 cup flour
2 large onions, peeled and diced (1/4 inch)
5 cups diced celery
2 medium green bell peppers diced
2 medium red bell peppers diced
6 cloves garlic chopped
1/2 teaspoon cayenne pepper
4 bay leaves
1 teaspoon salt
1/8 teaspoon each dried oregano,
    basil, and thyme
2 quarts fish stock or water
1 pound andouille sausage, sliced
1 pound okra, sliced 1/2 inch thick
1 pound medium size shrimp, shelled
    and deveined
1 pound lump crabmeat
6 cups cooked white rice
Tabasco sauce

Clean the crabs by removing the gills. Cut the crabs in half, and crack the claws with a mallet.

Heat the oil in a heavy duty saucepan, gradually add the flour and cook over high heat, stirring constantly, until the roux is light brown: do not let it burn, or the gumbo will taste bitter. Stir in the vegetables, herbs, garlic, bay leaves, salt and cayenne pepper; cook another 5 minutes with the roux. Gradually add the fish stock, stirring constantly, and bring the mixture to a boil.

Add the crabs, sausage, and okra. Cover the pot, reduce the heat to moderate and simmer for 1 hour; stir the gumbo from time to time and skim often. Add the shrimp, crabmeat and boil for two minutes. Serve immediately, passing the rice and Tabasco sauce separately.

Texas Tortilla Soup
Yield: serves 10

1 large onion, peeled and diced
1 large carrot, peeled and diced
6 sticks celery, diced
1 jalapeno pepper, seeded and
    chopped finely
3 bell peppers, seeded and diced
5 cloves garlic, peeled and minced
12 ounces chicken meat,
    cut into small cubes
2 tablespoons tomato paste
2 tablespoons flour
3 large tomatoes, seeded and cut
    into cubes
2 quarts chicken stock
1/2 teaspoon dried thyme
1/4 teaspoon cumin
1/2 teaspoon chili powder
1/2 cup vegetable oil
1/2 cup cilantro, chopped
6 corn tortilla, cut into thin strips
    and fried to a crisp
1 cup grated cheddar cheese
3 ripe avocados, cut into cubes

Heat the vegetable oil in a six-quart soup pot, add the diced chicken meat and brown lightly. Add the diced vegetables, and cook over low heat for 5 minutes. Add tomato paste and seasoning, mix well. Dust the mixture with flour, and then add the heated chicken stock. Bring to a boil and simmer for 25 minutes, stirring from time to time. Just before serving add the diced tomatoes and chopped cilantro. Dice the avocados and place equally into the soup cups or crocks, ladle the soup over it. Top with crisp tortilla chips, grated cheese and serve.

Creamy Garlic Soup
Yield: serves 6

10 cloves garlic, peeled
2 tablespoons butter
1 teaspoon flour
1 slice slab bacon
1 bay leaf
1 stalk leek, white and tender green,
    cut half lengthwise, wash and dice
1 medium size onion, cut into chunks
4 cups chicken stock, fresh or canned
1 medium size potato, peeled and cut
    into 2 inch chunks
2 slices white sandwich bread, crust removed,
    cut into 1/4 inch cubes
1 1/2 cups half and half
1 tablespoon olive oil
Salt and white pepper
Freshly chopped chives for garnish

Preheat the oven to 400°F. In a saucepan, heat the butter; add the slice bacon, leeks, onions, garlic and cook over moderately high heat, stirring occasionally until just softened. Dust the vegetables with flour and mix well. Heat the chicken stock, and whisk into the vegetable – flour mixture. Add the potatoes, bay leaf, salt, and pepper. Bring the soup to a boil, reduce the heat and simmer for 40 minutes.

In the meantime toss the bread cubes with the olive oil in a medium size bowl. Spread the cubes on a cookie sheet pan and toast in the oven until crunchy and golden brown. Remove the bacon from the soup, and puree the rest in a food processor. Return the soup to the pan and stir in the cream. Over moderate heat bring the soup just to a simmer, taste for seasoning and ladle into heated bowls. Garnish with bread croutons, chopped chives and serve.

Pan Roasted Gulf Red Snapper with Tomatillo Salsa

Yield: serves 4

    4 red snapper fillets (7 ounces each)
    1/2 cup vegetable oil
    1/2 cup flour
    1/4 stick soft butter
    1 teaspoon fresh lemon juice
    1 teaspoon Worcestershire sauce
    Ground black pepper and salt to taste

Wash the fillets under running cold water, and dry with a paper towel. Season with salt, pepper, Worcestershire sauce and lemon juice. Heat the oil in a heavy-duty frying pan, dip the fillets in flour and sauté evenly for about 2 minutes on each sides until cooked and golden brown. Do not overcook; the fish should be very moist.

Ladle Tomatillo Salsa over the bottom of each of four heated dinner plates and place a red snapper fillet in the middle. Discard the vegetable oil from the frying pan, and then add the butter. Brown the butter over high heat and spoon lightly over the snapper fillets. Serve with seasonal vegetables and boiled potatoes.

Tomatillo Salsa:
    1 pound tomatillos, husks removed, and diced
    1/2 cup diced jicama or joyote
    1/2 cup diced mango
    1/2 cup diced red pepper
    1/4 cup diced yellow pepper
    1/4 cup chopped fresh cilantro
    2 Serrano chilies, seeded and finely chopped
    1 cup peanut oil
    1/4 cup virgin olive oil
    1/4 cup white vinegar
    2 tablespoons balsamic vinegar
    1 teaspoon fresh lime juice
    2 teaspoons fresh lemon juice
    2 cloves garlic, minced

Combine tomatillos, jicama, mango, red and yellow peppers, and cilantro in a medium size bowl. In another bowl whisk together the peanut oil and olive oil, vinegars, lime, lemon juice and garlic. Pour over the tomatillo mixture. Add salt and fresh ground pepper to your taste.

Piñón

Stuffed Whole Gulf Flounder

Yield: serves 4

12 ounces fresh lump crabmeat, picked over
1/2 red bell pepper, cut in half, seeded and diced
1/2 green bell pepper, cut in half, seeded and diced
1 stalk celery, washed, and diced
1/2 cup soft breadcrumbs
1/2 cup mayonnaise
1 whole egg
1/2 teaspoon mustard powder
3 drops Tabasco sauce
Salt and pepper to taste.

4 whole flounders, 14 to 16 ounce each
3/4 cup melted butter
1 cup dry breadcrumbs
1 teaspoon seasoning salt

To make the stuffing, combine the crabmeat and vegetables in a ceramic mixing bowl, and add the seasonings. Using a rubber spatula, carefully blend the egg and mayonnaise with the crabmeat/vegetable mixture. Refrigerate until ready for stuffing the flounders.

Preheat the oven to 450°F. With a pastry brush, spread 1 tablespoon of the melted butter evenly over the bottom of a shallow baking-serving dish large enough to hold the fish side by side. Set aside. Wash the flounders under cold running water and pat dry with paper towels. Place each flounder one at a time on a cutting board (dark colored side up). With a sharp kitchen knife remove the head and discard. Using a smaller boning knife, make a 4 to 5 inch long slit completely through the dark skin and top surface flesh to the backbone of each flounder. With the point of the knife cut along the bones to loosen the top fillet on each side to create a pocket. Season the inside and outside with salt, and fill equally each flounder with the stuffing.

Brush the entire surface of the fish generously with the remaining melted butter; sprinkle the breadcrumbs over the entire fish. Place the flounders on the baking dish, and bake in the middle of the oven for 15 minutes, reduce the heat to 300°F and bake another 5 minutes until nicely brown and the fish feels firm when prodded with the finger.

Pot Roasted Texas Longhorn
Yield: serves 6

     5 pounds chuck roast
     6 strips of bacon, diced
     2 onions, diced
     2 stalks celery, diced
     2 large carrots, diced
     4 cloves of garlic, minced
     2 bay leaves
     1/2 cup flour
     1/4 cup tomato paste

Marinate the meat for 2 days. Preheat the oven to 450°, place the beef roast in to a roasting pan, add the bacon and brown the meat on all sides (do not burn the bacon). Add the onions, garlic, celery, and carrots, and roast for 1/2 hour, turning the meat occasionally. Remove the meat, dust the vegetables with flour, then add the tomato paste and combine well, add two cups strained marinade, two cups of water and bring to a boil. Return the meat to the pot, and cover tightly with foil, place into the oven at 300°F and bake for two hours, (or until the meat is tender). Turn from time to time. Remove the roast, and slice the meat. Strain the gravy, season to your liking and serve separately.

Meat Marinade:
     3/4 bottle zinfandel red wine
     1/2 cup vegetable oil
     2 ribs celery, diced
     1/2 onion, diced
     2 cloves garlic, minced
     1 cup red wine vinegar
     8 crushed juniper berries
     2 slices oranges
     2 sprigs rosemary
     2 tablespoon brown sugar

Place all ingredients in a stockpot, bring to a boil and simmer for 20 minutes. Let the marinate cool, then place the meat in to it.

Southwestern Meat Loaf

Yield: 6 servings

1 1/2 pounds ground lean beef
1/2 pound lean ground pork
1/4 cup vegetable oil
1 medium onion, chopped finely
1 red bell pepper, cut in half, seeded and diced
1 tablespoon chopped parsley
4 cloves garlic, minced
2 fresh jalapeño peppers, cut in half, seeded and chopped very fine
2 tablespoons chili powder
2 teaspoons salt
1 teaspoon oregano
2 teaspoons ground cumin
1 can (28 ounces) peeled tomatoes, crush and well drained
1 cup dry bread crumbs
2 whole eggs beaten
1 cup sweet corn kernels, well drained
3 scallions, thinly sliced,
1/2 cup barbecue sauce
2 tablespoons Dijon mustard
1/2 pound grated sharp cheddar cheese

In a large skillet, heat the vegetable oil over high heat. Add the chopped onions, red peppers, garlic, jalapeno peppers, parsley, chili powder, salt, oregano and cumin. Cover the pan, reduce the heat to low and cook, stirring once or twice, until the vegetables are soft, about 10 minutes. Add the drained tomatoes, and continue to simmer for another 5 minutes.

Preheat the oven to 350°F. In a large bowl, combine the beef and pork, add the tomato / vegetable mixture, bread crumbs, eggs, and mix very well. Add the kernel corns and scallion, and blend together to form a firm meat mixture. Transfer the meat mixture to a shallow baking dish and form to a loaf. Mix the Dijon mustard with the barbecue sauce and brush generously over the meat loaf.

Bake the meat loaf for about 1 hour, or until a thermometer inserted in the center registers 160°F.

Sprinkle the cheddar cheese over the meat loaf and return to the oven for a few minutes until the cheese is melted. Slice and serve with garlic mashed potatoes.

Barbecued Cabrito
(Young Goat)
Yield: 6-8

1 young goat 8-10 pound
2 quarts dark beer
2 jalapenos, seeded and chopped
1 medium size onion, chopped
8 cloves garlic, crushed
1/2 cup cilantro, chopped
3 cups Texas barbecue sauce

Cut the goat into large pieces, and wash under running cold water. Place the meat in a ceramic bowl, add jalapenos, cilantro, garlic, onions and cover with dark beer. Cover the bowl with plastic wrap and marinate for 24 hours, turning often. Heat coals in a grill, add a piece of mesquite wood if possible and let the coals burn to a low fire. Remove the meat from the marinate, season with garlic salt and place over the fire.

Slowly brown on all sides over indirect heat at 350°F and baste often with the barbecue sauce to keep the meat moist. After grilling for about one hour place the meat in a Dutch oven, add two cups of marinade, cover and finish in the oven at 300°F for 2 hours. (The meat should be tender and easy to remove from the bones). Serve with extra barbecue sauce and Mexican red beans.

Texas Barbecue Sauce:
1/2 cup balsamic vinegar
1/2 teaspoon ground black pepper
1/2 teaspoon dry mustard
3 tablespoons brown sugar
1/4 cup tomato ketchup

1/4 cup molasses
1/2 cup espresso coffee
1/4 cup Worchestershire sauce
1/2 cup Dijon mustard
1 cup vegetable oil

Combine all ingredients in a casserole and simmer over low heat for 10 minutes, stirring constantly.

Mexican Red Beans:
1 pound red beans, soak in cold water
   for 12 hours
2 large onions, chopped
3 cloves garlic minced
5 slices bacon, chopped
1 smoked ham hock
1 cup cubed ham
1 (16 ounces) can tomatoes

2 tablespoons chili powder
1 teaspoon cumin
2 bay leaves
1 teaspoon dried thyme
1 teaspoon salt
1 1/2 teaspoons sugar

Drain the beans. Sauté the bacon in a heavy-duty pot over high heat, but do not brown. Add the onions, garlic, chili powder and cumin, combine well. Add the beans, tomatoes, ham hock, thyme, bay leaf, sugar and salt, cover with water and simmer slowly for 4 hours. Stir occasionally and add more water if necessary. Remove 1/2 cup of beans, purée in a blender, then return to the pot, add cubed ham, bring to a boil and serve.

Chalupas

Texas Hot Open Face
Ground Beef Sandwich

Yield: 4 to 6

1 pound ground beef
1/2 stick butter
1/4 teaspoon chili powder
1/2 teaspoon cumin
1 teaspoon salt
6 corn tortillas
1 cup vegetable oil
1 1/2 cups bean dip
2 cups grated cheddar cheese
1 cup diced ripe tomatoes
3 cups finely sliced iceberg lettuce
1/2 cup green bell peppers
3/4 cup guacamole
1/2 cup sour cream
1 medium size onion, chopped fine

Preheat oven to 350 ° F. Heat the oil in a heavy-duty pan, and fry each tortilla on both sides until light brown and crisp. Drain on a paper towel and set aside. In another frying pan melt the butter, add the ground beef and sauté over low heat until the meat is cooked. (Drain the grease if necessary) Add cumin, chili powder and salt, combine well and remove from the stove.

Spread each tortilla with a generous portion of bean dip, and top with 3 tablespoons of meat mixture and two tablespoons grated cheddar cheese. Place on a cookie sheet pan and bake for 5 minutes, or until heated through. Place the piping hot tortillas on individual plates, and sprinkle with lettuce, diced tomatoes, bell peppers, guacamole, chopped onions and sour cream.

Serve immediately.

For large parties, prepare each tortilla with bean dip, meat, and cheese. Place the garnishes in separate bowls, and let each guest build their own chalupa.

Venison Tenderloin with Bell Peppers
Yield: serves 4

12 venison medallions (2 ounces each, from the back-strap if possible)
4 egg whites, whipped
2 teaspoons light soy sauce
2 tablespoons cornstarch
1 tablespoon honey
2 cloves garlic, minced
1/4 cup butter
1/2 cup vegetable oil
1/2 cup flour for dusting

Sauce:
1/2 medium onion, finely diced
1/2 red bell pepper, cut in half, seeded and diced
1/2 green bell pepper, cut in half, seeded and diced
1/2 jalapeno pepper, seeded and minced
1/4 teaspoon cumin
1 teaspoon flour
1/2 teaspoon chili powder
2 cups fresh Portobello mushrooms, sliced
2 cups chicken stock, fresh or canned
3 strips lean bacon, chopped finely
1 cup zinfandel wine
1/4 cup cranberry jelly
1 cup heavy cream
2 bay leaves
4 juniper berries

Pound the medallions with a mallet and place into a ceramic dish. Whisk the egg whites in a bowl; add soy sauce, honey, garlic and cornstarch. Spoon the mixture over the venison, combine well and refrigerate for 24 hours. Heat the oil over high heat in a large frying pan, dust the medallions with flour and cook (6 medallions at a time) on both sides until golden brown. Do not overcook the meat, it should be a little pink in the center). Drain the oil; add a little butter, which gives the venison a delicious nutty taste.

Remove the medallions from the skillet, place on a serving platter and keep warm. Lower the heat, but keep the frying pan on the stove.

To make the sauce, sauté the chopped bacon in the venison rendering, add the onions, peppers, mushroom and sauté until glossy. Dust with flour, cumin, chili powder and combine well. Add the chicken stock, red wine, cranberry jelly, bay leaves, juniper berries and bring to a boil. Simmer over low heat for about 5 minutes, then add the cream, heat but do not boil. Season with salt and black pepper to taste, strain the sauce over the venison and serve with wild rice or any kind of pasta.

Grilled Pork Tortillas with Tomatillo Salsa
Yield: serves 4

1-pound pork tenderloin
8 flour tortillas
1/2 pound tomatillos, husked, cored and cut into halves
1/2 medium onion, quartered
4 cloves garlic
2 medium serrano chilies, cut in half and seeded
1/2 cup fresh cilantro, chopped
1 tablespoon fresh lime juice
1 tablespoon olive oil
1 teaspoon ground cumin
1/2 teaspoon crumbled dry oregano
1/2 teaspoon freshly ground black pepper
1/2 cup scallions, chopped
1/4 teaspoon salt

Light the grill or preheat the broiler. In a small saucepan, combine the tomatillos, onions, garlic cloves, chilies, and 1 cup water. Bring to a boil over moderately high heat. Lower the heat and simmer for 8 minutes until most of the liquid has evaporated and the tomatillos are cooked. Add the lime juice, olive oil and a dash of salt. In a food processor pulse until coarsely pureed. Transfer the salsa to a medium ceramic bowl, cover and let stand at room temperature for up to one hour.

In a small bowl combine the cumin, oregano, 1/2 teaspoon salt, and black pepper. Trim the pork tenderloin, then cut into 4 diagonal slices and pound with a mallet to 1/2 inch thick, Rub the seasoning mixture on both sides of the pork medallions. Grill or broil the pork for about 5 minutes per side, until nicely brown and fully cooked. Transfer to a plate, cover with foil and keep warm.

Grill or fry the tortillas for about 30 seconds, until light brown. With a sharp knife slice the pork medallions against the grain into 1/2 inch wide strips and place the meat equally in to the center of each tortilla. Spoon a generous portion of the salsa over the pork, sprinkle with scallions and cilantro, roll and serve at once.

Texas Pecan Tart
Yield: serves 6 – 8

3 large whole eggs
1 cup white sugar
1 cup white Karo syrup
1/4 stick butter
1/8 teaspoon salt
1 teaspoon vanilla extract
9-inch pie crust, uncooked
1 1/4 cups pecan nuts

Preheat the oven to 400°F. Whisk eggs; add sugar, syrup, butter, salt and vanilla. Place the pecans into the unbaked pie crust, and pour the syrup mixture over it. Bake for 15 minutes until the pecans have risen to the top. Reduce the temperature to 325°F and bake for another 35 minutes until the center is cooked and the pie has a nice crusty top.

Texas Strawberry Tart
Yield: makes one 9 inch tart

Sweet pastry dough:
>   2 cups cake flour
>   1 1/2 stick soft butter
>   1/2 cup sugar
>   1 1/2 teaspoon vanilla extract
>   1/4 teaspoon salt
>   1 large whole egg
>   1 egg yolk
>   Grated rind from 1/2 lemon

Sift the flour on a flat surface. Place the butter, sugar, eggs, salt, ground lemon rind, and vanilla extract in the center of the flour and knead the mixture from the outside until the dough masses together. Wrap in plastic and refrigerate for one hour.

On a well-floured working surface roll the dough with a rolling pin, rotating the dough as you gradually form a thin circle. Press the dough into a well-greased removable bottom tart pan, and cut the edges with a knife. Bake in the middle of a 350° oven for 15 minutes.

The leftover scraps can be used to make sugar cookies of your choice

Cheesecake filling:
>   Preheat the oven to 350 °F
>   4 ounces cream cheese, softened
>   2 tablespoons butter, softened
>   1 teaspoon cornstarch
>   1/4 cup sugar
>   1/4 cup sour cream
>   1 1/2 teaspoons vanilla extract
>   1 large egg

Strawberry topping:
>   1 cup apricot glace
>   3 tablespoons white rum
>   2 tablespoons water
>   2 pints large strawberries , washed, stemmed and cut in half

Using a handheld electric mixer, beat the cream cheese until smooth, then add the butter, sugar, egg and vanilla. Continue to mix until frothy, slowly blend in the cornstarch. Pour the filling into the tart shell and bake on the lower shelf for 20 minutes until the cheese filling is firm and slightly brown. Set aside and let the tart cool. Remove the tart from the tart form and place on a serving platter. Arrange the strawberries in a circle on top of the cheesecake filling.

In a small saucepan heat the rum, water and apricot glace until smooth. Simmer for a few minutes until thick, and then brush the strawberries generously. Cut the tart in wedges, serve with fresh whipped cream and garnish with a sprig of fresh mint.

Tex-Mex Wedding Cookies
Yield: 36 cookies

1 stick unsalted butter, room temperature
1/2 cup finely chopped pecan nuts
1/2 teaspoon vanilla
1 1/2 cups confectioner's sugar
1 cup all purpose flour
Pinch of salt

In a medium bowl, beat butter, pecans and vanilla until fluffy and creamy. Beat in half of the confectioner's sugar. Stir in the flour and salt, mix well. Roll the dough into two 8-inch long logs, wrap in plastic and refrigerate for several hours or overnight. Preheat the oven to 350° F. and line a large cookie sheet with parchment paper. Using a sharp knife, quarter each log of cookie dough lengthwise, and then cut it crosswise into four equal slices. Roll each piece of dough into a 3/4 inch ball and arrange one inch apart on the cookie sheet.

Bake in the middle of the oven for about 15 minutes, or until golden brown. Let the cookies cool slightly, then roll in the remaining confectioners sugar. Transfer on a serving platter, garnish with fresh mint and a few ripe strawberries.

Trail Ride Oatmeal Cookies
Yield: 7 dozen 2-inch cookies

1/2 pound butter softened
1 cup granulated sugar
1 cup dark brown sugar
2 whole eggs
1 teaspoon vanilla extract
1 1/2 cups cake flour
1 teaspoon baking soda
1/2 teaspoon salt
3 cups quick-cooking oatmeal
1/2 cup finely chopped pecan nuts

In a deep bowl, cream the butter, vanilla extract and the brown sugar with an electric mixer, add the eggs one at a time and whisk until the mixture is light and fluffy. Combine the flour, baking soda, and salt in a sifter and sift together directly in to the bowl. With a wooden spoon blend the mixture together until smooth, then mix in the oatmeal by the cup full. Stir in the pecan nuts.

Divide the dough in half and transfer to a lightly flowered surface, roll each half into a cylinder about 2 inches in diameter and 14 inches long. Wrap the dough in plastic wrap and refrigerate over night. Preheat the oven to 350°F. Remove the plastic wrap and with a sharp kitchen knife slice the dough into rounds 1/3 inch thick. Arrange the rounds 1 inch apart on a cookie-baking pan and bake in the middle of the oven for 10 minutes, or until the cookies are light brown and firm in the center. Transfer them to wire racks and cool the cookies at room temperature before serving.

DREAMS
REALIZED

I loved being food and beverage director at the Hyatt Regency in Houston. After 30 years, I could finally take off my white chef's uniform and put on a nice pinstriped suit and some shiny new shoes. Sometimes people still ask me what it felt like to not be a chef anymore, but these are usually people who know little about the real profession. They picture me one day standing on the line with a sauté pan in my hand, putting out steaks and seafood for a roomful of hungry diners – and then, the next day, never doing that again. As you have seen, however, my job as food and beverage director had been many years – not one night – in the making. The more restaurants you have under your wing, the more meals you serve each day and the more staff you have depending on decisions you have to make, the less truly rides on your genius with that sauté pan. I got a raise, of course, and the chance to walk around in a suit, but in most ways I was still me and still worried about the same sorts of things. I'd learned years earlier at Disney that some things are just about changing your costume!

It was no accident that my success occurred with Hyatt, since this particular hotel company was a bit of an upstart when it came to food and beverage. Seeing the amount of investment and sheer work it took to keep one or more restaurants going day after day, a lot of other companies simply leased restaurant space out to a variety of operators – Trader Vic's being one of the best known in the '60s and '70s. Still, Hyatt embraced the European model, in which a fine hotel required fine dining. In Europe, as many travelers know, some of the very finest dining rooms are located in multi-starred hotels. The two go hand in hand, though it took Hyatt to see things that way in this country. They hired some of the very best people, including European chefs, food and beverage directors and wine stewards to operate restaurants in their flagship properties. I'm very, very proud to have worked for such a great company.

One of the most important components of my job in Houston wasn't in Houston at all. As assistant to our big boss Dick Nelson, I found myself getting involved in the creation of Hyatt Regency after Hyatt Regency all across America, from Atlanta to New Orleans to San Francisco. We designed and built different restaurants in each city, all the while seeking ways to achieve the economy of scale without having our places seem boring or cookie cutter in any way. Through every opening, I took notes on things I learned from the people I worked with – recipes that interested me, of course, but also ideas for design and efficient operation. I could learn something from just about everybody, it seemed, and everything I learned in hotel after hotel, I wrote down for my future. You see, even with the best job in the world, I knew that sooner or later I would follow in Rudi's path and open a restaurant of my own. It didn't bother me that La Quiche was about 20 years ahead of its time, that Americans weren't ready for a whole concept built around quiche. Rudi quickly changed the concept to a place under his name, Rudi Lechner's, specializing in German and Austrian cuisine. The success of that restaurant spurred me on. It was the kind of success I wanted for my own life. I wasn't sure how to begin, but I was confident I had the lessons I would need stashed away in all my Hyatt notebooks.

One day I was standing in our revolving rooftop restaurant Spindletop when I was struck not only by the beauty of Houston but by its sheer crazy energy expressed in new construction. As the restaurant turned slowly, I realized that in every direction I faced the horizon was filled with cranes erecting new highrise buildings. I knew, as I watched the dreams of so many other entrepreneurs get built, that someone would someday build my dream too. I raced right back to my office and started building my own restaurant – only on paper, of course. I used all I'd learned about layout opening Disney World and of course all those Hyatt Regencys to create a design that would work, from the way the kitchen was laid out to how the dining tables would be situated, with room for staff to plow from one to the other. For looks I borrowed heavily from Anthony's Pier 4 in Boston, since it was one of the nation's most successful restaurants and my heart still belonged there to some degree. I drew in a wonderful rotisserie, since we'd been making sure that each of the Hyatts we built included one of those. The whole restaurant was built around my entire life experience, around everything I'd ever seen that worked. I factored in 180 seats, figured out the average guest check to see how much money we could take in, and then subtracted 38 percent for food cost and 26 percent for labor cost. It was a lovely business plan, perfect for presenting to the bank as well as to any potential investors. After all, the first thing I figured I'd need to build my dream was some money.

When I went to visit my first bank, I was the picture of hope and confidence. I showed the loan officer all the figures I'd drawn up, all my brilliant calculations about how this mythical restaurant of mine was supposed to make a ton of money. I told him how much sense it would make for his bank to lend me the entire $350,000 I'd need – and how happy they'd all be at the end of the day, what today we'd call a "win-win" situation. But after listening to me for quite some time, the banker said there was one thing missing from my proposal – a financial statement. "Well," I said, "it's just me, and I don't actually have much money." I still figured the absolutely clear vision on paper would carry me through this, but the banker rather politely told me "thanks but no thanks." The next banker I visited wasn't so polite; he practically threw me out for wasting his time. So on my third try, I went to a friend in banking. At least he sat me down and told the way things have to work. No, some bank probably was never going to lend me $350,000. I'd have to go and find some investors and save up a chunk of money myself. And finally, when I had maybe $250,000, some bank might lend me the last $100,000. As many people have observed since: You can't borrow money unless you almost don't need to. I was disappointed but not crushed. That was simply how it was going to be.

I tried the investor route among my friends at that time; but even though everybody said they were impressed with my presentation and with the potential for my restaurant, every last one of them had some reason he couldn't invest. There were some big hospital bills, or a kid had just gone off to college, or he'd just lost a bundle in the stock market. So that wasn't working. Next, I turned to all the big builders in Houston, figuring they might want to build my restaurant as a kind of investment, that they might want to partner with me that way – for the building and a little bit of seed money. The vast majority of builders never even told me thanks for thinking of them. So that plan wasn't working either, even after a year of sending out my proposals. But then, in a way I couldn't have foreseen, a cooking school opened in Houston, a place called Gourmet World, and they asked if I wanted to teach some classes. It was through teaching these classes that I met Rosemary and Frank Malone. Both were in construction and, as we became friends through various gourmet societies, they agreed to take a look at my proposal. They both said it made a lot of sense, but mostly we concentrated on having wonderful food, wine and conversation together as often as we could. Every time I did something fun at the Hyatt, I made sure to invite Rosemary and Frank.

One day out of the blue, Frank called me up and asked if I was still interested in building my own restaurant. "More than ever," I said, thinking of all my friends who had done so well by venturing out as entrepreneurs. "Well," Frank said, "I just bought this piece of land out on Wilcrest Drive. It's pretty far west and there's not too much there right now, but with the way this city is growing, I think this is the place you need to be." Of course I agreed to go see the place. We drove, and we drove, and it was pretty much a wilderness. Based on the movies I'd seen about Texas, in fact, it looked a lot like Indian Territory. Frank still had my proposal, and he assured me it would fit perfectly into a collection of condominiums and apartments he was hoping to build. Time passed. We saw each other now and then, and neither of us really mentioned the idea of building my restaurant. So after a while I started to figure it was just another of those things business people talk about. You know, things that would make sense but nobody ever quite gets around to doing.

Then Frank called me and invited me over to have dinner and meet with his attorney and his architect about my lease. Construction had already begun on the apartments and condominiums, he said, and within about 90 days I should be able to move into my restaurant. I was stunned. I was delighted. I was upset. And I told Frank I had to talk to him before the other guests arrived.

"I am so happy you like my idea," I told him, once we'd both poured a glass of wine at his house. "But honestly, if I ever gave you the impression I had the $350,000 I would need to open this restaurant, I'm so sorry. I don't, Frank. But there is one way we still might be able to do this. You could build me the restaurant as collateral, you could be my partner in this, and I'm sure the bank would then lend us the money we need to finish."

"I don't know, Joe. At my age, I'm not so sure I ought to be going into the restaurant business. But we're not going to talk about this tonight. We're going to have a nice dinner and some wonderful wine. We're going to talk over the details with the lawyer and architect, then I'll talk with Rosemary tonight, and I'll give you my answer in the morning."

To my undying amazement and gratitude to Frank, who was such a father figure to me in every way, that's what we did. We talked over dinner, and he talked to Rosemary. The next morning he called me and told me YES.

What a crazy three months those were. All the time keeping my plans to myself, I went through the motions I'd gone through a dozen or more times before – choosing tablecloths and silver, outfitting the kitchen, starting to interview potential staff – except this time I was doing it for me. Part of the way through the building of my restaurant, Dick Nelson asked me to go to Dallas for a month, to help open the Hyatt Regency there, so of course I did. I felt already this would be my last big project for Hyatt. Even had I stayed, I knew the company was looking to make me a general manager somewhere,

With Frank Malone, friend and investment partner in Rotisserie for Beef & Bird

thus taking me yet another step farther from the kitchen. I was almost certainly leaving Hyatt, as only I knew, but I never would have wanted to let Dick Nelson down. In your working life, if you're lucky as I have been, people come to believe in you. They see you as part of their team, and even if you move apart and work for different companies in different cities or countries, and even if you don't talk for years – they know you're there. They know you can do the job for them. They call you, as Dick and a handful of others had always done for me. When people are that in your life, when they believe in you that much, you'll do practically anything not to let them down.

When I came back from Dallas, Dick called me into his office and told me how happy he and Hyatt were with my work there. They didn't, he said, know exactly where they wanted to send me as a general manager, so he asked me where in the rest of the United States or even overseas I would like to go. And sitting there that day, I realized a lot of things more than I ever had before. First and foremost, in my life, I had never really had a home. When you start out as a child driven from your homeland as a refugee, when you spend your life going from job to job, the idea of home doesn't seem to matter – until you realize it matters more with each passing day. As no one, including me, could ever have predicted, Texas had become my home. And I had no interest in ever leaving.

"Mr. Nelson," I said, "I really have to tell you. I will be leaving the company within six weeks."

"Oh come on, Joe," he shot back. "We're prepared to offer you virtually anywhere you want, virtually everything you could ever want. You have a great future with us, wherever in the world you decide to go. What company could offer you more than Hyatt?" He paused for a moment, surely studying my resume in his head and thinking of Paris, London or Rome. Maybe Hong Kong, Buenos Aires or Sydney. "Where in the world are you thinking of moving now?"

I could only smile. "Well, sir, I'm going to go out to Wilcrest!"

It was right before Thanksgiving in 1978 that my restaurant Rotisserie for Beef and Bird opened its doors. The name had come about naturally, simply taking shape from the things we placed on the menu. A rotisserie would be the center of everything, I knew, and in addition to the beef I knew Texans would demand, we'd roast chickens and ducks and game birds with the changing seasons. As I say, the name pretty much configured itself.

You really need to hear, right from the start, that almost nothing about owning my own restaurant was the way I expected it to be – or the way I wanted it to be for my personal happiness. For one thing, remember that all the places I'd worked for other people during my 17 years in America had been hugely successful. Either they were that before my arrival, like The Stork Club in New York or Anthony's Pier 4 in Boston, or they became that way as quickly as they opened, like the Hyatt Regency in Houston. I was proud of all I'd accomplished, and more than a little arrogant. I thought that from the moment the world heard about Rotisserie for Beef and Bird, we would have every table full and lines reaching out the front door. Oh how little I really knew about opening a restaurant of your own.

Additionally, the relationships impacted by the opening became very difficult very fast. All the time leading up to Rotisserie, Frank and Rosemary had been among my very best friends. Yet there is nothing like going into business together – after all, I was this huge celebrity in my own mind, but only a small shareholder in the business – to take a nice friendship and toss it right into the dumpster out back. If doing business dooms a friendship, what can I possibly say about my marriage? Gigi was happy at first, to be in a city as big as Houston, but also to have what she thought would be her own "theater." What better place than a restaurant for someone who always fancied herself an actress! After all, we did two shows daily and called them lunch and dinner. Gigi immediately came to work at Rotisserie for Beef and Bird and tried every second to be the star of the show. What she didn't realize – what *we* didn't realize – was that there's room for only one star. That star is the chef, and that chef was me. We argued about everything at work, and of course took almost every argument home with us. Neither of us had anyplace to go to escape the arguments, until at last we decided it just wasn't working. The restaurant part, anyway. Gigi had to leave Rotisserie and find someplace where she could be the star she so wanted and needed to be, and she has resented me for that ever since.

I also was misguided enough to think that as a restaurateur, I would be just like a food and beverage director. As you recall, it had actually been many years since I'd cooked on the line and that was something I felt I'd graduated from. But now it was my restaurant – and in my restaurant, shortly after opening, I realized the food was horrible and the service was even worse. I'm grateful to those close friends who drew me aside to tell me these things. In this business, you hear horror stories about places that hear nothing but "Oh, everything was great" until they have no customers left at all. Everybody wants to hear praise, but in a business that depends so heavily on customer satisfaction, you can't afford to hear too much empty praise. You need to hear about the problems too, or else you'll never make time to fix them. To that end, after a few weeks, I went out and bought myself some nice chef whites and went to work in the kitchen.

It was hard, starting with only two other cooks and increasing that to four, since otherwise I had to spend all my days cutting up chickens and filleting whole fish. There was never a day off, and of course I did everything. One day it was pouring down rain and I looked out at all these well-dressed business people trying to get to their cars, and of course we couldn't afford a valet. So… I put a plastic bag over

Awards from Rotisserie's 26 years

my head and went up to the front of the line. "Sir," I said, "please give me your keys. I will go get your car!" I cut the lawn in the afternoon. I peeled all the potatoes. After we closed each night, I kept one guy at minimum wage to help me clean the whole restaurant, front and back. Even with all this, we lost money every day we opened, each month falling behind another $20,000 or $30,000. I had to keep going to Frank for this money to pay for things, and very quickly he got tired of throwing good money after bad.

Within six months, I was at the end of my rope. Day and night, all I could think of was that one phone call – the one to Hyatt that would lift me out of this nightmare and take me back where working hard made sense. Where I could get a good job in no time, where Dick Nelson could watch over me, where I could afford qualified staff and the best ingredients. Oh, how many nights did I stare at that phone thinking I would make the call, wishing I could bring myself to make the call – and asking how I'd let my pride and my arrogance get me into this horrible, doomed situation. All my life I've believed in spiritual things, without talking about them much or trying to convince people to believe things my way. At the end of all this misery, when everything I'd dreamed of for 20 or even 30 years had failed me and vice versa, the only thing I could do was say a prayer. I learned a lot about miracles from what happened next, about how miracles happen to us at the same time we are active in making them happen.

The very next day, jogging as I did every morning in hopes of keeping my sanity, I felt myself fill with peace and confidence and ideas for how to make Rotisserie for Beef and Bird work. All my life I'd had ideas that made things work for others. How could I let my dream die without having ideas that made things work for me?

I gathered the staff, including the 12 who were now cursing me and themselves for following me from the Hyatt. I told them we were not going to let this thing fail. And that, starting that day and starting with me, everybody who might be hungry in Houston was going to know about Rotisserie for Beef and Bird. Dressing up in my chef whites with the tall toque blanche balanced on my head, I grabbed a couple of chickens and started doing cooking demonstration at Foley's and all the rest of the local department stores. I went to the Jewish Community Center in Meyerland and started teaching cooking classes, inviting anyone who came to join me at my restaurant for lunch or dinner. I even called up all the ladies I knew in garden clubs and invited them to come for lunch on Mondays. They, of course, were worried about the cost, so I said, "Look, I'll cook your group a fine lunch and you just pay what you think it's worth – if it's $1 fine or if it's $10 fine. But the thing is, each lady has to bring her own car." This may have sounded like an odd request, but on that first Monday 40 ladies from a garden club came in for lunch – complete with 40 cars in my parking lot. Everybody who drove by on Wilcrest Drive had a great view of a new restaurant so popular its lot was full even on a Monday. The very next day, we were packed!

My staff could not believe the change that had come over me. No, I hadn't "found religion," enrolled in some new motivational scheme or, as one or two employees must have wondered, started using some recreational drug. All I'd found was the truth, a truth I'd lived with in one way or another as long as I'd been working. I'd always done whatever it took to

drive the business – come on now, you must remember me raising those rabbits and making all those jars of strawberry preserves! For years, I'd been fearless and in some ways a bit shameless to bring business to my employers. But there it was, undeniably – when I became an entrepreneur, I figured business would just come to me. Quite the opposite is true, of course. When you're an entrepreneur, every penny someone gives you is because you make them give it to you. You should be honest and faithful and moral about it, and probably work harder for that penny than a penny is really worth. But you have to make them give it to you. Every day for the rest of your life, if you remain an entrepreneur, you're going to wake up thinking of new ways to make new customers come in and old customers come back. You'd better love it, learn to love it or pretend to love it, because as the next two decades of success bore out at Rotisserie for Beef and Bird, it's never going to get easy.

Within a few years, Rotisserie for Beef and Bird was solidly established as one of the finest restaurants in Texas and even in the entire South. Our awards came to cover the walls, for both the food that came from the staff I handpicked and trained in our kitchen and to the wine collection we built up slowly. This was during the same time that more and more Americans were learning to enjoy the wonder of wine, so before long I was taking requests from my customers – plus making several trips with Frank and Rosemary to the traditional hotbeds of wonderful wine, Bordeaux and Burgundy. With each year of greater success came no easing up in our work but considerable easing up in our financial worries. In the beginning, it was all about Frank being able to bail the place out, to make up the shortfall of this or that month's revenues versus our expenses. But in time, I'm sure he enjoyed the fact that I didn't have to ask him for money anymore. Houston's love for the Rotisserie for Beef and Bird spurred me on with its enthusiasm to try new things all the time. We were one of the first restaurants to have live lobsters because some customer found out I used to work in Boston. We were one of the first restaurants to explore wild game cookery in the wintertime, because somebody figured out that since I was European I'd probably know about that. We had special seasonal menus, we had festivals and celebrations of every sort – and we had food editors writing about each one in the pages of the Chronicle and the Post.

Things changed in the late '80s, though. The first blow was when Frank Malone died, and I realized I'd lost far more than an investor, far more than my own personal "money guy." I had lost a man of great taste and culture, whose understanding of food and wine always kept me seeking the latest and best, never resting on anything that looked like a laurel. Yes, I'd lost far more than that, and I didn't realize what Frank had been until he wasn't anymore. He had been a father figure. Just think of my life – all the years of my childhood when my father was away at war, so many years that by the time he found his way home from the refugee camps it was almost time for me to leave home to find work. Then all those years with a family a distant memory that seemed ever farther away.

How else could it seem from all over Europe, from South Africa? From New York? From Bermuda and the Caribbean? From Boston, Orlando or Houston? In that journey, I had become a man with a family of his own, but somewhere deep inside me there was emptiness – the place I always wanted my mentors to fill, each and every one. The place that Frank Malone filled for me so profoundly.

Then, what do those boxes of salt all say: When It Rains, It Pours? About the same time, Gigi finally got serious about filing for divorce. She had talked about it for years, and it was probably best for both of us. But it was still a shock when she filed. I didn't feel there was anything I could do but go down to the courthouse and sign the divorce decree. The harder part, in many ways, stretched before me. As one shareholder among four, I had already decided to buy out Frank and Rosemary after his death; now I had to buy out Gigi's shares too. There was something painful about lifting your restaurant out of financial stress by years of hard work – only to plunge your personal finances into incredible strain by buying out not one, not two but three partners. I did it, though – at the same time Monique was in college studying fashion and Erika was in college for hotel/restaurant management. I was single again, but it felt as though the two most important relationships in my life had ended and left me alone. This was emotionally the lowest point in my life.

By the 1990s, some amazing things had begun happening on the international scene. For decades since the end of World War II, the part of the world that I had left behind and always thought of as Pomerania had existed only behind the Iron Curtain. Visiting had been difficult to dangerous to impossible, depending on the diplomatic intrigues of the moment, and of course nobody could get out. But beginning with the opening of the Berlin Wall and the birth of democracies in many Eastern European countries, the place I knew as Pomerania but the world knew as Poland was available to me for the very first time since we ran to that harbor and escaped the fires and explosions. I determined I would go and got two friends named Bob and Antje

Onofrey excited to go with me.

Still, as we went through the months of planning, one idea formed inside me and wouldn't leave me alone. I didn't want to return to my homeland alone. I had been divorced for several years and had, up till then, no intention of entering any serious relationship – after all, I'd seen what those were about. Besides, there wasn't time to get one of those, so I knew I should just quit fretting and go with my friends. But I couldn't. Then, about a week before we were scheduled to leave, two pretty ladies came into my restaurant for dinner and I really liked one of them so I asked her out on a date. And at the end of that date, after a couple bottles of wine, I asked her a question.

"Would you go to Poland with me next week?"

"Yes, of course I will," she said.

Then, the next day, after the wine wore off, she called me and asked if we'd really talked about going to Poland and if she'd really said she'd go across an ocean with a man she knew virtually nothing about. In fact, she said, she couldn't even remember my last name! Doing that would be crazy, she said. She couldn't just run off to Poland with me. Surely I could understand that. Well, of course I couldn't! I asked her to have lunch with me to talk about it, assuring her everything would be proper and safe for her every step of the way, and that I was an all-around decent guy who would keep all his promises. She was reluctant, but she agreed. That wasn't the first time I was happy I was good at talking people into things.

The trip was extraordinary for Bob and Antje – and for Connie and me. We traveled through the countryside and the cities, many buildings replaced entirely after being destroyed in the war, others thrilling me with the faintest memories that I'd seen them or someplace just like them as though in a dream. Though we've talked about it many times since, I still can only imagine what it was like for Connie, traveling inside the homeland of a man she'd barely met, sharing with him some of the most emotional experiences of his life. At one point, in the city of Kolberg – or Kolobrzec as it's called in Polish – the four of us found ourselves in front of a charming little chapel built by Catherine the Great of Russia. Almost

before we could think about it, Bob and Antje had maneuvered Connie and me in front of that chapel so they could take a photo. A happy couple photo! We smiled for the picture, and I held Connie's hand. And I swear to you that I knew, standing in front of that chapel, that Connie and I would be married. We returned to Houston, dated for four years and then did precisely that.

When you are happily married, the whole universe looks different. Since the day I waved goodbye to my childhood in war-ravaged Europe, my life had been about work – and my work had made me happy, I thought. Yet as Connie and I enjoyed the first few years of our marriage, the most bizarre thought started entering my mind at the oddest moments – retirement. No, it wasn't the retirement a lot of men my age were thinking about, full of golf or tennis or coin collecting. Connie and I wanted to travel, to be sure, and some form of retirement would make that easier. But what really baffled us was that I seemed to be wishing for two things that didn't exactly go together. I wanted one more challenge as a restaurateur, yet I also definitely wanted to slow down. As for the first, Rotisserie for Beef and Bird was a well-oiled machine. It had a steady stream of customers in good times and bad, and from the dining room to the kitchen, every employee knew what he or she was doing. You see, as the advertising slogan goes, it was everything I'd ever dreamed of in a restaurant - and less. I wanted to create something, to build something new again, probably for the last time. Yet I wanted to create and build it in such a way that never again would I be its slave. Typically, I knew what I had to do.

I took my initial inspiration from the bistros of France, a country Connie and I loved to visit. I know, in America, the word "bistro" means anything somebody wants it to mean – like just about every other word in America. But in France, where things tend to be set in stone even when there's no need, a bistro is a comfortable city or probably country restaurant, serving fresh, simple, straightforward foods that have as much in common with Mama's home cooking (if Mama is a very good cook) as with the self-expressions of some highly trained chef. We loved that kind of food in France, and we felt confident that a welcoming, unpretentious wine bar that served the best bistro food could be a kind of "semi-retirement" for me. I'd never want to not own a restaurant, after all – it kind of tells me who I am. But now, with so many other wonderful things, my two grown daughters and one wonderful wife to tell me who I am, I didn't feel the need to work myself to death every single day. I designed Bistro Le Cep to be such a place, starting out much as I would have had my friends at Disney said, "Joe, we need a bistro for our new attraction called Franceland." But I made sure it was never corporate, always personal, always exuding the feeling of a true Mom and Pop. If you go to a bistro and don't at least feel the influence of Monsieur and Madame, you're not in much of a bistro.

We found a nice location on Westheimer, the busiest road in Texas with 85,000 cars going by our front door every day. We built our little bistro and before long people were coming in for lunch, for dinner, for Sunday brunch, and still others to rent the Alsatian Room when they had an even more special occasion in mind. Many of our first customers were people who already knew me from Rotisserie for Beef and Bird, and since the Bistro was newer and needed my attention more, they knew they could find me there. After 26 years at the Beef and Bird (serving 1.8 million meals), it felt so good to be doing something new – not to mention something that happened to fit perfectly with nearly every business trend I

With my daughters Monique and Erika

read or heard about. People wanted their dining experiences to be less formal… well, a bistro was the perfect place for that. People wanted comfort food, well, a bistro was the perfect place for that too. Best of all, being a bistro is more about how the place feels than what it's forced to serve. We can cook almost anything that's hearty, that's soul-satisfying, that fills some great void in the lives most of us live now, rushing around from place to place. There is freedom in the warm reassurance that is a bistro.

Some of my customers brought their children to dine with me at Rotisserie, and now some of those children are bringing *their* children to dine with me at Bistro Le Cep. Eventually, time came to close the Rotisserie. We'd been open more than a quarter-century, and I knew the job before me of renovating and repairing that building would be larger and more expensive than even building a new place. I decided it was time to sell the restaurant that had brought me success in Houston, to let someone else deal with those challenges.

As at so many other times in so many other places, I could look back sadly at a form, a function, an identity, even a way of living that was passing away – yet only for a moment.

I have my bistro, I have many terrific friends, I have a pair of talented daughters, and I have a wife who is happy to share all these things with me. As you must have noticed by now, I can never look back sadly for long. There are too many wonderful reasons to look ahead. Besides, there's simply no future in the past.

With my wife

1996

DiRoNA
Award Recipient

183

MY
TRAVELS

BORDEAUX
An Unforgettable Wine Experience

Wine touring has always been a perfect holiday for my wife and me. The rolling hills of the vineyards, the scents of old cellars, the enthusiasm of the growers, and a tasting direct from the barrel have left many fond memories of our travels. One of these wine trips found us in the world's premier wine destination, Bordeaux.

The word Bordeaux has many applications: it is a city, a wine region, a wine event, as well as a symbol of exceptional quality in the world of wine. We started our culinary adventure with a gastronomical feast at Le Chapin Fin restaurant. The following day we crossed the Gironde River to the medieval town of St Emilion. This romantic village was founded in the 8th century and has been declared a historical monument with ancient churches, caves, and crumbling walls. We settled in at Château Grand Barrail, a fine hotel with a grand view of the most famous wine-growing estates in the world. Since it was Sunday and most of the estates were closed, we visited our friends, Olivia and Neil Donnan, at Château Masburel in Bergerac, sampled many wines and enjoyed a spectacular dinner.

On Monday, we returned to the Left Bank city of Bordeaux and toured the legendary Château Haut-Brion, which in 1855 produced the only wine from the Graves region to be admitted into the Grands Crus Classés. We finished the day with a tasting and dinner at the historical Château Pape Clement. The estate takes its name from Clément V. Archbishop of Bordeaux, who was elected to be the French Pope in 1305 during the reign of Phillipe Le Bel.

Returning to St. Emilion on the Right Bank, the following day was a memorable experience. We toured the village before leaving for Château Cheval Blanc, which was established in 1764, for a sampling of one of the finest wines in this region. The vineyards border the Pomerol appellation with their

most famous vineyard, Château Petrus. We stopped for a short visit before leaving for lunch at Château L'Angelus. This estate is just half a mile from the famous Saint-Emilion bell tower. The property owes its name to a plot of land among the vines where the Angelus bell can be heard ringing from all three local churches simultaneously. In the afternoon, Monsieur Vauthier invited us to his Château Ausone. The estate was named after Roman consul and poet, Ausonius. It is the showplace of the Côtes and one of only two Premiers Grand Crus Classés A. The cellars of Ausone are built into an ancient stone quarry and is the only natural cellar in Bordeaux. It was the perfect place to celebrate our farewell from St.Emilion.

Next, we traveled along the Gironde with a destination of Pauillac, the capital of the most Grand Cru Châteaux. We settled in with our long time friend Jean-Michel Cazes, at his Château Cordaillan-Bages Hotel next to his well-known estate, Château Lynch-Bages. The Lynch family owned this

Château for three-quarters of a century. They descended from John Lynch, a young Irishman from Galway who was chased out of his country in 1691. The estate has been in the Cazes family since 1934. The vineyards are located on the Bages plateau overlooking the Gironde Valley, which is one of the finest areas in the Pauillac appellation.

We had several tastings, including one at their other property Château Pichon-Longueville before leaving for our next destination: Château Latour. This estate entered the annals of history as early as 1378 and was a fort during the hundred-year war in France. After a succession of sales and inheritances, Latour finally became the property of Alexander de Ségurin in the 18th century. It was the beginning for Grand Cru Classé wine production, so awarded with the classification of 1855. This outstanding Château also produces a second wine called Les Forts de Latour at a more reasonable price. Additionally, other chateaux produce reasonable second labels such as Comtesse de Lalande, Petit Batailley and Saint Anne. Our last tasting for the day was at Château Mouton Rothschild and a tour through their spectacular wine museum. Their Pauillac Premier Grand Cru is regarded today as one of the world's greatest wines. The greatness of this wine is brought together by the abundance of sun and rich soil along with the passion of one man, Baron Philippe de Rothschild (1902-1988). When we returned to Château Cordaillon-Bages a six-course dinner, which included Pauillac lamb, was waiting for us in their award-winning restaurant.

Our destination the next morning was the village of Saint-Estèphe with a tasting hosted by Mr. Jean-Guillaume Prats, the owner of Château Cos d'Estournel. It is the first château on the boundary from Pauillac to St. Estèphe, built in pagoda style architecture, and producing this communes finest wine. In the afternoon, we drove to Margaux, visited the famous Château Margaux and tasted the new releases at Château Rauzan-Ségla. The wine was classified a second growth in 1855 and will satisfy even the most demanding connoisseur, thanks to its finesse, distinction and full bouquet. In 1661, P. des Mesures de Rauzan, an important wine shipper, owned the vineyard which was split up during the French Revolution. The last descendant of the Rauzan, Baroness de Ségla received 2/3 and added her name, and today it is the house of Rauzan-Ségla. The remaining 1/3 went to a politician named Gassies, who then added his name to this portion, Chateau Rauzan-Gassies. The highlight of our wine tour through Bordeaux was a tasting and festive dinner with the family Xavier Gardinier at Château Phélan Ségur, overlooking the Gironde River. Following the sale of their Champagne houses Pommery and Lanson, Mr. Gardinier and his three sons purchased Phélan-Ségur in 1985.

On our last day we visited the legendary Anthony Barton at Château Léoville Barton for an early morning tasting. Thomas Barton left his native Ireland in 1722 and settled in Bordeaux. He started a trading company, which still exists today under the name of Barton et Guestier, B & G. He also started a family, or rather a dynasty, which is one of the oldest and most alluring among the Bordeaux wine-growing fraternity. We accepted an invitation from the Borie family for lunch and wine sampling at the spectacularly landscaped Château Ducru Beaucaillou in St. Julien. This charming Victorian mansion overlooking the meadows to the river has an attraction all of its own.

Our wine tour had come to an end. We returned to Bordeaux, stayed the last night at the Relais Le St-James overlooking the city and left the next morning with the TGV fast train to Paris. As we glided at 150 miles per hour through the French countryside, we thought about the long wine producing tradition in this region. It takes persistence and dedication to produce first-class wines that have lived up to their world class reputation for centuries.

Bordeaux Theme Dinner

Bourride de Provence

Yvecourt 2000 Bordeaux Blanc

Bar Poché au Beurre Blanc

Château Tour de Mirambeau, Entre-Deux-Mers Blanc

Escalope de Veau à la Dijonnaise

Château Tertre de Turenne 1998, Côtes de Castillion Rouge

Steak au Poivre

Château Tour Blanche 1996, Medoc Cru Borgeois

Fromage de France

Château la Commanderie 1998, Saint Estèphe

Tarte aux Poires

Château de Richaud 1996 Loupiac

Café et Petits Biscuits

Provençal Fish Soup with Garlic Toast
Yield: 8 to 10

3 pounds fish heads and bones
6 cups water
1 cup dry white wine
2 medium sliced onions
1 leek, white part only
2 carrots, peeled and diced
1 stalk celery, diced
1/4 cup white vinegar
2 bay leaves
6 juniper berries
2 teaspoons salt
1 cup heavy cream
5 egg yolks
1 pound fresh fish fillets each of:
Red snapper, halibut and cod, cut into 2 inch serving pieces
1 tablespoon fresh chopped parsley

Rinse the fish bones under cold running water and place in a 6-quart saucepan. Add all the seasoning, vegetables, white wine, cover with water and bring to a boil over high heat. Lower the heat and simmer the fish stock for one hour, skimming the top from time to time. Strain the fish broth through a sieve into another pot, pressing down firmly on the vegetables and trimmings with a wooden spoon before discarding them.

Add the fresh fish, bring to a boil and simmer uncovered for 4 minutes. With a slotted spoon transfer the pieces to a heated serving platter and keep warm. Start boiling the broth again to reduce to about 8 cups, taste for seasoning. Mix the egg yolks and heavy cream in a 2 quart bowl, whisk 2 cups of the hot fish stock into the egg-cream mixture, then return to the pot stirring constantly. Cook over low heat, until the soup is thick enough to coat the back of the wooden spoon. Do not boil the soup. Season with lemon juice, salt and pepper, ladle over the fish pieces, and sprinkle with fresh chopped parsley. Serve with Aioli Croûtes.

Aioli Croûtes:
4 egg yolks
1/4 teaspoon salt
6 cloves garlic
1 1/2 tablespoons lemon juice
1/2 teaspoon Spanish paprika
1/8 teaspoon ground red pepper
1/8 teaspoon ground white pepper
1 cup olive oil
10 (1/2 inch thick) slices crusty French bread, toasted

Smash the garlic cloves with a wooden spoon and the salt on a small cutting board to a smooth paste. Transfer to a mixing bowl, add the egg yolks, paprika, cayenne and white pepper. With an electric mixer whisk in the oil, first drop by drop until the mixture resembles thick cream, then add in a thin stream. Add the lemon juice. Spread the croutons generously with the aioli.

Poached Bass with Butter-Caper Sauce
Yield: serves 6

2 1/2 pounds bass fillets cut into 6 pieces
1/4 stick melted butter
Salt and pepper to taste
10 fresh sprigs of dill
10 slices lemons

Court Bouillon:
1 quart water
1 cup dry white wine
1 tablespoon vinegar
1 tablespoon lemon juice
1/2 onion chopped
1 carrot chopped
1 bay leave
5 crushed peppercorns

Place all the Court Bouillon ingredients in a casserole and bring to a boil, then reduce the heat and simmer for 45 minutes to reduce the liquid to about two cups. Strain through a sieve and set aside.

Preheat the oven to 400°F. Place the fish fillets into a fireproof ceramic dish 8 X 8 inches, side by side. Ladle the court bouillon over the fish, season with salt and pepper, and dot with the butter. Seal the pan tightly with foil and bake for 10 minutes, or less, in the middle of the oven, depending on the thickness of the fillets. Using a spatula transfer the fish on to serving platter and keep warm. Serve with Beurre Blanc. Garnish with fresh sprigs of fresh dill and lemon slices. Serve with new boiled potatoes.

Beurre Blanc:
1/2 cup fish stock
1/4 cup white vinegar
1/4 cup dry white wine
1/4 teaspoon salt
2 tablespoons caper
3 drops Tabasco sauce
1/2 pound chilled butter, cut into small pieces

Strain 1/2 cup of the fish stock into a 2 quart saucepan, add 1/2 cup white wine, 1/8 cup white vinegar and bring to a boil, Remove from the heat and with a wire whisk immediately stir in 3 pieces of the chilled butter, beating constantly until the butter is completely absorbed into the liquid. Return the saucepan to very low heat, and add the rest of the butter, piece by piece. The finish sauce will be thick, cream colored. Add the capers and spoon over the fish.

Sautéed Veal Medallions
in Mustard Sauce

Yield: Serves 6

12 (3 ounce) veal scallops, pounded
    with a mallet 1/4 inch thick
1 cup flour
1/2 teaspoon Spanish paprika
1/2 stick butter
1/2 cup vegetable oil
5 shallots finely chopped
1 red bell pepper, cut in half,
    seeded and diced finely
1 green bell pepper, cut in half,
    seeded and diced finely
3/4 cup dry white wine
1 1/2 tablespoons Dijon mustard
1 cup heavy cream
1/4 cup chopped fresh parley
Salt and fresh ground black pepper

Mix the flour and paprika in a small bowl. Season the veal scallops with salt and pepper and dip them in the flour mixture, and then shake them vigorously to remove any excess flour. In a 10 to 12 inch non-stick skillet heat the oil over moderate high heat. Brown the veal scallops for 3 to 4 minutes on each side, until nice and brown. (You may have to sauté them in two batches), Remove them from the pan and set aside.

Pour off the fat and heat the butter in the same pan. Add the shallots and peppers and sauté over low heat until cooked but not brown. Pour in the wine and bring to a boil over high heat, stirring and scraping the browned bits from the bottom of the skillet. Reduce the heat, add the Dijon mustard and heavy cream, and simmer for 5 minutes until the sauce thickens. Return the veal scallops to the skillet, baste with the sauce and heat just long enough to heat through. Arrange the veal scallops, overlapping them slightly on a heated platter, pour the sauce over them, and sprinkle with chopped parsley. Serve with pasta.

Escalope de Veau Dijonnaise

Sautéed Sirloin Steak
with Peppercorns
Yield: serves 6

6 well trimmed sirloin steaks,
    about 1 inch thick (8 oz each)
1 tablespoon salt
5 tablespoons whole black pepper, coarsely crushed
3 tablespoons clarified butter
3/4 cup cognac
1 1/2 cups beef broth, fresh or canned
2 bay leaves
1/4 stick butter, chilled and cut into 1/2 inch cubes
1/4 cup heavy cream.
1 teaspoon cornstarch, dissolved
    with two tablespoons cold water

Season the steaks generously with salt. One side at a time sprinkle each steak with the crushed black peppercorns, pushing them firmly into the meat with your hands. In a 12-inch cast iron or heavy-duty skillet, heat the clarified butter over high heat. Place the steaks in the pan (3 at the time) and sauté them 4 minutes on each side, or until they are done to your taste. Transfer the steaks to a heated platter and set them aside while preparing the sauce.

Remove the pan from the stove, add the cognac, let warm for a minute, then ignite with a match. Pour in the beef broth, bay leaves and cream. Bring the mixture to a boil over high heat, whisk in the cornstarch and blend well. Remove the pan from the heat and whisk in the chilled butter bits one at a time. Strain the sauce with sieve over the steaks, and serve at once.

Pear Tart
Yield: makes 1 (9 inch) tart

Pears:

> 4 cups water
> 2 cups sugar
> 3 cloves
> 1 stick cinnamon
> 3 large ripe Bosc pears, peeled, cut in halve, remove the stem and core
> 2 tablespoons lemon juice

In a 3-quart casserole, bring the water to a boil, add the sugar, cloves, cinnamon and lemon juice, simmer for 5 minutes. Add the pears and poach over low heat until soft. With a slotted spoon remove the pear halves and arrange cored side down on a wire rack to drain.

Piecrust:

> 1 1/2 cups cake flour
> 1/4 teaspoon salt
> 1/2 stick butter, chilled and cut into 1 inch cubes
> 2 tablespoons vegetable shortening
> 4 tablespoon chilled water

Sift the flour and salt on to a working surface; add the chilled butter and vegetable shortening. Knead with your hands and add the water one spoon at the time. Gather the dough into a ball, dust with a little flour and wrap in wax paper. Refrigerate for one hour. On a lightly floured surface roll out the dough and line a 9 inch fluted false-bottom pie pan. Line bottom with foil, and cover with two cups of beans to hold the foil down. Bake at 400 ° for 15 to 20 minutes. Remove the foil and beans, and you are ready for the filling.

Filling:

> 1 pound almond paste, room temperature
> 3 eggs
> 2 egg yolks
> 3/4 cup flour
> 1/2 stick soft butter
> 1/2 cup sugar
> 2 teaspoons vanilla extract
> 1 1/2 cups apricot jam
> 1/4 cup kirsch (cherry brandy)

Place almond paste into a large mixing bowl. Using a rotary electric mixer combine one egg at a time with the almond paste. Add the sugar, vanilla and mix until nice and smooth without any lumps. Add the egg yolks and butter and blend well together. Using a wooden spoon, fold in the flour. Heat the apricot jam with the kirsch in a small pan over low heat.

To assemble the tart, spread half of the apricot mixture in the bottom of the pastry shell. Arrange the pear halves in the tart shell like the spokes of a wheel, spread the almond paste over the pears and bake for 45 minutes at 375°, until firm in the center and nice and brown. Glaze the tart with the remaining apricot mixture. Serve at room temperature with whipped cream.

RENDEZVOUS IN BURGUNDY

The route to Burgundy, land of France's greatest wines, home of Dijon mustard, Charolais cattle, and fine cuisine, begins for Houston residents with a great leap across the Atlantic. Then from Paris, this region of rolling hills and valleys laced with streams is within quick reach thanks to the TGV or "Tres Grande Vitnesse," France's high-speed rail line. The overall lengthy travel from Houston

Intercontinental to Burgundy's gateway gives the traveler time to mentally prepare for the great gastronomical feasts that await.

As a restaurateur and chef, I was looking forward to the coming days of sampling quantities of wine and fine Burgundian food. On my first evening in Beaune, I settled in at the famed Hotel de la Poste, one of the grand old historical hotels. Relaxing in the hotel's garden, even though it was close to 10 p.m., I could still discern the ancient towers of old world Beaune, structures built by the rich medieval Duke of Burgundy. I sipped a glass of chilled Meursault from the golden hills of the Côte d'Or. The fading light, the quiet garden and the delicate white wine put me in the proper mood; a grand start to an even grander holiday.

Walking the streets of Beaune, I could

almost feel the enormous maze of cellars that wind for miles beneath the city. Imagine that just under our feet were some of the greatest and rarest vintages in the world. Burgundy is known for its wines, but marrying good food with wine is nothing new to this region. It certainly is a fine art that has been practiced here for more than a 1,000 years.

The chicken from Bresse, the heavy Charolais beef and the Burgundian snails are known throughout the world. Dijon is the capital of fine mustard. Blackberries are plentiful and made into Cassis. Other fruits and great vegetables thrive in the gentle climate, particularly south of Lyon. Burgundy can justly claim to be the birthplace of the gastronomical revolution, the place where good French eating began. The region was always a very desirable place to be. The Romans appeared here in 52 B.C. conquering the land, and calling it their own. By the end of the 5th century, the Burgundians, who came from the region of the Baltic Sea, stormed in, giving this part of the country its name. Centuries later, the first Capetian duke was appointed from there.

Burgundy prospered as a stronghold of Christianity. Monasteries were founded, and massive churches built. But it was not until the takeover by the Valois in 1364, that the grand dukes of Burgundy made their resplendent mark on the landscape. The territory expanded to include portions of Belgium, Holland, and Luxembourg. Burgundy became the center of art and architecture, a sophisticated culture flourished.

The Burgundian court at Dijon became the center of enlightenment, hospitality and fine dining. Luckily for generations to come, especially ours, the talented hands of the church successfully extended to include the refinement of wine production and food preparation.

Beaune's famous Hospice was founded as a charity hospital in 1443 and today the institution owns the finest parcels of land and most famous vineyards in the region. Wine Connoisseurs and buyers from around the world make annual pilgrimages here the third Sunday in November for Beaune's renowned wine auction. Great feasts are enjoyed during this time and the gastronomical societies put on a colorful show, dating back to medieval time.

The region's rich culinary heritage is evident in the Chevaliers du Tastevin, an organization that spread worldwide from Dijon. Likewise, culinary gurus and the famous chefs such as Bocuse, Dumaine, Point and Troisgros made

ever-lasting history in Lyon.

Burgundians are very adventurous with their food. Charcuteries offer a large selection of pâtés, sausages, terrines and quenelles along with dry-cured hams and bacon. The fish markets are sensational, particularly during the very early morning hours. Fresh fish from the fishermen's net, you will find different species of fish, many varieties of fresh oysters, crayfish, and young eels. Beside wonderful produce, wine and seafood, Burgundy is also a splendid place for chocolate lovers. The addictive treat was developed by craftsmen from Italy in the 18th century and soon evolved into an art form handled exclusively by the Pâtisseur. The choice of pastries in Burgundy is almost sinful, from the famous Petits Fours filled with nougat; a delicious cream made from chocolate and ground hazelnuts to chocolate truffles of every kind.

Considering the quantities of calorific food and wine consumed on this visit to Beaune, I was obligated to continue my Houston regimen of morning exercise. Jogging around the old walled city of Beaune at sunrise, I felt very American; but the mouthwatering aromas of freshly baked croissants, brioches and crusty long French breads placed me in the very lap of Burgundy.

Burgundy Theme Dinner

Terrine de Queue du Boeuf

Aligote Pierre Morey 1999

Darne de Saumon Grillé Sauce Vierge

Macon la Roche-Vincuse 2001

Lapin à la Moutarde

Hautes Côtes-de-Nuits Domaine Moillard Bourgogne 1999

Gigôt d'Agneau Braisé

Volnay-Vielles Vignes Nicolas Potel 2000

Fromages Assortis

Givry Remoissenet 1999

Mousse Au Chocolat

Crémant de Bourgogne-Verget N/V

Oxtail Terrine

Yield: Serves 8

3 pounds oxtail, cut into 3 inch pieces
1 tablespoon coarse salt
4 carrots, peeled and cut into 3/4 inch pieces
2 leeks, white part only, cut in half and washed, then sliced
2 celery ribs, coarsely chopped
1 medium size onion, coarsely chopped
4 cloves garlic, mashed
2 tablespoons chopped capers
1/2 cup chopped chives

Bouquet garni: (place the seasoning in a cheesecloth and tie with twine)
2 bay leaves
10 peppercorns, crushed
1/4 teaspoon thyme
1/4 teaspoon fennel seeds
10 sprigs fresh parsley
10 juniper berries

Place the oxtail in a heavy-duty stockpot or Dutch oven and cover completely with cold water. Bring to a boil over medium heat. Simmer, skimming very carefully with a ladle to remove all of the foam and fat. When the impurities have returned to foam, skim again. Continue cooking for 20 minutes. Season the broth with salt, and add the vegetables, garlic and bouquet garni. Return to simmer, skim again and boil over low heat for 3 to 4 hours until the meat is falling off the bones. Transfer the oxtail and liquid into a large bowl, cool, and then refrigerate overnight to allow the fat to solidify.

The next day, carefully spoon off and discard all of the fat from the top. Remove the pieces of oxtail from the bowl and place on a cutting board. Using a fork separate the meat from the bones. Remove and discard the bouquet garni, Return the shredded meat and liquid to a saucepot, add the capers and bring to a boil to melt the gelatinous liquid. Check the seasoning and add salt and pepper to your taste. Transfer the meat, and vegetables to 2 quart terrine mold, pressing down the meat to make a compact terrine. Cover and refrigerate for 24 hours.

To serve, remove the terrine from the refrigerator 10 minutes before serving. Cut into thin slices, sprinkle with chives, and serve with cornichons, pickled onions and horseradish on a bed of Boston lettuce.

Grilled Center Cut
Salmon Fillets with Salsa
Yield:Sserves 6

6 boneless cuts of salmon, 6 ounces each
2 tablespoons extra-virgin olive oil
1 tablespoon Chinese oyster sauce
Salsa:
    3 tomatoes, peeled, cored,
        seeded and chopped
    1 green bell pepper, cut in half,
        seeded and diced
    1 red bell pepper, cut in half,
        seeded and diced
    1/2 onion, finely chopped
    3 cloves garlic, minced
    1/2 cup olive oil
    1 tablespoon cider vinegar
    3 tablespoons freshly squeezed lemon juice
    3 tablespoons chopped fresh cilantro
    Salt and freshly ground black pepper

Combine all the Salsa ingredients in a ceramic bowl, season with salt and pepper, cover and set aside for two hours to allow the flavors to blend. Preheat the broiler, prepare a grill for grilling, or heat a cast iron skilled over high heat. Brush the salmon fillets with a mixture of olive oil and oyster sauce, and place under the broiler. Cook the fish for about 8 minutes until firm and brown on the top, but still rosy in the center. Remove the salmon fillets to a large preheated platter and top with the salsa. Serve with boiled new potatoes.

Darne de Saumon Grillé "Sauce Vierge"

Oven Roasted Rabbit in Mustard Sauce

Yield: Serves 6

4 pounds fresh rabbit, cut into large pieces
1/2 cup vegetable oil
1/2 cup Dijon mustard
2 tablespoons butter
1/2 bottle dry white wine
1 1/2 cup chicken stock, fresh or canned
1/2 cup heavy cream
2 medium size onions, finely chopped
2 cloves garlic, minced
2 carrots, finely diced
2 celery ribs, finely diced
1/2 cup flour
1 teaspoon Spanish paprika
1 teaspoon dried thyme
2 bay leaves
1/4 chopped fresh parsley
Salt and freshly ground black pepper

Preheat the oven to 400°F. Place the rabbit pieces on a sheet of parchment paper, and season with salt and pepper. Combine the flour and paprika, then coat each piece generously with the flour-paprika mixture, reserve the rest of the flour. Using a heavy skillet, heat the vegetable oil over high heat. When the oil is hot but not smoking, add several of the rabbit pieces, do not crowd the pan. You will have to cook this in several batches, cook until brown about 10 minutes. Turn the rabbit and cook the other side until golden brown. Transfer the rabbit to a large platter and continue cooking in this manner until all the rabbit is browned.

Melt the butter in the same frying pan; add the onions, garlic, carrots, celery and the rest of the flour. Cook over low heat for 3 minutes, stirring constantly. Add 1 1/2 cups chicken stock to the skillet and scrap up any browned bits that stick to the pan. Add the white wine, bay leaves, thyme, mustard and bring to a boil. Add all the rabbit pieces, cover the skilled and bake in the middle of the oven for 1 hour or until the rabbit is very tender and the sauce begins to thicken. Using a slotted spoon transfer the rabbit to a heated serving platter, add the cream to the sauce and season to your liking. Ladle the finished sauce over the rabbit, sprinkle with chopped parsley and serve with buttered noodle or rice.

Braised Leg of Lamb
Yield: 6-10

1 boneless leg of lamb (5 to 8 pounds)
6 medium size onions, peeled and quartered
6 carrots, peeled and cut into 1 inch long chunks
3 turnips, peeled and cut into 1/2 inch long chunks
4 rutabagas, peeled and cut into wedges
12 fingerling new potatoes
1 head of green cabbage, cut into wedges
1/2 bottle of red wine
2 cups beef broth, fresh or canned
3 bay leaves
1/2 teaspoon thyme
5 sprigs fresh rosemary
6 large tomatoes, peeled,
    seeded and coarsely chopped
16 cloves garlic, peeled
12 sprigs of fresh mint

Preheat the oven to 425°F. Using a small paring knife, cut several slits into the leg of lamb, press 10 cloves of garlic into the meat, season with salt and place into a Dutch oven or large roasting pan. Add 1 cup of water and roast for 1 1/2 hour, basting from time to time. Lower the heat to 325°, add all the vegetables, tomatoes, the rest of the garlic, thyme and rosemary, pour in the wine and beef broth. Cover the pan tightly, return to the oven and bake for another two hours, or until the meat is still juicy, but very tender. Slice the meat and transfer to a heated serving platter, arrange the vegetables around the meat, garnish with fresh sprigs of mint and serve at once.

Chocolate Mousse

Yield: serves 6

6 ounces semi-sweet chocolate (cut into pieces)
2 tablespoons instant coffee powder
2 tablespoons hot water
1/2 teaspoon vanilla extract
5 large eggs (separated)
1/2 cup sugar
1/2 pint whipping cream

1/4 cup whipping cream for garnish and 3 tablespoons chocolate shavings

Melt the chocolate in top of a double boiler until soft. Dissolve the instant coffee with the hot water and stir into the melted chocolate. Whisk until smooth, add the egg yolks, one at a time while beating.

With an electric mixer beat the 5 egg whites in a chilled stainless steel bowl. Gradually adding 1/2 cup sugar, beat until stiff. Gently fold the egg whites into the chocolate. In a separate bowl, whip the 1/2 pint whipping cream and fold into the mixture.

Ladle into individual stemmed glasses and refrigerate for at least 3 hours. Before serving, garnish with a dot of whipped cream and chocolate shavings.

LANDING IN NORMANDY

Arriving at Charles de Gaulle Airport, we began our journey by car on the Autoroute A13, with destination Deauville. In the 9th and 10th centuries marauding Vikings arrived from the east and invaded the rich valleys of Normandy. This province is a beautiful part of France, but the Normans retain a powerful sense of separate identity. Although the word Norman was derived from Northmen (as in Norsemen), these people never constituted more than a modest minority among the indigenous Celtic-Roman-Frankish majority.

The Normandy countryside took a battering during the Hundred Year's War, but in spite, the Normans settled down and built a prosperous country. Close to the sea, they also developed into great seafarers and built an impressive merchant fleet. Ships departed from the port of Honfleur to explore the coast of Brazil and also the St. Lawrence River in Canada. A long history is very visible in medieval abbeys (like the wonderful Mont-St-Michel), châteaux, and splendid castles.

Two of the best sections of Normandy's coast are the wild and beautiful head of the Contentin peninsula and the much more fashionable Northern Riviera, which starts at Cherbourg, peaks at Deauville, and ends at the charming fishing village of Honfleur. In between these two areas lie the D-Day landing beaches, Utah, Omaha, and Arromanches-les-Bains. On the coast nearby one can see the Musée du Débarquement above the beach and the chain of floating concrete slabs that constituted a Mulberry Harbor. Near Vierville-sur-Mer the United States Military Cemetery commemorates the soldiers who perished during the landing at Omaha beach. Just a few miles inland off Autoroute A 13 is the city Caen, the home of the ancient Abbey aux Hommes which bears testimony to the historical links with William the Conqueror. Bayeux, only a few miles north is another city on the history trail famous for its tapestry.

Late in the afternoon, we arrived in St. Gatien a small country village, surrounded with apple orchards and lush green meadows. The inn Le Clos Saint Gatien was comfortable with charming rooms and a fine dining room.

Normandy by no means has the culinary temples of Lyon, Provence or Paris, but it is a land of bounty in its own right. A region of orchards and plenty, the province is also bordered by several hundred miles of coastline. The bounteous products of pasture and farms complemented by gifts from the sea. Faced with such an abundance of riches, the Normans have always had the good sense to keep their cooking techniques simple. The traditional dishes of the region are unpretentious, seasoned only with a little fresh chives, chervi, or shallots, but showcase the riches of cream, cheese, butter, apple cider, plus their famous apple brandy Calvados.

Normandy is also the perfect place to acquire a taste for fresh seafood. Dover sole sauté meunière in brown butter or a bowl of tiny crevettes can turn into a feast at Les Vapeurs on the main street near the market in Trouville-sur-Mer. Ever since the original Normans brought with them their sturdy cattle from Scandinavia, dairy products have been the foundation of the cooking of the region. Le plat de fromages is a must to sample the many fine local cheeses, accompanied with a slice of crusty french bread.

In France a good meal always calls for a bottle of good wine, preferable local "une bonne petite bouteille." For a region with so strong a tradition of culinary excellence, Normandy is unique in not having its own vineyards. The domestic beverage is apple based. Cider, sweet or dry, is made from carefully mixed different varieties of cider apples. Calvados is the celebrated spirit of Normandy, distilled from apple cider, golden to amber in color and high in alcohol. The finest of all Calvados is an "appellation d'origine contrôlée" from Pays d'Auge in the département of Calvados. Here it is made from local cider, twice distilled. In the spring there is a public tasting and grading in the town of Cambremer on the "route du cidre." Every producer hopes to win awards presented during the annual competition in order to receive the Cru de Cambremer.

The gastronomical highlight during our trip was our farewell dinner at Au Petit Coques aux Champs, a very charming inn near the village of Campicny. Route du Fromage-Calvados.

Normandy Theme Dinner

Crème de Crevettes

Paul Blanck Pinot d'Alsace 1999

Flétan Vallée d'Auge

Barrique Réserve Bourgogne Chardonnay 1995

Carré de Porc Normande

Cuvée Prestige Hugo Château L'Escart 1997

Côtelettes d'Agneau Grillées Comptoises

Lalande de Pomerol Château Fleur de Jean Gue 1996

Fromages Assortis de Normandie

Remoissenet Père et Fils Bourgogne Rouge 1995

Charlotte aux Pommes

Sauternes Château Grillon 1996

Cream of Shrimp Soup

Yield: Serves 6

1 pound small to medium size raw unpeeled shrimp
1/4 stick butter
1 small carrot, peeled and diced
1 small onion, sliced
1 stalk celery, diced
1 1/2 cups white wine
3 1/2 cups water
2 sprigs of fresh thyme
2 bay leaves
2 tablespoons dry sherry
2 drops Tabasco sauce
1/2 cup heavy cream
1/2 teaspoon salt
1/4 cup chopped fresh chives

Béchamel Sauce:
3 tablespoons butter
5 tablespoons flour
3 cups milk

To prepare the Bechamel Sauce, heat the milk in a small pot. Melt the butter in another pot, add the flour stirring constantly for one minute over low heat. Whisk in the boiling milk, simmer for a few minutes to make a smooth sauce and keep warm.

Wash the shrimp under cold running water. In a heavy duty 3 quart casserole melt the 1/4 stick butter over medium heat, add paprika, onions, celery, carrots, raw shrimp, bay leaves, and thyme, sauté the mixture for 2 minutes stirring from time to time, or until the shrimp are turning pink. Add the white wine, salt and 3 1/2 cups of water; simmer for 10 minutes over low heat. Using a slotted spoon remove the vegetables and cooked shrimp.

Peel half of the shrimp for the garnish and set aside. Crush the shells and the rest of the shrimp/vegetable mixture in a food processor and return to the shrimp broth. Simmer for another 10 minutes to reduce the stock to 3 cups. Strain the liquid into the béchamel sauce, add the cream, Tabasco sauce, dry Sherry season with salt and pepper to your taste. Heat the cream of shrimp soup, and ladle over the shrimp, garnish with chopped chives and serve.

Halibut Steaks
with Apple and Cider
Yield: Serves 6

3 pounds boneless halibut (6 steaks, 8 ounces each)
2 leeks, white part only, cut in half, washed and sliced
2 apples, peeled, cored, cut in half and sliced
3 tablespoons melted butter to grease the pan
Salt and pepper to taste
1 1/2 cups apple cider
1 1/2 cups dry white wine
1 pound small mushrooms (champignons de Paris), washed
3 tablespoons lemon juice
1 cup heavy cream
1/4 stick chilled butter, cut into bits
1/4 cup chopped fresh chives

Set the oven to 400°F. Wash the halibut steaks under running cold water and pat dry with paper towels. Butter a large fireproof ceramic or stainless steel pan and sprinkle the bottom with the sliced leeks and apples. Lay the halibut on top, season with salt and pepper and pour the cider and white wine over it. Bring to a boil on top of the stove, then bake in the stove for 35 minutes, basting the steaks often. Using a spatula, carefully transfer the fish to a serving platter and keep warm.

Strain the liquid through a sieve into a smaller saucepan, pressing hard on the leeks and apples to extract the juice. While the fish is cooking, put the mushrooms into a small pot, add 1 cup water, the lemon juice, cover the pot and steam the mushrooms for 5 minutes. Drain, reserving the liquid, slice the mushrooms and spoon over the halibut, keep warm.

For the sauce, combine the fish stock with the mushroom liquid and bring to a boil, simmer over low heat until reduced to half. Add the cream to the fish-mushroom reduction and continue to boil until thick enough to coat the back of a wooden spoon. Whisk in the butter bits, one by one, keeping the pan over low heat. Taste for seasoning, and then spoon half of it over the fish, sprinkle with chopped chives and serve. Serve with the remaining sauce on the side.

Pork Loin with Apples and Calvados
Serves 6

3 pounds boneless pork loin
1/4 cup vegetable oil
3 tart apples, peeled, cored and sliced
2 medium onions, sliced thinly
1/4 cup Calvados
3 tablespoons flour
1 tablespoon butter
1/4 teaspoon Spanish paprika
1 cup chicken broth, canned or fresh
1 cup dry white wine
Salt and pepper to taste
11/4 cups heavy cream

Caramelized apple slices:
3 tablespoons butter
1/4 cup sugar
3 tart apples, unpeeled, but cored

Preheat the oven to 375°F.

Mix the flour with the paprika and dust the pork loin generously, then season with salt and pepper. Reserve the remaining flour mixture. Heat the oil in a shallow casserole on top of the stove, and brown the pork loin on all side over medium heat. Remove the pork loin, add the onions and apples and cook until light brown. Add the Calvados, carefully ignite with a match and then add the chicken broth and wine. Return the pork loin to the juices, cover and bake for one hour, or until the meat is tender, basting occasionally.

When the meat is almost tender, prepare the apple garnish; core and thickly slice the apples, leaving the skin. Heat the butter in a frying pan. Dip each slice in sugar and place in the hot butter. Cook over high heat for 3 minutes on each side, then transfer to a heated serving platter, add the remaining sugar to the pan, heat and pour over the apples.

Once the pork loin is tender, remove it from the pan and carve diagonally in medium slices. Arrange the slices overlapping on the platter cover and keep warm while finishing the sauce.

Strain the cooking juices into a small saucepan, pressing to purée the apples and onions. Skim off the fat from the top and bring to a boil. Combine 1 tablespoon from the remaining flour with 1 tablespoon soft butter and whisk in to the sauce. Add the cream and bring the sauce to a boil, simmer until thickens.

Spoon some gravy over the pork and garnish the dish with the caramelized apples slices. Serve the remaining sauce separately.

Grilled or Broiled Lamb Chops
Yield: Serves 6

12 lamb chops, (4 ounces each)
2 large onions, thinly sliced
2 tablespoons butter
1 tablespoon rice
1 cup heavy cream
1/2 cup chicken broth (fresh or canned)
1/4 cup fresh mint
6 sprigs fresh rosemary
Salt and freshly ground pepper for seasoning

Melt the butter in a sauté pan, add the onions and cook over low heat until light brown. Add the rice and stir in the cream and chicken broth. Simmer over low heat until the onions are cooked and the rice has thickened the sauce, set aside and keep hot.

Heat the grill, broiler or cast iron skillet. Seasoned the lamb chops with salt and pepper, and grill on each side for 5 minutes, or until well browned, but still pink in the center.

Spoon the onions into a serving platter and set the chops on top, sprinkle with fresh mint and garnish with rosemary sprigs.

Baked Apples Charlotte
Yield: Serves 6

5 pounds apples, preferably Golden Delicious
1 1/2 stick butter
1/2 cup dry white wine
3 tablespoons Calvados
3 tablespoons lemon juice
3/4 cup sugar
4 tablespoons apricot jam
12 slices white bread, crust removed
Pinch of cinnamon and ground cloves

Peel, core and slice the apples. Melt half of the butter in a heavy-duty casserole, add the apples, wine, cloves, cinnamon, lemon juice and sugar. Cover and cook over low heat, stirring occasionally for 20 to 25 minutes, or until the apples are reduced to thick pulp. Stir in the Calvados and ignite with a match, add the apricot jam and mix well.

Preheat the oven to 400°. Butter a charlotte mold. Meanwhile, clarify the remaining butter. Cut some oblong pieces of bread the same thickness and the same height as the mold, dip into the butter and line the sides of the mold. These pieces should also overlap.

Fill the mold with the apple mixture, taking care it is well filled, mound the center slightly (it will sink during the baking process). Cover with another two pieces of bread dipped in melted butter.

Bake in the oven for 20 minutes, until the bread is golden brown. Lower the heat to 350° and bake for another 40 minutes longer or until the charlotte is firm. When baked, leave the mold for 15 minutes before unmolding, then transfer to a heated platter and serve with ice cream or whipped cream.

A TASTE OF PIEDMONT

By no means is the Piedmont region on the slopes of the Italian Alps some stronghold of rustic mountain cooking; it is a very sophisticated area developed and cherished by the aristocratic families of Italy. The upper class Piedmontese were blessed with long periods of peace in their land and had the time and money to

devote to the pleasure of fine dining. It is said that when Italy was united in 1861, its first ruler, Victor Emanuelle II, came to Piedmont's House of Savoy and was the founder of a gastronomic Italy.

The region is blessed with rolling hills, mild summer days and cold nights, which is very suitable to grow the finest Nebbiolo grapes to make the famous Barolo wine. The mountain grass is rich and the dairy farmers produce some of the most delicious cheeses in the world, such as Bel Paese and Gorgonzola. Rice farming also plays an important role and the farmers are very proud of their products. Turin is the capital of Piedmont, and because of the early foresight of the kings court, two culinary academies add to the advantage of this gastronomic world, one in Coconato and the other in La Morre.

With connecting flights from Chicago via Rome, we arrived in Milan. A fast traveling train with a great view quickly brought us to a most beautiful resort town, Stresa. Our destination was the Grand Hotel Des Borromees overlooking the scenic Lake Maggiore. The hotel was built during the 18th century with all the beauty and charm of a first class European establishment.

The first introduction to our culinary exposition was Ristorante Piemontese, with Gnochetti and Cosiotto d'agnello con insalatina, accompanied with a bottle of Banfi Brut 1989 and a great Barolo Enrico VI 1990. The next day we visited a rice processing plant and were told that at the end of the 18th century, Piedmontese rice was so precious that U.S. President (and gastronome) Thomas Jefferson smuggled the rice seeds into our country. Our next stop was the small winery Antichi Vigneti di Cantalupo with a tasting of Ghemme wines and a great lunch at Restaurant Macalle. Chef Sergio Zuin is a master of the local products such as Gorgonzola cheese and rice.

Back in Stresa, several friends made dinner reservations at L'Emiliono, which places its reputation among the best in Italy.

Shopping in the village of Stresa is limited, but climbing the steep hills surrounding the lake and enjoying a breathtaking sunset was a memorable event. Dinner the following day was at

"Evetia" on the charming island of Isollo Bella, which can only be reached by boat. The fresh fish pâté went very well with a fine bottle of Gahmpenois Barbero. Next dish was the pansicia alla novarese, a stew made with rice, beans, salami and fresh vegetables, playing an excellent accompaniment to a well-balanced Roero Arnais 1994.

A visit to Martini & Rossi was a great experience. The story starts in 1847 and this winery quickly became the largest exporter of Piedmont. With plenty of good wines in the surrounding hills and abundance of aromatic plants on the slopes of the Alps, Turin was well placed to become the biggest production center for vermouth in the world. A must in this city is a visit to the café Barratti & Milano, in continuous operation since 1875, and also the historical restaurant Del Cambiao, which opened across from the king's residence in the year of 1757.

Our next destination was the little town of Asti with a memorable dinner at Ristorante Gener Neuv. With the most pleasant spring weather, we ventured out in the countryside to the mountain village Costigliole d'Asti. At the highest point we noticed the Castello di Costigliole, which soon will be the home of a new culinary school for chefs from foreign countries who wish to study the culinary arts and philosophy of Italian food preparation. Lunch was at Ristorante Guido, which was selected by Wine Spectator magazine in 1994 as having the best wine list in Europe.

Next stop was the town of Canelli to visit the house of Gancia, with a tasting of fine sparkling wine. The following day brought more sparkling wine during a visit and tasting at the house of CINZANO. Lunch was served with gracious hospitality at the most beautiful restaurant Belvedere on top of the mountain in La Mora, also the home of the white truffles.

The highlight of our culinary adventure through Piedmont was a visit and dinner in the ancient hunting lodge in Serralunga d'Albert, called Fontanafredda. It is also one of the leading wineries in the area and produces some of the famous Barolos and Barbarescos. This castle is in the middle of nowhere, with a succession of vineyards stretching out in perfect harmony over gentle hills within a beautiful setting. It is surely a place to remember. The history of Borolo, the authentic jewel of Italian winemaking, is also firmly linked to the long history and experience of Fontanafredda, which was founded over 120 years ago.

On our long flight home to Houston, we thought about our enrichment from the gastronomic experience of the trip, the many nice people with whom we dined and wined, and the gracious hospitality of our Italian hosts. With great interest, I also studied many recipes I collected from my colleagues in the old world, and desire to share my experiences with our Texas friends.

Piedmont Theme Dinner

Tonno sott'olio alla Borghese

La Seoleo Gavi 1993

Conchiglie di Scampi Lucullo

Roero Armeis 1992

Anatra alle Prugne

Barbaresco 1991

Fettuccine Piemontese

Marchesi di Barolo 1991

Caprolo alle Ribes

Barolo 1990

Pere al Vino Bianco

Folinari Asti Spumante

Tuna Salad a la Borghese

Yield: Serves 4

2 cans chunk tuna fish (6 ounces each)
3/4 cup tomato catsup
1 tablespoon finely chopped parsley
1/2 tablespoon finely chopped tarragon
6 anchovy fillets, washed free of salt, chopped
1 red bell pepper, cut in half,
    seeded and chopped in large chunks
1/4 cup olive oil
1/2 medium onion, diced
4 cloves garlic chopped
1/2 cup diced carrots
1/2 cup small mushrooms, sliced
1/2 cup frozen peas
1/2 cup pitted ripe black olives
2 ripe Roma tomatoes cut into wedges
2 hard-boiled eggs cut in quarters
8 Bibb lettuce leaves
Sprigs of fresh dill

Heat the olive oil in a heavy-duty casserole. Add the onions, garlic, bell peppers and cook until glazed but not brown. Add the tomato catsup, and bring to a boil. Add the parsley, anchovies, tarragon, carrots, peas, mushrooms, and black olives. Simmer the mixture for about 4 minutes, then add the tuna fish chunks, and bring to a boil. Transfer the tuna salad to a bowl, and refrigerate overnight. Place the Bibb lettuce leaves on 4 individual serving plates, spoon the tuna salad into the center, and garnish with tomato, egg wedges, and sprigs of fresh dill.

Tonno sott'olio alla Borghese

Baked Shrimp in Scallop Shells

Yield: serves 6

30 small raw shrimp, peeled, and de-veined
2 tablespoons butter
3 shallots, peeled and chopped
1 1/2 cups sliced mushrooms
2 tablespoons Madeira wine
1 1/2 cups Béchamel sauce (recipe below)
1/2 teaspoon Dijon mustard
1 dash of Tabasco sauce
Salt and black pepper to taste
1 large carrot, peeled and cut into fine juliennes
1 large zucchini, washed and cut into fine juliennes
2 ribs of celery washed and cut into juliennes.
2 teaspoons salt

In a saucepot, bring 3 quarts of water to a boil; add the salt and fresh vegetables. Simmer for two minutes, and then drain the hot water. Rinse the vegetables with cold water, then dived equally into 6 coquille shells. Transfer the shells on to a cookie sheet and set aside. Preheat the oven to 400 °F.

Melt the butter in a frying pan, add the shallots, shrimp and sauté over low heat just until the shrimps turn pink and loose their transparent look. Add the sliced mushrooms, Madeira wine and cook the mixture, scraping the pan well with a wooden spoon, until most of the liquid has evaporated. Add the béchamel sauce, Dijon mustard and mix gently until the shrimps are well coated. Season with salt, pepper and Tabasco to your liking.

Spoon the shrimp and mushrooms on top of the vegetable juliennes. Top with a thin coating of the remaining sauce and sprinkle generously with Parmesan. Place the cookie sheet pan in the middle of the oven and glaze until light brown. Garnish with fresh parsley sprigs and serve on a bed of rice.

Béchamel Sauce:
    4 tablespoons butter
    1 teaspoon chopped onions
    3 tablespoons sifted flour
    2 cups hot milk
    1/2 teaspoon salt
    1 bay leaf
    Pinch nutmeg and white pepper

Melt the butter in a heavy saucepan over medium heat. Add the onions and cook until transparent but not brown. Add the flour, and stir for 1 minute. Gradually add the hot milk, stirring constantly with a wire whisk until smooth. Bring the sauce to a boil, lower the heat and simmer for 15 minutes, stirring occasionally. Strain the béchamel though a fine sieve into a bowl, and keep hot.

Roasted Duck
with Prunes and Fava Beans
Yield: Serves 4

1 duck, about 4 to 5 pounds
2 cups pitted, dried prunes
1 lemon, sliced
1/2 cup dry white wine
1/2 cup orange juice
1 teaspoon cornstarch dissolved in 1/4 cup cold water.
2 pounds fresh fava beans, shelled
1/2 stick butter
4 strips bacon, diced
1 can Roma tomatoes (15 ounces)

Soak the prunes in lukewarm water to cover. When they are nicely swollen and soft, drain them.

Preheat the oven to 375° F. Wash the duck under cold running water, pat dry, and discard the liver and gizzard. Rub inside and outside with salt and pepper. Stuff the duck with the prunes and lemon slices. Sew up the cavity and place in a flameproof baking dish and add 1/2 cup of water.

Roast for two hours or until the joints rotate easily, basting the duck frequently with the fat that melts in the baking dish. Lift out the duck; remove the prunes from the cavity and place in the center of a heated serving platter. Cut the duck into serving pieces and arrange on top of the prunes. Ladle the fava beans around the meat.

While the duck is roasting, fry the bacon in the saucepan. Add the tomatoes and the shelled beans, season with a little salt, cover and cook over low heat for a few minutes until the beans are almost tender, dot with butter and set aside and keep hot. Discard the fat from the baking dish and pour in the wine, orange juice, scraping up the browned bits and stirring over moderate heat. Whisk in the corn starch and heat until slightly thickened. Pour sauce over the duck and serve.

Fettuccine Piemontese
Yield: Serves 6

1 pound top quality fettuccini
8 tablespoons softened butter
1 cup grated Parmesan
1 cup white truffles, sliced
Salt and freshly ground pepper to taste

Cook the fettuccini in plenty of vigorously boiling, salted water; drain them, then transfer onto a heated platter. Dot with butter, sprinkle with half the Parmesan and top with the sliced truffles. Serve the rest of the Parmesan cheese and the pasta sauce on the side.

Italian Pasta Sauce (Yield: 4 cups)

4 strips lean bacon
1/2 cup diced ham
1/2 cup ground salt pork
1 cup chopped mushrooms
1 pound beef bones
1 tablespoon olive oil
1 pound veal or pork bones
1 teaspoon sugar
1/2 teaspoon salt
1/2 cup red wine
1 teaspoon black pepper
2 Roma tomatoes
1 tablespoon tomato paste (peeled, seeded and diced)
1/4 teaspoon dried thyme
1/4 teaspoon dried marjoram
1 teaspoons flour mixed with
1 bay leaf
2 teaspoons melted butter
1 medium size onion, coarsely chopped
1 carrot, peeled and coarsely chopped
1 stalk coarsely chopped celery
2 clove garlic, crushed

Set the oven to 400° F.

Place the bones, bacon, salt pork, carrots, onions, garlic and celery into a roasting pan and roast for 25 minutes, stirring occasionally. When the bones begin to brown add the tomato paste, then deglaze the pan with 2 cups of water, and transfer to a stockpot. Add another 6 cups of water, the salt, black pepper, bay leaf, marjoram, thyme, and simmer uncovered on top of the stove for 2 hours over low heat, until most of the liquid has evaporated. (You should have 2 1/2 cups of broth) Strain liquid into another pot through a fine sieve, add 1/2 cup of red wine, and the flour-butter mixture, continue to cook until the desired thickness has been achieved.

Heat the olive oil in a saucepan; add the ham, mushrooms, tomatoes, and sugar. Cook the mixture over low heat for 5 minutes, add the gravy and bring to a boil, ladle over the fettuccine pasta.

Roasted Leg of Venison with Red Currant Sauce

Yield: serves 6

1 venison leg, about 5 pounds
1 bottle dry red wine
1 cup beef broth
1 onion, sliced
1 carrot, peeled and sliced
1 celery stalk, sliced
1 tablespoon juniper berries
2 whole cloves
1 fresh rosemary sprig
2 bay leaves
8 ounces salt pork, cut into little strips
1/4 cup vegetable oil
1 cup flour
1 teaspoon Spanish paprika
1 jar red currant jelly
1/2 cup cream
1/4 cup brandy or grappa

Bone the meat, and cut into large cubes. Place in a ceramic or stainless steel bowl with the wine, beef broth, vegetables and flavorings. Cover the bowl and refrigerate for at least 24 hours.

Drain and dry the meat with paper towels, reserving the marinade. Lard the meat with half the salt pork with a larding needle or pressing a piece of fat into a slit cut in each meat cube. Melt the remaining salt pork in a casserole over high heat, and add the vegetable oil. Mix the flour with paprika and dust the meat cubes generously.

Place the meat in the casserole and brown the cubes on all sides. Pour the marinade over the venison and cook, uncovered for 1 to 2 hours or until the meat is tender. Transfer the meat with a slotted spoon to a heated bowl and keep hot. Strain the sauce into another sauce casserole and stir. Stir in the currant jelly, brandy and continue cooking until sauce is reduced to desired consistency. Add the cream, heat but do not boil. Season to your liking and ladle over the venison cubes. Serve with risotto or creamed potatoes.

Poached Pears
in White Wine alla Italiana
Yield: serves 6

6 large, ripe pears, peeled and cored but left whole
1 cup sugar
2 cups dry Italian white wine
1 tablespoon grated orange rind
1 teaspoon grated lemon rind
2 cloves
1 stick cinnamon
3 tablespoons toasted and chopped pistachios
1 dozen Italian almond macaroons

Place the pears in an enamel fireproof baking pan small enough so that they can stand upright.

In a separate saucepan bring the wine, cloves, cinnamon and sugar to a boil, simmer for 5 minutes. Strain over the pears, seal the dish with foil and poach over moderate heat until the pears are pierced easily with a fork. Remove them with a slotted spoon and place them in a glass-serving bowl. Raise the heat and reduce the liquid to about 3/4 cup. Pour though a fine sieve over the pears, and refrigerate until well chilled. Just before serving, sprinkle them with the toasted pistachios and serve almond macaroons on the side.

EMILIA ROMAGNA
The Land of Balsamic Vinegar and Parma Ham

Two ancient provinces were wed in 1860, when the lush and prosperous coastal Romagna joined the seriously artistic plain of Emilia. The city of Bologna is the capital of this wonderful region, and it rivals with Milan in architectural achievements and high standard of living.

Our gastronomic expedition started in Miami on Alitalia flight #631, which left the U.S. at 6:30 PM and arrived in Rome at 10:20 AM with a connecting flight to G.Marconi Airport in Bologna. Our travels continued by motor coach on the modern

Autostrada, passing the romantic villages of Modena, Rubiera, and Reggio nell'Emilia with our destination the Toscanini Hotel in Parma.

With great expectations, we entered Italy's richest regional cuisine. The city of Parma was founded in the sixth century and has the most beautiful architecture from medieval times.

Parma is also the home of the famous Parma ham, prosciutto di Parma. Dry cured, pink in texture and thinly sliced, it is known all over the word. In the Enza Valley, just outside of Parma, is Italy's largest dairy community producing an abundance of cream, milk, butter and all kinds of cheeses. The most famous is Parmigiano Reggiano, the king of all Italian cheeses.

Our first dinner was at the Palazzo Calvi, a first class restaurant serving specialties of the region such as Salame della Bassa, Prosciutto di Langhirano e Torta Fritta. Wonderful Parma ham with traditional fried bread was followed by five courses and finished with Sfogliatina calda di mele con Zabaione, a thin apple tart with a whipped egg and wine sauce. The wines of Emilia-Romagna are not counted among Italy's best, but they do compliment the food of this region. Many are frizzante (slightly sparkling) and are meant to drink young. One of the best in this part of the country is the Lambrusco, which is dark red and fruity with a taste of cherries. Sangiovese is another fine red wine from this region in addition to two delicious white wines, Trebbiano and Albana di Romagna.

The next day we visited a local creamery and witnessed the production of their famous Parmesan cheese, from boiling of the milk in large copper cauldrons to the final molding of the "curd-mass". A final tasting of the unique aged and flavorful Parmigiano-Reggiano with a glass of local wine was the highlight of the morning.

A few miles outside of the ancient village of Modena, in the middle of the rolling hills and vineyards, we visited Acetaia del Cristo, the makers of Italy's most famous balsamic vinegar. Tradition and painstaking care followed by complex sequence of fermentation in large and small barrels made of different types of wood gives this vinegar a very explosive flavor. The vinegar has to mature from 12 to 25 years in the barrel before being bottled and sold. This balsamic vinegar is not sold by the gallon – only by the ounce – with a cost equal to some of the most exquisite French Cognac.

A fabulous dinner was waiting for us at one of Bologna's finest restaurants, Antica Trattoria, with a traditional fare of Carrello degli arrosti and Carrello dei bolliti, roasted and boiled meats, in addition to five other courses accompanied by well selected wines.

Our next destination was the coast of the Adriatic Sea and the city of Cattolica. A visit to the historical city of old Ravenna transported us back in time to the sixth century A.D. Almost every building or church could be a museum, presenting its rich past in marble, gold and ivory.

Ravenna was the headquarters of Caesar for his march on Rome and also the center of changes in the religious world. It always was a thriving community protected by swamps and criss-crossed by canals, an early version of Venice.

We finished the day with a classic dinner at San Domenicos, a two-star Michelin restaurant, which also houses one of Italy's finest wine and Armagnac selections dating back to the year 1804. A visit to the smallest republic in Italy, San Marino, and a tour through the castle San Leo was another great experience. The most memorable lunch was served in the castle of Montegridolfo, overlooking the coast of the Adriatic Sea. This castle is one of the best preserved in the area and is also a first class hotel with the highest standards.

The most sumptuous seafood dinner was at Lamparta in Cattolica. The memorable event was medieval farewell dinner in the picturesque Mastin Vecchio Castle. On our flight home to Texas, I was thinking about the wonderful hospitality of our gracious Italian hosts, the great tradition of food accompanied with fine wines, and the art of dining and conversation.

Emilia Romagna Theme Dinner

Rollatini di Melanzane e Zucchini

Santa Margherita Pinot Grigio 1994

Scampi alla Griglia

Coltibuono Cetamura 1994

Quaglie in Umido

Del Falegname Chianti 1992

Straccoto al Barolo

Toscana IGT Campo del Bosco 1993

Torta di Susine

Moscato d'Asti 1990

Cascinetta

Eggplant and Zucchini Rolls

Yield: Serves 6

2 large eggplants, unpeeled
2 large zucchini
5 tablespoons extra-virgin olive oil

Stuffing:

1 cup dried breadcrumbs
3/4 cup chopped pine nuts
2 tablespoons diced chives
1/4 teaspoon oregano
3 ounces provolone cheese, rind removed, chopped
1/4 cup chopped fresh parsley
1/2 pound smoked ham, diced
1 whole egg
3 tablespoons soft butter to grease the baking pan

Topping:

2 cups tomato sauce (recipe below)
8 ounces grated Parmesan cheese
Salt and pepper to taste.

Preheat a broiler. Slice the eggplant lengthwise into 12 slices each, 1/4 inch thick. Cut the zucchini the same way, only 1/8 inch thick each slice. Brush each slice generously with olive oil on both sides, place on a baking pan and broil under the broiler for 5 minutes. Turn the slices over and broil until light brown 4 minutes longer. Remove from the baking pan, transfer to a plate and let cool.

Preheat the oven to 375° F. To make the stuffing mix all the ingredients in a mixing bowl, including salt and pepper, until blended. To assemble the rollatini: on a clean working surface, lay 1 eggplant slice and place 1 zucchini slice on top of each. Place two teaspoons of the stuffing into the center, and roll up the sliced eggplant and zucchini overlapping the ends. Place the rolls, seam down in a buttered baking dish. Repeat with the remaining slices and stuffing.

Spoon the tomato sauce over the rollatini, sprinkle the top with parmesan cheese and bake in the oven for 25 minutes until cooked, and the top has a nice golden brown color.

Place 2 rolls to each warmed individual plate and serve with crusty Italian bread.

Quick tomato sauce:

6 cups, peeled, seeded and chopped ripe Roma tomatoes, or 2 cans, 15 ounces each
1 medium size onion, chopped very fine
5 cloves garlic, minced
1/4 teaspoon dried herbs
2 bay leaves
1/2 teaspoon sugar
1/2 cup vegetable oil

Heat the oil in a casserole, add the onions, garlic, and herbs and sauté until translucent, but do not brown. Add the tomatoes, salt pepper, sugar and simmer over low heat, until thickened and most of the liquid has evaporated, stirring occasionally. Season with salt and black pepper to your taste.

Sautéed Shrimp in Garlic Butter
Yield: Serves 6

2 1/2 pounds large shrimp in the shell
2 tablespoons olive oil
2 cloves garlic, minced
1/2 green bell pepper, cut in half, seeded and diced finely
1/2 red bell pepper, cut in half, seeded and diced finely
1/4 cup shallots, peeled and chopped finely
1 tablespoon fresh lemon juice
5 tablespoons chopped fresh parsley
2 drops Tabasco sauce
1 teaspoon salt
1/2 teaspoon dried oregano
1/4 cup dry white wine
2 lemons cut into wedges
1 stick butter

Peel the shrimp, being careful not to remove the last small segment of the tail. With a small knife, slit each shrimp down the back and remove the dark intestinal vein. Wash the shrimp under cold running water and pat them dry with paper towels. Place all ingredients except butter in a large ceramic or glass bowl. Cover and refrigerate over night, stirring from time to time.

Using tongs, remove the shrimp from the marinade and place on a plate, reserving the marinade. Melt the butter in a large heavy duty or cast iron skillet, add the shrimp and stir-fry over high heat until pink and firm to touch. Be careful not to overcook them. Arrange the cooked shrimp nicely on a heated serving platter. Add the marinade to the skillet and heat thoroughly, then spoon over the shrimp. Sprinkle with chopped parsley, garnish with lemon quarters and serve piping hot.

Scampi alla Griglia

Stewed Quail with Pancetta

Yield: Serves 6

12 quails, cleaned and trussed
1/4 cup olive oil
1/2 cup flour
1 teaspoon Spanish paprika
1/2 teaspoon salt
1/8 teaspoon black pepper
1 cup chopped pancetta
1/2 cup dry white wine
4 ripe tomatoes, peeled, seeded and chopped
1 medium size onion, chopped finely
4 cloves garlic, minced
1 cup white grapes, cut in halves
3 pounds green beans, snapped and cut

Season the quail with salt and pepper. Combine the paprika with the flour and dust the quails generously with the mixture. Heat the oil in a large casserole over high heat and brown the quail on both sides, add the onions, garlic, chopped tomatoes, and white wine. Cover the casserole and simmer for 25 to 30 minutes.

While the birds are cooking, fry the pancetta in another saucepan. Add the beans, grapes and a little salt, cover and cook over low heat for a few minutes until the beans are almost tender. Spoon this mixture over the quail and continue cooking for another 5 minutes to blend the flavors. Transfer to a serving dish and serve.

Quaglie in Umido

Chuck Roast Braised in Barolo

Yield: Serves 6

3-4 pounds chuck roast
2 carrots, peeled and cut into large dice
1 onion, coarsely chopped
2 celery stalks, cut into 1/2 inch long pieces
2 bay leaves
4 cloves garlic, crushed
1 tablespoon juniper berries
1 teaspoon crushed black peppercorns
8 ounces salt pork fat, cut into small strips
1 1/2 cups aged red Barolo wine
1/2 teaspoon salt
1/4 cup tomato paste
1 cup beef broth, fresh or canned

Combine the meat, all the vegetables, the herbs and the wine in a large bowl. Cover and marinate in the refrigerator for at least 24 hours, turning the meat from time to time. Remove the meat and dry well, reserving the marinade. Using a small knife make little cuts into the meat and force the pork strips into it. Heat the olive oil in a casserole or Dutch oven and brown the meat thoroughly on all sides. Strain the marinade, add the vegetables to the meat and reserve the liquid.

Preheat the oven to 350°. Place the Dutch oven in to the oven and roast the meat with the vegetables for 1/2 hour stirring occasionally. Add the tomato paste, then the marinate liquid, 1 cup beef broth, cover the Dutch oven and braise the beef for about 2 1/2 hours. Adding more wine as needed to keep the meat from drying out. Remove the meat when done, slice with a sharp knife and place on a heated platter. Discard the bay leaves, and puree the vegetables and wine in a food processor. Reheat the sauce, season to your taste and pour over the meat. Garnish with fresh sprigs of Italian parsley. Serve at once with your favored pasta.

Plum Cake
Yield: Serves 8

1 1/4 cups flour
1/4 stick butter, at room temperature
2 tablespoons soft butter to grease the cake pan
2 large eggs, separated at room temperature
1/3 cup granulated sugar
1/4 cup heavy cream
1/4 cup milk
1/8 teaspoon salt
2 tablespoons sugar for whipping the egg whites
2 1/2 teaspoons baking powder
2 teaspoons vanilla extract
24 Italian plums, pitted and cut into sixths
1/2 cup sliced almonds
1/2 teaspoon sugar, combined with 1/4 teaspoon cinnamon
1/2 cup confectioner's sugar

Preheat the oven to 375°. Butter a 9-inch cake or tart pan with a removable bottom. In a bowl, using an electric mixer set at medium speed, beat together the butter and sugar until smooth and fluffy. Add the egg yolks and beat until creamy. In a small bowl, sift together the flour, salt and baking powder. In another bowl whisk together the milk, cream and vanilla extract. Pour the milk-cream mixture into the flour, then add the butter-egg mixture and combine with a wooden spoon. Do not overmix.

In anther bowl, using a clean beater, whip the egg whites until they form soft peaks. Sprinkle in the 2 tablespoons sugar and continue to beat until semi soft peaks form. Using a rubber spatula, fold the beaten egg whites into the cake batter, breaking apart any lumps. Pour the batter into the prepared cake pan and level the surface. Arrange the plums in a circle on the top of the batter, sprinkle with the sugar-cinnamon mixture, top with the sliced almonds and bake for 35 to 40 minutes. Remove the pan sides and let cool on a cake rack. Dust with the confectioners' sugar and serve at room temperature with whipped cream.

SPAIN: A Triumph of Culture and History

My first introduction to the Spanish culture, history, and food was in 1964 on the beautiful island of Puerto Rico. At the time, I was a young executive chef at the El Miramar Hotel in San Juan. During my stay I was fascinated with the language, food, architecture, and the everyday way of life. Since then, it had been my desire to visit Spain to explore the museums, medieval castles, vineyards, and spectacular cities. Four decades later, my wife Connie and I finally arrived in Barcelona, capital of Catalonia, with its 2000 years of history. We settled in at the new Hotel Arts overlooking the Mediterranean Sea and soon we were on our way to discover modernist Barcelona via a Gaudi Tour. Antonio Gaudi, the world-renowned architect of the Sagrada Familia Church, went beyond academic rules with his incredible imagination and his influence can be seen in the construction of many buildings in the Art Nouveau Era.

Restaurant Botafumeiro, the best known Galician restaurant in Barcelona, was our destination for lunch. We enjoyed an abundance of fresh seafood, well prepared by the legendary chef/proprietor Moncho Neiras. A local Catalan sparkling wine, Méthode Champenoise from the nearby Penedès, was a fine selection for this feast. The Mediterranean diet back home in the USA has made headlines over the years and therefore our next destination was the food market La Boqueria. Here we found the secrets to a healthy and long life in a spectacular variety of goat cheese, olives, and virgin olive oils and the finest in fresh and exotic fruits, vegetables and seafood.

We spent the rest of the afternoon strolling along Las Ramblas, the liveliest place in Barcelona. This promenade is a constant and colorful flood of humanity strolling past flower stalls, bird vendors, musicians, newspaper stands, and outdoor cafés. The port city of Barcelona is also the home of many interesting museums, including one featuring the early paintings and artwork of Picasso from 1881-1973. The highlight during our stay in Catalonia was a tour through the grand "Torres Vineyards" which included a luncheon served in the gracious hospitality of the Miguel Torres Family.

We departed Barcelona by Air Iberia to Seville, the city that played an important role in the voyage of Christopher Columbus. With the discovery of the New World, Seville reached it's height of splendor, outshining Madrid in riches and culture as Spanish ships loaded with booty from the Americas sailed upriver past the Torre de Oro (Tower of Gold). Seville is a river port on the Guadalquivir, and is Spain's fourth largest city. We stayed at the gracious, and well managed Hotel Alfonso XIII, and soon were discovering the splendid monuments, cathedrals, palaces and the cross-cultured Spain that is both Christian and Moorish. The Southern peninsula of Andalusia attracted the Muslim people from the deserts of North Africa. Andalusia was a place where they could live a life of sensuality and repose, which attracted them for eight centuries.

We visited the 15th century Gothic Cathedral Giralda and Alhambra, the former palace of the

Islamic rulers in Granada which is an architectural gem built by Syrian craftsmen in the 11th century. A wonderful traditional Spanish luncheon was served at the famous Restaurant Enrique Becerra. We finished the day at the Hacienda Benazuzu in the village of Sanlúcar La Mayor. The Moors built the estate in the 10th century. King Alfonso X took possession in the 12th century after the Moors departed and later the estate belonged to the crusading Knights of Santiago. Needless to say, we were happy to be here, dining in style, almost a thousand years after its founding.

The next day we visited the Spanish Equestrian School featuring a show of precision and beauty. Old Spain was the center of Andalusian breeding, one of the oldest and most revered horse breeds, as long ago as 200 BC. In the sun-scorched southern frontiers, Carthusian monks preserved the purity of the equestrian legacy with dedication for decades. Lunch was at the well-known Osborn Cellar with a tasting of sherry and a tour though the ancient cellars. The proper name for this delicate aperitif is Jerez de la Frontera but was later changed by an English nobleman who had problems with the Spanish spelling to simply "sherry." Dinner was casual with a "Tapas Crawl" in the Barrio de Santa Cruz. Tapas are another legacy of the Moorish taste for small and varied delicacies, similar to French hors d'oeuvres or Italian antipasto.

After visiting the Maria Louisa Park with its pavilions from the 1929 exhibition, the Plaza de America, and Plaza de España, it was time to depart by high-speed bullet train to Madrid. We traveled for about four hours along endless olive orchards, through the tunnels of icy mountains, and past ancient castles to the high plains of the Castilian plateau. Arriving at the Atocha Madrid Station, the capital of Spain since 1561, we experienced the artistic legacy of one of the greatest global empires ever assembled. Madrid is a young city by Iberian standards, a mere millennium old compared to Barcelona. This city never sleeps; it is a moveable feast of medieval lanes, broad avenues, spectacular palaces, museums, housing resplendent paintings, and an infi-

nite number of irresistible restaurants and taverns. We started our gastronomical feast with lunch at Restaurante Botin, established in 1723, and one of the oldest restaurants in the world. Their specialties are Roasted Segovia Suckling Pig and Aranda Lamb, cooked slowly over wooden logs in century old ovens. The setting and ambiance is similar to arriving on a stagecoach and dining in the cellar of an old country inn. This was a great beginning.

Our Hotel was the Westin Palace, situated between the Parliament and the Prado Museum in the heart of Madrid. Restaurant Zalacain, was our dinner destination. Under the guidance of master chef Benjamin Urdain, we enjoyed Basque style cooking, and certainly had to agree with the three stars Michelin rating of this luxurious, fine restaurant.

By crystal blue sky, we left Madrid en route to Toledo, a city of genuine Spanish culture and civilization. We strolled through the Gothic Cathedral of the Cardinal Primate, visited the royal tombs, the enormous golden altar, and the 14th century Santa Maria la Blanca synagogue. We enjoyed a traditional Paella Feast, in addition to a spectacular Flamenco Show at El corral de la Moreria before leaving the next day for Segovia. It was here that Isabelle the Catholic was proclaimed Queen of Castile in 1474 and it is also a showplace of historic Roman architecture. The Aqueduct with 118 arches, which span a total distance of 728 meters in the Plaza del Azoguejo, is proof of the grandeur during the occupation of the Roman Empire. The Cathedral of San Martin and the castle museum with an elaborate display of armor from Castilian knights left an everlasting impression on us. Alcázar also inspired my former employer, Walt Disney, to build a duplicate in Orlando at the Magic Kingdom.

Spanish Theme Dinner

Gazpacho Andaluz

Muga Rosé 2001

Bonito con Aceitunas y Alcaparras

Vega Sindoa Chardonnay 2000

Codorniz con Higos

Vina Alarba "Old Vines" Garnacha 2000

Cordero a la Moruna

Emilio Moro Red 1999

Queso de Cabrales

Borsao Ribera del Duero Garnacha/Tempranillo 2001

Tarta de Santiago

Marques de Gelida Cava N/V Brut

Chilled Gazpacho
Yield: serves 6

3 large ripe tomatoes, peeled, cut in half, seeded
    (reserve 1/2 tomato for garnish)
1 green bell pepper, cut in half, seeded
    (reserve 1/4 for garnish)
1 cucumber, peeled and seeded
    (reserve 2 inch slices for garnish)
2 stalks celery
1 onion, chopped
1 can tomato juice, (12 ounce can)
2 cloves garlic, peeled and finely chopped
4 tablespoons tomato purée
1/4 teaspoon thyme
1/2 teaspoon salt
1/4 teaspoon savory
1/8 teaspoon freshly ground black pepper
2 tablespoons wine vinegar
2 tablespoons olive oil
5 drops Tabasco sauce
2 tablespoons chopped parsley
2 boiled eggs, chopped

Wash and dry the vegetables, chop them and place them in a blender with enough tomato juice to partially cover. Add garlic, tomato purée, savory, thyme, pepper, salt, vinegar, oil and Tabasco sauce and then purée until smooth. Pour the mixture into a bowl and stir in the remainder of the tomato juice. Chill for two hours. Serve the gazpacho in individual soup cups, dice the remaining bits of tomato, green bell peppers, and cucumber separately and sprinkle them separately with the chopped parsley and boiled eggs on top of the soup.

Gazpacho Andaluz

Baked Tuna Steaks
with Olives and Capers
Yield: serves 6

6 tuna steaks (7 ounces each)
1/2 cup dry white wine
2 tablespoons sherry vinegar
2 tablespoons lemon juice
3 cloves garlic,
    peeled and chopped
1 bay leaf
2 sprigs fresh thyme
6 black peppercorns, crushed
1 large onion,
    cut in half and sliced
1/2 cup pitted olives
1/2 cup olive oil
1 tablespoon capers
1 tablespoon chopped parsley
Salt to taste
3 tablespoons oil for baking dish

Preheat the oven to 400°F. Wash and dry the tuna steaks. In a bowl combine the white wine, vinegar, lemon juice, garlic, bay leaf, thyme, peppercorns and a little salt. Place the tuna steaks side by side into a ceramic dish, pour the marinade over it and refrigerate for two hours.

Remove the tuna steaks from the marinade and drain. Keep the marinade, removing the sprigs of thyme and the bay leaf. Heat the olive oil in a frying pan over high heat, add the onions and cook until translucent, but not brown. Pour in the marinade and 1/4 cup water. Add the olives, capers and parley and bring the mixture to a boil, simmer for 3 minutes. Place the tuna steaks into a well-oiled, fireproof baking dish, ladle the sauce over the steaks and bake uncovered for about 20 minutes, basting the steaks occasionally. Serve the fish in the baking pan.

Roasted Quail with Figs

Yield: serves 6 as an appetizer

6 whole quail, cleaned
1/2 cup olive oil
1 large onion, finely chopped
1/2 cup flour
1/8 teaspoon each oregano and thyme
1 tablespoon butter
1 bay leaf
8 fresh figs, peeled
3/4 cup white wine
Salt and pepper to taste
1 tablespoon chopped
    semisweet chocolate

Preheat the oven to 450°. Rinse the quails and pat dry. With a sharp knife remove the backbone, flatten the birds with a mallet and rub them with salt and pepper. Heat the olive oil in a frying pan, dust the quails generously with flour and brown over high heat on both sides. Remove the quails and transfer to a casserole. Add the butter to the same frying pan and cook the onions until light brown, add the white wine, oregano, thyme and bay leaf. Simmer for 1 minute, and then pour over the quails. Add the figs, stir in the chocolate, seal the pan and bake for 30 minutes. Serve in the casserole.

Moorish Baked Lamb Shoulder

Yield: serves 6

2 lamb shoulders (2 1/2 pounds each)
1/2 teaspoon cinnamon
1/2 teaspoon cumin
1 teaspoon freshly ground black pepper
1 teaspoon salt
1/2 cup olive oil
4 sprigs fresh rosemary
2 large onions, diced
4 cloves of garlic, minced
2 cups chicken or beef broths,
    fresh or canned
1/2 cup raisins, soaked in
    1/4 cup sherry wine
1/2 cup almonds, roughly chopped
1/4 cup chopped mint
1 tablespoon cornstarch dissolved
    with 2 tablespoons water

Preheat oven to 375°. Wash the meat and pat dry. Place the shoulders on to a large platter, and then rub thoroughly with salt, pepper, cinnamon and cumin. Heat the olive oil in a braising pan or Dutch oven on top of the stove and brown the meat on all sides. Add the onions, garlic, and rosemary and cook until they are translucent.

Pour the broth over the meat, and add enough water to just cover the lamb shoulders. Seal the baking pan with foil and braise in the oven for 1 1/2 hours, basting from time to time or until the meat is tender. Remove the meat from the roasting pan, slice and transfer to a heated serving platter. Strain the sauce through a sieve into a small saucepan and skim off the fat. Add the chopped mint, raisins and almonds. Bring the sauce to a boil, remove from the heat and whisk in the cornstarch. Heat the sauce, stirring constantly until thicken, pour over the lamb and serve.

Galician Almond Tart

Yield: one 9-inch tart

Pastry shell:
>   1 cup flour
>   1/2 cup sugar
>   1/2 stick butter softened
>   1 whole egg
>   2 drops vanilla extract
>   Extra butter to grease a loose-bottomed fluted tart pan

Filling:
>   4 whole eggs
>   2 1/2 cups finely ground almonds
>   1 1/4 cups sugar
>   Pinch ground cinnamon
>   Lemon zest from one lemon

Preheat the oven to 375°. Sift the flour on to a work surface and make a well in the center, add the sugar, egg, vanilla extract and butter, knead to make smooth dough. Wrap in wax paper and set aside for 1/2 hour. To prepare the filling, beat together the eggs, lemon zest and sugar until creamy. Fold in the ground almonds, and cinnamon. With a wooden spoon beat the filling until all the ingredients are well mixed together.

Roll out the pastry on a floured surface and line the pie tart with the pastry dough, prick it all over with a fork and spoon the filling on top. Bake in the middle shelf in the oven for about 30 minutes, until golden brown. Leave the almond tart to cool in the pan. Once cool, transfer it to a serving plate and dust with confectioners sugar before serving.

GREEK ISLANDS

We arrived via Lufthansa and started our journey in Venice at the Hotel Bauer on the Grand Canal. The hotel was built in the late 18th century, and it represents elegance with its majestic marble columns in the lobby and a sincere welcome to its visitors. Dinner on the terrace at this prestigious hotel, which overlooks all the activities on the main waterway, was a memorable event to start our Mediterranean culinary journey. Venice is not just another city, but it was an independent empire for over 1000 years with a fantastic skyline seeming to float on the surface of the Adriatic Sea.

The city is a vast communal work of art starting with the Piazza San Marcus, the world's most beautiful square. A gondola ride through the side canals and the Grand Canal can be expensive but grand. There is always the more economical "vaporetto" (water-bus). To experience the art of Venetian glass blowing, a visit to the nearby island of Murano is a must. The cuisine is mostly Italian starting out with an antipasto consisting of sardines, cheese, and sausage and smoked Parma ham. A large variety of fresh seafood is always available, cooked mostly in olive oil and lemon juice.

Our evening departure was on a small ship The Seadream, with our first destination the island of Hvar off the Croatian coast. We arrived the next morning at 7:30 AM. The rising sun added to the beauty of this ancient place with traces of the Spaniards, Greeks and its 3000 years of turmoil. The well-preserved historical town is small with highlights such as the sixteenth-century Cathedral, St.

Stephen. Inviting, romantic restaurants along the harbor offer local octopus, mussels, fresh fish and domestic wines. Situated in the very south of the Croatian Republic, the walled city of Dubrovnik was our next destination. The existence of the town was recorded for the first time in the year 667, and it was called the "queen of the Adriatic". With its magnificent fortifications, medieval churches, palaces and plazas, it is an architectural monument to its days as an affluent merchant state.

We set sail at sunset to enter the small port of Corfu the next morning, with its history of torturous invasions and changing rules in government. The Seadream, however, came in peace with its Texan sailors to enjoy the rich heritage of fine food, domestic wines and feta cheese. The highlight was a visit to the Achilleon Palace which was built over 100 years ago for the Empress Elisabeth of the Habsburg Empire and Kaiser William of Germany, who used it as a summer retreat. A statue of the Greek god Achilles is a reminder of a great civilization from a long time ago.

We set sail again in the evening, to arrive just before breakfast in the small port town of Itea on the Gulf of Corinth, about 200 Km northwest of Athens. The landscape has a natural beauty with rugged mountains, combined with ancient ruins. The village itself is not noteworthy, but surrounding it are millions of olive trees, which provides the main employment in the area. Tucked away high up in the mountains is Delphi, with the Sanctuary of Apollo. During medieval times it was one of the world's most important religious centers to consult with the gods. Even today in the 21st century the area is shrouded in mystery with a well-preserved stadium, and spacious amphitheater exposed on the rocky slopes. The Delphi Museum has many treasures, plus a magnificent bronze Charioteer from the 5th century BC.

We boarded the Seadream again with a world of new impressions and knowledge of Greek history. The highlight of the day was the passage through the magnificent Corinth Canal. Our next destination was Mykonos. Unfortunately the sea was very turbulent, so we changed our destination into calmer waters with plans to arrive in the morning at the beautiful island of Paros. The town is built around the port, and has about 3,000 year-round inhabitants. Paros is a very lively town with many restaurants, bars and hotels. It is also the main port with many connections to other islands, and for that reason it attracts thousands of visitors every summer.

Santorini was the last island we visited on our eight-day Mediterranean venture. The village of Fira with a sensational setting on top of the volcanic cliffs was our first stop. As good old Texans we saddled up on a herd of mules and climbed up the steep slopes to the top. Everybody in our group will remember Santorinis most scenic road from a mule. To calm down our nerves we stopped at the Antoniou Winery for a tasting of local wines. The island has been a major topic of discussion among archaeologist as to whether Santorini was the site of the legendary lost continent of Atlantis. We returned by cable car to our tender, which transferred us to the "Seadream" for a spectacular sunset dinner. As we departed for Athens we admired one more time the dramatic little pastel painted village's dwellings nestled in niches hewn into the volcanic rock.

After a night's rest we arrived bright and early on the docks in Piraeus and boarded a bus for the Intercontinental Hotel in Athens. A day of visiting several historical sites positioned us well for a quiet dinner with traditional home cooked food. We started out with a Greek salad, topped with virgin olives, followed by oven-roasted lamb with porcini risotto accompanied with local wines. We enjoyed local musical entertainment as well. The restaurant of our choice was Sholarhio on Tripodon 14 Street. The next day was our last day, and it was time to say goodbye. As a group we dined at the Dionysos restaurant with a sumptuous multiple-course Greek dinner in the open garden. The restaurant is directly opposite the Acropolis, and it was a great setting for a farewell dinner with wonderful old and newfound friends.

Mediterranean Theme Dinner

Avgolemono

Santorini 2002 Boutari, Greece

Ameijoas na Cataplana

Pinot Grigio 2003 Prædium, Italy

Horiatiki Salata

Conde de Valdemar 1999 Martinez Bujanda Reserve, Spain

Lombo de Porco con Pimentas

Paros 1999 Boutari, Greece

Arroz Dulce

Moscato d'Asti 2004 Andrea Faccio, Italy

Chicken Lemon Soup with Rice
Yield: Serves 6 - 8

1 whole chicken
2 celery ribs, cut 1 inch long
1 carrot, peeled and cut 1 inch long
1 onion, peeled and cut into quarters
1 tablespoon salt
2 bay leaves
3 large eggs
1/4 cup fresh lemon juice
5 tablespoons long-grain white rice
1/4 cup chopped parley
Dash of black pepper

Place the chicken into a large pot, cover with water and bring to a boil over high heat. Reduce the heat, skim off the foam and add the salt, carrots, onions, celery and bay leaves. Simmer for 1 hour, or until the meat and skin can easily be removed from the bones. Chill the chicken under cold water, discard the bones and skins. Dice the meat into 1/4 inch cubes and set aside. Simmer the chicken stock to reduce the liquid to 7 cups, skimming off the fat often, then strain through a fine sieve into another clean pot, bring to a boil.

In a separate casserole cook the rice in plenty of water until tender, drain and set aside. Beat the eggs in a small bowl gradually whisk in the lemon juice. Whisk 2 cups of the hot chicken stock into the eggs to heat them. Continue to beat until lightly thickened, and then slowly whisk the egg, lemon mixture into the very hot chicken stock. Add the diced chicken and rice and taste for salt and pepper. Heat but do not boil the soup. Ladle the Avgolemono into individual cups, sprinkle with chopped parsley and serve.

Stewed Clams with Sausage
Yield: Serves 6

4 pounds little neck clams
1/4 cup olive oil
2 tablespoons butter
3 ripe tomatoes, peeled, seeded
    and cut into large chunks
1 Spanish onion, peeled and diced finely
1 small jalapeno chili, seeded
    and chopped very fine
6 cloves garlic, finely chopped
1 bay leaf
1/2 teaspoon dried thyme
8 ounces prosciutto, diced
8 ounces chorizo sausage,
    casing removed and crumbled
1 cup dry white wine
1/4 cup chopped cilantro
12 lemon wedges

Scrub the clams under cold running water, discard any clams that do not close to the touch and set aside. In a large sauté pan over medium heat, warm the butter and olive oil. Add the onions, and sauté until tender but not brown. Add the garlic, jalapeno, bay leaf, thyme and sauté another 2 minutes longer. Add the ham, sausage, wine and tomatoes. Stir well and simmer over low heat uncovered for 20 minutes. Add the clams, cover the pan and raise the heat to high and cook until the clams open, stirring occasionally. Discard any clams that have not opened. Ladle into warm soup bowls, sprinkle with cilantro and serve with lemon wedges.

Amêijoas na Cataplana

Traditional Greek Salad
Yield: Serves 6

Dressing:
- 1/4 cup fresh lemon juice
- 1/2 cup extra virgin olive oil
- 1 tablespoon dried oregano
- 2 cloves garlic, minced
- Dash of freshly ground black pepper

- 6 cups assorted salad greens of your choice
- 6 small ripe tomatoes cut into wedges
- 2 cucumbers, peeled, cut in half, seeded and sliced
- 1 red Spanish onion, sliced very thin
- 2 green bell peppers, cut in half, seeded and diced
- 2 ribs celery, diced
- 3 hard-boiled eggs cut into quarters
- 6 large slices feta cheese (2 1/2 ounce each)
- 30 Kalamata olives

To make the dressing; whisk the oil together with the lemon juice, add the oregano, garlic and black pepper. Cover and set aside. In a large bowl, combine the greens, cucumbers, bell peppers and celery. Drizzle two thirds of the dressing over the top and toss gently to mix. Place the sliced feta cheese on top of the salad and nicely arrange the tomatoes, red onions, tomatoes, olives and eggs around the feta cheese. Pour the remaining dressing over the feta cheese. Serve on chilled plates with crusty bread.

Pork Ragout with Sweet Red Peppers
Yield: Serves 6

- 4 pounds boneless pork shoulder, cut into 1 inch cubes
- 2 tablespoons ground cumin
- 6 cloves garlic, minced
- 1 tablespoon salt
- 1/2 cup olive oil
- 1 onion, chopped coarsely
- 2 tablespoons tomato paste
- 1 teaspoon ground black pepper
- 1 1/2 teaspoon Spanish paprika
- 1/4 cup flour
- 4 large red bell peppers, cut in half, seeded and cut into 1/2 inch strips
- 1/2 cup chicken stock, fresh or canned
- 1 cup dry white wine
- 1/2 cup chopped fresh cilantro

Place the pork cubes into a large bowl, season with salt, pepper, paprika, cumin and garlic, and mix well. Cover and let marinade overnight in the refrigerator. Bring the meat to room temperature and dust with flour. In a large sauté pan heat the olive oil over high heat. Working in batches, add the pork and brown quickly on all sides. Using a slotted spoon, transfer the pork to a large casserole. Add the chopped onions, tomato paste and simmer for 5 to 10 minutes. Return the sauté pan to high heat, pour in the white wine and deglaze the pan by stirring to dislodge any browned bits from the bottom of the pan.

Add the pan juices to the pork. Add the chicken stock and bring to a boil. Quickly reduce the heat to low, cover the casserole and simmer for 20 minutes. Add the red bell peppers, stirring from time to time cook until the meat is very tender. Stir in the cilantro, then taste and adjust the seasoning. Spoon into a heated serving dish and serve with rice or pasta.

Rice Pudding with Raisins
Yield: Serves 6

4 cups milk
3/4 cup sugar
1 tablespoon butter
2 lemon zest strips
1/4 cup raisins, soaked in warm water
1 cinnamon stick
1/2 cup short grain white rice
4 egg yolks
1/4 cup sliced almonds, toasted
1/2 teaspoon ground cinnamon
Sprigs of fresh mint, and ripe strawberries for garnish optional

In a saucepan over medium-high heat, combine the milk, sugar butter, lemon zest and cinnamon stick. Heat until small bubbles appear along the edge of the pan. Stirring constantly, add the rice and simmer over low heat until the rice kernels have swelled and are tender. Squeeze out any liquid from the raisins and add to the milk rice mixture. Discard the cinnamon stick and lemon zest.

In a bowl, using a whisk beat the egg yolks until light frothy. Gradually add 1 cup of the hot pudding to the yolks, beating constantly.

Gradually pour the warmed yolks into the remaining pudding, stirring constantly with a wooden spoon. Cook over very low heat until the rice pudding thickens, but do not boil. Spoon into 6 individual dessert bowls, dust with cinnamon, garnish with a ripe strawberry and a sprig of fresh mint. Serve at room temperature.

On the Road of Marco Polo
T H R O U G H   S Y R I A

Damascus is one of the world's oldest continuously inhabited cities. For centuries, it was the overland gateway between Europe and the Far East. Caravans arrived daily and traded dried fruits, silks, wool, spices and livestock. During its thousands of years of history, Damascus has seen many invasions and much destruction, including at the hands of King David during Biblical times, the Assyrians and Alexander the Great. Later invaders included the Romans in

64 BC, the European Crusaders in 1096, the Turks under the Ottoman Empire in 1516, and the French in 1920. Each group left its mark on the language, religion, architecture and agriculture. Ruins from these civilizations are highly visible: the ancient city wall, the Roman Arch, and the massive 7th century Omyyad mosque, housing what's said to be the severed head of John the Baptist. The underground Chapel of Ananias, named for the early Christian who restored the Apostle Paul's sight, reminds us of the religious struggle in this part of the world.

The bazaars in this bustling city are very colorful. Being a chef, naturally my first visit was to the food market. Despite a hostile climate, Syria produces a wide variety of unusual crops in the Baradda River Valley, in addition to an abundance of olives, dates, grapes, apples and fresh vegetables. Live chickens are traded, while sheep, goats and camels are butchered in the marketplace. Bedouins are selling goat cheese by the pound, and the bakers are cooling their flat bread on the sidewalk.

Arab cooking is vivid, exotic, and enchanting. It is with food that the natives express their generosity and hospitality. A simple lunch can consist of over a dozen dishes, called Mazza, and becomes a feast that can last for hours. Many recipes were introduced and refined during the ebb and flow of the conquest of other nations. Pistachios, olives, lentils, artichokes, eggplant, garlic, cumin, turmeric, and lamb make up a cuisine that has been evolving for over a thousand years.

Our next destination was the ancient city of Palmyra (City of Palms) now located on the outskirts of the town of Tadmor (an oasis in the middle of the desert). Palmyra was the capital of Syria at the time of Christ, and served as an important political and commercial center of the silk route between the Orient and Europe. The city was also the home of Queen Zenobia and Cleopatra. We visited the impressive temples, bath house, theater, and the Valley of Tombs before having a picnic dining on goat cheese and watching a spectacular sunset between several hundred colonnades and ancient arches.

After staying at the Cham-Palace Hotel and having a hearty breakfast, we left for Homs, outside of which lies the majestic crusades castle Krac des Chevaliers, built by the Knights of St. John. This crusades fortress took a hundred years to build, and commanded the only significant pass between Turkey and Lebanon. It housed a garrison of 4,000 men and 1,000 horses. Set on a high hill amid the mountains, it offers a scenic view over the entire valley making it a strategic asset. Before leaving this area we stopped for gas. Not only did the owner fill our tank, but he also invited us, with a friendly gesture, for tea. Soon the rest of his large family joined us. And to our surprise, we noticed everybody had large blue eyes. Later, we were informed that this is not unusual in this part of the country.

In the late afternoon, we arrived in Hama, an ancient city, within a rich agriculture region. The Roman waterwheels and irrigation system are the main attractions, which date from several thousands of years ago, and are still in working condition. Our journey continued on to Aleppo. Once a stopping point for caravans, Aleppo is one of the oldest settlements in Syria. Tourists come to admire the markets, the Bahramiye Mosque, and the gate of Antioch.

The following day we visited Busra, with 2nd century Roman and Arab ruins. A well-preserved classical Greco-Roman amphitheater, a medieval Arab citadel, a Roman bath and the Omayyad Mosque of Omar made this an interesting day. Soon we headed out into the desert to the Qulamoun mountain region of Maaloula. The breath-taking panoramic view and the village fascinated us, with closely built wall-to-wall houses, covering the southern slope down to the valley. Maaloula is an Aramaic word, which means, "entrance". Many caves and grottoes are visible on the mountainside. Some are the work of nature, others were dug long ago to serve as shelters for Christians in hiding. The Aramaic dialect is still spoken here. During the time of Christ, it spread all over the Near East. At the Convent of St. Serges, we visited with the priest, who took us on a tour through the monastery. The highlight was a tasting of his homemade wine.

On our last day, we arrived in Ras Shamara, a city dating back to 6,000 BC. It was a major stronghold of the Phoenicians, who developed the first alphabet.

Invaders destroyed the city about 1200 BC. Two temples and ancient tablets containing valuable information about Old Testament religion around 1500 BC were uncovered in 1929. Syria is a treasure chest of history and archeology, but undiscovered by tourists. It was a pleasure to drive through the countryside, drink tea with the natives, and experience their humble way of life.

Syrian Theme Dinner

Mazza: Hummus, Dolmeh, Tabbouleh
Vielles Vignes Chasselas 1996

Samak bil Tahineh
Milburn Park Chardonnay 1997

Kibby bil Sanie
Le Soleil des Terres du Sud Red Table Wine 1995

Lubya Khadra bil Lahma
Black Sea Cellars Cabernet Sauvignon 1996

Khyar bil Laban
Hebros Valley Merlot 1997

Baklava with French Vanilla Ice Cream and Honey-Brandy Sauce
Marquis des Roys Pecher Brut N/V

Hummus
(Chickpea Purée)
Yield: Serves 6

1 cup cooked chick-peas
1/2 cup tahini (sesame seeds purée)
3 cloves garlic, chopped
3 tablespoons water
3 tablespoons fresh lemon juice
1/8 teaspoon salt
Dash of freshly ground black pepper
12 fresh radishes
2 tablespoons extra virgin olive oil
1 tablespoon chopped parsley
1/2 teaspoon Spanish paprika
6 large black olives

Place the chick-peas, tahini, garlic, lemon juice, pepper and salt and a little water in a blender or food processor. Process until smooth and creamy, add a little more water, if necessary. Spoon the mixture into a shallow serving dish, dust with paprika and drizzle with olive oil. Serve radishes, olives and Syrian bread on the side.

Stuffed Grape Leaves
Yield: Serves 8

1 1/2 pounds ground lamb meat
1 jar (9 ounces) grape leaves
3 medium size onions, finely chopped
3 cloves garlic, minced
1 teaspoon salt
3 tablespoons olive oil
3/4 cup long grain white rice, uncooked
1/4 teaspoon black pepper
2 tablespoons chopped fresh mint
1 1/2 cups beef broth, canned or fresh
3 tablespoons fresh lemon juice
3 whole eggs, whisk with a dash of salt and pepper
Lemon slices

Wash and drain the grape leaves and place double layer on to a work surface.

Heat the oil in a casserole over high heat, stir in the onions, garlic and sauté until tender.

In a mixing bowl combine the ground lamb, onions, rice, salt, pepper and chopped mint.

Place a rounded measuring tablespoon meat mixture on the center of the grape leaves. Fold stem ends over the filling; fold in sides. Roll up tightly and place side-by-side, seam side down in a 12 X 12 inch skillet. Repeat with the remaining meat mixture and grape leaves. Add the beef broth, heat to boiling, reduce the heat and cover the casserole.

Set the oven to 375° and bake in the middle shelf for 45 to 50 minutes until the meat and rice are cooked. Drain and reserve the liquid. In a small bowl whisk together the eggs, lemon juice, a dash of salt and pepper until fluffy. Add enough water to the broth from the skillet to measure 1 full cup if necessary, gradually whisk in to the egg mixture. Pour the egg mixture over the grape leaves and bake uncovered for another 12 minutes. Garnish with lemon slices and serve.

Tabbouleh
Wheat and Parsley Salad

Serves: 6

1 1/2 cup fine bulgur wheat
1 tablespoon fresh lemon juice
1/4 cup olive oil
1/2 cup finely chopped fresh parsley
4 tablespoons fresh chopped mint
3 scallions, white part only, chopped
2 green bell peppers, cut in half
    and chopped finely
Dash of salt and black pepper
2 large ripe tomatoes, diced
8 large black olives

Put the bulgur wheat in a small bowl cover with cold water and soak for two hours.

Drain and squeeze with your hands to remove excess water. The wheat will swell to double the size. Spread on paper towels to dry completely, and then transfer to a large mixing bowl. Add the lemon juice, olive oil, mint, bell peppers, parsley and scallions. Season with a little salt and pepper. Cover the bowl and refrigerate for 1 hour in order for the flavors to develop. Stirring from time to time. Top with the chopped tomatoes, black olives and serve chilled.

Tahini Baked Fish

Yield: Serves 6

6 cod or haddock fillets, 6 ounces each
2 tablespoons fresh lemon juice
1/4 cup olive oil
1/4 stick butter
2 onions, finely chopped
1 large red bell pepper, cut in half,
    seeded and cut into juliennes
1 large green bell pepper,
    cut in half and cut into juliennes
1 1/2 cup tahini (sesame seed purée)
2 cloves garlic, crushed
1/2 cup dry wine or sherry
1/4 cup chopped parsley
2 lemons cut into wedges
Salt and pepper to suit your taste

Preheat the oven to 375°. Wash the fish fillets under running cold water and dry with paper towels. Arrange the fillets side by side in a fireproof ceramic baking dish. Combine the olive oil and lemon juice and pour over the fish. Season with salt and pepper and bake for 15 minutes (depending on the thickness). Meanwhile heat the butter in a heavy-duty frying pan and sauté the onions, red and green bell peppers until well browned and almost crisp.

Put the tahini and garlic in a small bowl and slowly whisk in the white wine, a little at a time, until the sauce is light and creamy. Arrange equally the onion-pepper mixture on top of the fish fillets, pour the tahini sauce over it and bake for another 15 minutes. Sprinkle with fresh chopped parsley and garnish with lemon wedges. Serve at once with white rice.

Stuffed Meat Loaf
with Pine Nuts
Yield: serves 6 to 8

1 1/2 pounds lean ground lamb or beef
1 1/2 cups bulgur (cracked wheat)
1 3/4 teaspoons salt
1/8 teaspoon black pepper
1/8 teaspoon cumin

Stuffing:

1/2 pound ground lamb
1 small onion, finely chopped
3 tablespoons pine nuts
1/8 teaspoon ground cinnamon
1/8 teaspoon salt
Dash of nutmeg
2 tablespoons olive oil
3 tablespoons melted butter

Cover cracked wheat with cold water; let stand for 10 minutes. Drain, and press the wheat to remove excess water. Mix the ground lamb meat with salt, pepper, and cumin, add the wheat and knead with your hands until well-combined. To prepare the stuffing, preheat the oven to 350° and heat the olive oil in a casserole over high heat, add the onions and sauté until tender but not brown.

Add the meat, cinnamon, nutmeg, pine nuts, salt and cook until light brown, stirring constantly. Press half of the lamb-wheat mixture evenly into an 8x8x2 ungreased baking dish and cover with the stuffing. Then spread the remaining lamb-wheat mixture over the stuffing. Cut diagonal lines across the top to make a diamond pattern. Pour the melted butter over the meatloaf and bake in the oven for 40 minutes. Cut into diamond shapes and serve.

Roasted Leg of Lamb
with Green Beans
Yield: Serves 6

1 leg of lamb, bone in (4 — 4 1/2 pounds)
1/4 cup olive oil
6 cloves garlic, chopped
1/2 teaspoon cumin
1/2 teaspoon Spanish paprika
3 sprigs fresh rosemary
1 teaspoon salt
1/8 teaspoon cayenne pepper
3 baking potatoes, peeled and cut in quarters
2 onions, peeled and cut into quarters
2 pounds fresh green beans, snapped
Fresh cilantro leaves for garnish

Trim excess fat and make several shallow cuts into the meat. Combine the olive oil, garlic, cumin, cayenne pepper and salt and spread over the surface of the lamb, pressing the mixture into the slits. Cover, and refrigerate over night.

Preheat the oven to 450°. Place the leg of lamb in to a roasting pan and cook for 15 –20 minutes, turning the meat occasionally to brown on all sides. Reduce the heat to 325°. Deglaze the pan with 1 1/2 cups water, add the rosemary, and cover tightly with a lid or foil and braise for 2 hours basting the meat from time to time. Add the potatoes, onions and beans, cover again and cook for another 40 minutes (add more water if necessary) until the meat is very tender and almost falls off the bones. Place on a heated serving platter; arrange the potatoes and beans around the meat. Garnish with fresh cilantro and serve.

Lubya Khadra bil Lahma

Cucumber Salad with Yogurt
Yield: Serves 6

2 whole cucumbers,
    peeled and diced
2 cloves garlic, minced
1 medium size onion, diced
2 cups plain yogurt
1/2 cup feta cheese
1 large ripe tomato cut in half
    seeded and diced
1 tablespoon chopped chives
2 tablespoons sliced almonds,
    toasted
1 tablespoon chopped chives
Fresh mint leaves

In a bowl beat lightly the yogurt, add the cucumbers, tomatoes, onions, and garlic and feta cheese, toss gently and refrigerate for 1 hour. Sprinkle with chives, toasted almonds, garnish with fresh mint leaves and serve.

Baklava
Yield: serves 6 to 8

1 pound phyllo dough
3 1/2 cups chopped walnuts
1 teaspoon ground cardamom
1 1/4 cups confectioner's sugar
1 stick melted butter

For the syrup;
1 1/2 cups honey
1 1/4 cups water
1 stick cinnamon
4 whole cloves
2 tablespoons rose water

Place the honey, cinnamon, cloves and water in saucepan and bring to a boil, reduce the heat and simmer for 5 minutes, stir in the rose water. Set the syrup aside and let cool.

Mix together the walnuts, confectioner's sugar and ground cardamom.

Preheat the oven to 325°. Brush a large rectangular baking pan with a little melted butter.

Carefully, taking one sheet of phyllo at a time, and keeping the remainder covered with a damp cloth, brush with melted butter and lay on the bottom of the pan. Continue until you have six buttered layers in the pan. Spread half of the nut mixture over, pressing down with a spoon.

Take another six sheets of phyllo, brush each with butter and lay over the nut mixture. Sprinkle over the remaining nuts and top with a final layer of six phyllo sheets each brushed again with butter. Cut the pastry diagonally into small diamond shapes using a sharp knife. Pour the remaining melted butter over the top. Bake for 20 minutes, and then increase the heat to 400° and bake for about 15 minutes until light golden brown and puffed. Remove from the oven and strain the syrup over the baklava; let rest for 1/2 hour before serving.

Khyar bil Laban

THROUGH CHINA

After graduating from the Hotel School in Munich in the mid-1950s, it was my desire to travel as a young chef all over the world. After I read "The Travels of Marco Polo", he became my mentor and I wanted to explore the Far East, visit the Great Wall, the Forbidden City of Beijing, the Grand Canal and experience the unique treasury and cultural timeless tableau of China.

This far eastern land has a history as long, eventful and productive as the combined histories of ancient Egypt, classical Greece and Rome, plus that of Europe up to the Renaissance. The history of China begins 5,000 years BC, when peasants built settlements in the fertile Yellow and Wei river valleys, where people lived in well-ordered protected farming communities, worshipped animist gods and produced fine painted pottery. During the next four millennia, the art of war was developed and such peacetime skills as the production of silk, porcelain, flood control and irrigation were mastered. As the farmers domesticated animals and planted fruits and fresh vegetables, the culinary arts had its beginning. Over the next several centuries, the cooking of China

became one of the most famous cuisines in the world. Around the time of the first dynasty, the SHANK (1766-1066 BC), writing was invented and the earliest cities were developed. The capital CHANG'AN located on the site of today's XIAN, became a great cosmopolitan center with traders from all the known world.

The best artists, musicians, architects, teachers and scientists came to the capital and left their mark. Gunpowder was invented, porcelain making was refined, and fine silk was used for trade. Half a century of warlord rule followed the fall of the TANG Dynasty. In 1279 BC, the weakened SONG regime was unable to hold back the MONGOL horde of Kublei Khan which conquered China and founded the YUAN Dynasty (The yuan is today's currency). The invaders built their new capital, DADU, on the site of today's Beijing. Marco Polo describes the splendors of this city in his travels.

The MING Dynasty was China's Renaissance and an era of prosperity and territorial expansion. Chinese fleets explored trade routes to Arabia and Africa, while Portuguese merchants settled in the enclave of Macao.

During this time, Jesuits were honored in the court for their skill in astronomy, the use of a compass, map making, cannon casting, and less so for their Christian message. The Silk Road, established by Marco Polo in 1260 AD, was a trade route for 1000 years that crossed deserts and mountains to take China's luxury goods to Europe. The only commodity the British and other Western powers could find to balance Europe's huge demand for China's tea was opium. This led to the addiction of countless Chinese and the government in alarm destroyed a year's supply of the drug in 1839. The British sent gunboats and demanded compensation. The resulting Opium War and Boxer Rebellion was a disastrous defeat for China, which forced the cede of Hong Kong to the British and opened several treaty ports, including Shanghai to foreigners.

During the civil war in 1911, the country became very vulnerable and was invaded by the Imperial Army of Japan in 1937. When World War II and the civil war from 1946-1949 ended, China was economically, politically and emotionally in need of a new leader and government. It came in the form of the Chinese Communist Party and Chairman Mao Tse Tung who, in 1949, proclaimed the founding of the People's Republic from Tiananmen Gate in Beijing. Since then the country has endured years of hardship during the GREAT LEAP FORWARD and cultural revolution.

While carrying out land and industrial reform, every sort of luxury disappeared, and also the golden age of ancient Chinese cooking was over. The reform destroyed the art of imperial dining, in which lay some of their country's greatest assets. Chinese cuisine was destroyed in China, and would be dead today if it were not for the many custodians of its secrets who got out in time, taking with them priceless knowledge in the culinary art of China.

Needless to say, I never traveled to China as a young chef. Instead, in 1956, I went to the Edward Hotel in Durban, South Africa, were I worked side by side with a master in genuine imperial cooking. As time went by, in New York City, Bermuda and also at the Polynesian Village in Disney World, I had the pleasure of working with Chinese chefs and was fascinated with their simple techniques and seasonings. A European chef needs dozens of pots, pans, molds and skillets to prepare a dish in addition to a large array of different knives, scoops and cutters. An Asian chef needs only two tools, a wok and a cleaver, and with these tools he can prepare several hundred different dishes.

However, nearly a half century later, my desire to visit China became reality. With great expectation, my wife Connie and I boarded flight 751 AIR CHINA from San Francisco to Shanghai. Leaving at 5 p.m., we crossed the Arctic, Siberia, lost one full day, and arrived at our destination the same time we left San Francisco. After going through customs and immigrations we checked in at the luxurious 5 Star Jing Jiang Tower Hotel. Across the river is Shanghai's new finance and business district, designed to be Asia's Wall Street in the 21st Century.

On what was once farmland now soar hundreds of gleaming skyscrapers and more are under construction. Dominating the skyline is the Oriental Pearl Tower, with fine restaurants, observation decks and great hotels. Super highways and belts connecting the city, and the dramatic Yangpu and Nanpu bridges link Pudong with old Shanghai, home of Yu Yuan Garden and the famous Jade Carving Factory.

The next day we visited the City of SUZHOU, nestled in lands of silk and rice and is one of the most romantic places in China. In the ornamental garden, nature is tamed to human scale with bamboo forests, miniature waterfalls splashing into ponds filled with colored fish and lotus leaves. Suzhou with its network of canals, crisscrossed with hump-backed bridges is wonderfully presented as a Tang-dynasty Venice.

Flight KA 803 took us to Hong Kong, where we landed at the new and largest airport in the world giving us a splendid first impression. We stayed at the Grand Hyatt, most likely one of the greatest hotels on this planet, built with marble, glass and rare wood. Hong Kong, like Las Vegas, is difficult to describe. You need to see it for yourself.

Flight WH 2340 with Dragon Air brought us to Guilin, my favorite place in China. Geologically, the peaks surrounding the city are pure limestone that have been eroded into strange formations over millions of years. Within the city the most distinctive hill is shaped like an elephant with its trunk in the river. It is also a favorite spot to take pictures of the local fishermen with their trained cormorants, fishing birds.

Flight WH 2340 with Dragon Air took us to the ancient city of XIAN, the home of the 8000 terra-cotta warriors. This city has an extraordinary history, making it one of the world's most outstanding tourist destinations, as well as the repository for much of China's 5,000 year heritage. Xian was the capital of China for over a thousand years, and is today a mirror of Ming China with its Pagodas, Palaces and the Great Mosque.

Our last destination was the capital of China; Beijing, also the home of the famous Peking Duck, the Forbidden City (ruled by the son of heaven), and business center of tomorrow. Skyscrapers rise above the old courtyards, competing with historic pavilions, temples, pagodas and church towers. Beijing retains so much history and romance. The life of the city is open to view; 6 million citizens cycling along the broad avenues, street vendors offering their home-cooked fast food, and men strolling through the parks carrying their pet songbirds. With a population of 13 million, Beijing is a world-class city. Must-sees include the Great Wall at Badaling and the Ming Tombs.

After two weeks in this ancient land, it was time to fly home to the USA. As our plane glided over Lake Conroe and approached Bush Intercontinental Airport, I just smiled and said to my wife, "It's nice to be in Texas again."

Chinese Theme Dinner

Ching Chiao Tze

Stoney Hollow Sauvignon Blanc/Chardonnay 1997

Dai Gee Ha Dung Woo

Willm Pinot Gris 1998

Gai Nga Choy

Lockwood Chardonnay Reserve 1994

Hui Know Jou

Chateau Timberlay Bordeaux Superior 1997

Chin-ch'ien-niu-pai

Cathedral Cellar Cabernet Sauvignon 1995

Hung Yum Cha

Emilio Lustau Pedro Ximenez Sherry

Shanghai Dumplings
Yield: 24 dumplings

Wrapper Dough:
    2 cups flour
    1 teaspoon baking powder
    1/2 teaspoon salt
    2 egg yolks
    1 teaspoon walnut oil
    3/4 cups water

Filling:
    10 ounces lean pork, finely ground
    4 whole green cabbage leaves
    1 tablespoon scallions, finely chopped, white part only
    3 cloves garlic, minced
    1 tablespoon light soy sauce
    1 tablespoon fresh ginger, chopped very fine
    2 tablespoons sesame oil
    1/4 teaspoon salt
    1 tablespoon bread crumbs
    1 tablespoon cornstarch
    1 teaspoon chopped parsley

Sift the flour with the baking powder and salt onto a work surface. Make a well in the center, beat the egg yolks with the water and pour in the well. Add the walnut oil and knead for 5 minutes to make a firm, elastic dough. Wrap the dough in plastic wrap and let rest for one hour while preparing the filling. In a 2 quart stockpot, bring the water to a boil, add 1/2 teaspoon salt and blanch the cabbage leaves for 2 minutes. Chill the leaves under cold water, squeeze out any excess liquid and chop very fine.

Place the ground pork into a large mixing bowl, add the rest of the ingredients and mix well. At last combine the chopped cabbage with the mixture. If the filling is too firm, add two teaspoons cold water. Roll out the dough into a shape of a sausage 21/2 inch thick and slice into 24 pieces. On a lightly floured work surface roll each slice to a 31/2 inch round. Place a spoon full of the filling into the center, and then close securely, pinching them into a point in the center. It is important that the filling is firmly enclosed. Transfer the dumpling in a Chinese steamer basket, close the cover and steam over boiling water for 20 minutes. Serve hot with your favorite Chinese dipping sauce.

Scallops and Shrimp with Mushrooms

Yield: serves 6

24 medium size fresh scallops
8 ounces small peeled raw shrimp
3 tablespoons dry sherry
1/2 teaspoon dark soy sauce
2 teaspoons light soy sauce
8 dried Chinese black mushrooms, soaked in cold water
1 cup fresh small button mushrooms, sliced
1 cup fresh or canned straw mushrooms
2 cloves garlic, minced
1 teaspoon honey
1 teaspoon fresh chopped ginger
2 green onions, washed and thinly sliced
3 tablespoons peanut oil
3/4 cup fish or chicken stock (canned or fresh)
1 1/2 teaspoons cornstarch
1/8 teaspoon salt
Dash of freshly ground black pepper
2 tablespoons chopped parsley

Rinse the shrimp and scallops under running cold water, drain well and transfer to a bowl. Add honey, ginger, light soy sauce, sherry wine and garlic, marinate for 1 hour.

Drain the dried mushrooms and squeeze out excess water. Trim off the stems close to the caps and discard, drain the straw mushrooms and set aside. Heat 1 1/2 teaspoon of the oil in a wok or large frying pan. Add all three kinds of mushrooms and toss over high heat for 1 1/2 minutes, then add 2 tablespoons of stock, cover the wok and steam the mushrooms for 2 minutes or until completely tender.

Pour the mushrooms and liquid into a bowl. Reheat the wok with the remaining oil and sauté the green onions briefly. Add the scallops and stir-fry until the meat is beginning to turn white and firm. Add the shrimp and continue to stir-fry until the shrimp are pink.

Mix the stock and cornstarch. Return the mushrooms to the wok with the scallops and shrimp, and then add the cornstarch. Stir in the dark soy sauce, season to taste with salt and pepper and cook over high heat until the sauce thickens. Transfer to a serving dish, sprinkle with chopped parsley and serve with steamed rice.

Shredded Breast of Chicken with Bean Sprouts

Yield: serves 6

1 pound boneless chicken breast
1 1/2 teaspoons brown sugar
1/2 cup dry sherry wine
1/4 cup vegetable oil
1 1/2 teaspoons cornstarch
1/8 teaspoon salt
1 teaspoon fresh shredded ginger
3 large green onions
8 ounces fresh bean sprouts
1 medium size carrot
1/2 cup frozen peas
2 tablespoons light soy sauce
1/2 cup shredded Chinese cabbage

Cut the chicken into thin slices, then stack the slices together and cut crosswise with a very sharp knife cut into narrow shreds. Place in a bowl, add the sugar, half of the sherry, 2 tablespoons vegetable oil and cornstarch. Mix well together, cover and refrigerate for half hour. Trim the green onions, cut lengthwise into quarters, and then cut into 2 inch lengths. Pick off roots and pods from the bean sprouts, rinse in cold water and drain well. Peel the carrot, cut into 2 inch lengths, then slice thinly lengthwise and slice again into thin juliennes.

Heat the remaining oil in the wok or frying pan over high heat. Add the chicken and stir-fry for 2 minutes, until the chicken changes color to a golden brown. Remove from the wok and set aside. Add the carrots and stir-fry for 1 1/2 minute, then add the green onions, ginger, sprouts, shredded cabbage and frozen peas. Sizzle the remaining sherry wine and the soy sauce over the vegetables, return the chicken and toss together quickly over high heat. Serve at once.

Twice-Cooked Loin of Pork

Yield: serves 6

1 1/2 pounds boneless pork loin
1 teaspoon salt
1 green bell pepper, cut in half, seeded and finely diced
1 small red chili pepper, seeded and chopped very fine
2 cloves garlic, minced
3 scallions, cut lengthwise to 2 inches, then quartered and washed
3 tablespoon vegetable oil
1 teaspoon sesame oil
2 teaspoons hot bean paste
2 teaspoons hoisin sauce
2 teaspoons light soy sauce
1/4 cup sherry wine
1/4 cup chicken stock
1/2 teaspoon cornstarch, dissolved in 2 tablespoons cold water
1 tablespoon honey

Place the pork loin in a skillet, cover with water, add salt and bring to a boil. Lower the heat and simmer for 25 minutes. Lift out from the stock, drain very well, and let cool. (The meat should be still rare in the center). Using a sharp knife cut into thin slices, then place 3 slices on top of each other, and cut into strips. Cut all the meat in the same manner and set aside.

Heat the vegetable oil in a wok, or cast iron frying pan with the sesame oil. Stir-fry the pork strips over high heat until it is slightly brown and crisp. Set aside. Stir-fry the peppers for 30 seconds, add the garlic, and scallions, stir-fry for another 30 seconds. Mix the remaining ingredients in a small bowl and pour into the wok. Stir well, then return the pork and toss together until the sauce thickens and evenly coats the pork, peppers and scallions. Serve with steamed rice or rice noodles.

Stir-Fried Beef Tenderloin
with Fresh Vegetables
Yield: serves 6

1 1/2 pounds beef tenderloin
6 dried Chinese mushrooms
1 pound fresh snow peas
1 teaspoon honey
2 tablespoons light soy sauce
2 tablespoons pale sherry wine
1/2 teaspoon grated orange rind
2 teaspoons cornstarch
1 egg white
8 water chestnuts, sliced 1/4 inch thick (canned or fresh)
3 tablespoons peanut oil
5 slices peeled fresh ginger
1/4 teaspoon salt, plus 1 teaspoon for the boiling water
1/8 teaspoon black pepper
1/4 cup chopped cilantro

Soak the mushrooms in warm water for 30 minutes. Squeeze out most of the excess water, and remove the tough stems, then cut each cap into quarters. Trim the beef tenderloin, remove any excess fat, grizzle and cut into 1/4 inch cubes, place into a ceramic or stainless steel bowl.

In a mixing bowl, whisk together the sherry, egg white, honey, soy sauce, garlic, black pepper and cornstarch and pour over the beef, marinate for 1 hour. Snap off the tips of the snow peas, and string the pea pods. Bring 3 quarts of water to a boil, add 1 teaspoon salt, immediately drop in the snow peas (they will turn bright green) for 1 minute. Drain the water and chill the peas with cold water.

Heat 1 teaspoon oil in a wok or cast iron frying pan. Add the mushroom, snow peas and water chestnuts, stir-fry over moderate heat for 2 minutes, or until all the ingredients are well coated with the oil. Stir in the salt, then remove the vegetables with a slotted spoon.

Pour in the remaining 2 tablespoons oil, add the ginger, orange rind and turn the heat to high. Drop in the beef cubes and stir-fry for 4 minutes, or until the meat is browned on all sides. Pick out the ginger and discard. Add the reserved vegetables and stir-fry with the beef cubes until well combined and steaming hot. Transfer to a serving platter, sprinkle with cilantro and serve at once.

Chin-ch'ien-niu-pai

257

Almond Curd with Fruits
and Raspberry Purée
Yield: Serves 6

1 1/2 teaspoons unflavored gelatin
1 pint fresh raspberries
2 tablespoons honey
1/2 cup boiling water
1 cup milk
1 cup heavy cream
2 teaspoons almond extract
1/2 cup sugar
1 1/2 cups fresh diced fruit or canned

Pour the boiling water into a small bowl and sprinkle on the gelatin. Mix well and let stand until the gelatin is soft. Bring the milk, almond extract and sugar to a boil stirring constantly. Pour over the gelatin, set the mixture aside and let cool, stirring occasionally.

Whisk the cream until stiff and blend gently with the milk-gelatin mixture. Pour in a mold and refrigerate over night. In a blender, purée the raspberries with the honey. Cut the almond curd pudding into squares, place on glass plates and top with fruit and raspberry purée.

SENTIMENTAL JOURNEYS

South Africa

It was one of the most exciting days in my life. I boarded Air France flight 432 in Paris: destination Johannesburg, South Africa. My spouse Connie and I had arrived earlier that morning from Houston. As our 747 climbed to 33,000 feet, my thoughts returned to the year 1956. I had just graduated from the culinary school in Munich and was on my first assignment as a young chef to the Edward Hotel in Durban on the Indian Ocean. Back then, our two engine DC 3 on Trek Airways with only 18 passengers, was flying at low altitude from Frankfurt to Johannesburg taking 5 days.

Now, after 40 years, it was my first return to the land where I had spent four glorious years of my youth. The world, my life and also air travel had changed dramatically over the years. As our jet roared through the night over Africa, I dined on Scottish smoked salmon with Russian caviar, accompanied by a glass of chilled French Pouilly-Fuisse and I was thinking of my past 37 years in America. My humble beginning in New York in 1960 was not always easy, but with hard work and dedication I have reached most of my goals in this great country.

Africa was also the birthplace of my father, so I always had an interest in its developments over the years. The union became a republic, the British pound became the rand, and then the final fall of apartheid and the dramatic change of government. The country that teetered on the brink of a civil

and racial war, then, as the world watched in growing fascination, drew back from destruction. South Africa entered a bewilderingly fast transformation to become planet Earth's trendiest democracy.

As we landed at Jan Smuts Airport, I realized, I was in for many new surprises. Our first night at the Sandton Sun Hotel was like staying at a first class hotel in the United States. A contemporary and spacious atrium with waterfalls, speedy elevators, excellent service, and a gourmet restaurant "Chapters" formed our welcome to a new South Africa. The next day we left by British Airways for the private game reserve Singita. In the native Shangaan tongue this means "The Miracle," and we had to agree breakfasting above the Sand River on a timber deck cradled in the branches of a towering jackalberry tree. Singita's cuisine is headed by a professional chef and worthy of its prestigious Relais et Chateux classification, and is complimented by one of South Africa's finest wine cellars. Most of all, this game reserve is renowned for its game-viewing; to witness lion, leopards and cheetah stalking their prey, follow elephants and white rhinos as they forage through lush green foliage, or revel in the colorful bird life of this idyllic wilderness.

After three days in the African bush, we were on our way to the capital Pretoria to board the Rovos Rail with destination of Cape Town. We returned to the golden age of luxury train travel in the heart of Africa. These beautiful restored trains consist of up to 19 sleeping coaches, plus a dining and observation car. Our train, also called the Pride of Africa departed from Pretoria, pulled by a rebuilt 1885 steam engine. Soon we joined the other 45 passengers in the elegant dining car and over a fine dinner and a chilled glass of local wine, we steamed through Eastern Transvaal with its history, myths and legends. For the next three days we traveled, without doubt, through the most romantic and challenging places of South Africa.

Vortrekkers made their way to a new life, battles were fought between the Boers and British, and King Shaka of the Zulus also left his mark on the Great Karoo. The Rovos Rail is by no means like the TGV of France, but after 3 days we completed our 1,000 mile journey and arrived on the most southern tip of the African continent in Cape Town. This city, with its landmark Table Mountain, is without any doubt one of the

most beautiful cities in the world. The Victoria & Alfred Hotel, overlooking the ancient harbor, was our next destination. The favorable exchange rate from the dollar to the rand was well used for the consumption of an abundance of Cape lobster and the finest in seafood in first class restaurants along the lively waterfront.

I enjoyed the abundance of excellent wines of the area. After decades of political isolation, Cape wines have now burst onto the world scene with all its splendors of the new kid on the block. There are 12 officially designated Wine Routes within easy distance of Cape Town, and about 4,647 wine farmers. The foundations were laid by Commander Jan van Riebeck, first Governor of the Cape, who produced the first wine in the year of 1659. The French Huguenots arrived in 1688 and left an enduring impression on the skill of fermenting grapes into fine wine.

Our first destination was the Estate of Saxonburg in Stellenbosch for a welcome luncheon. In the evening we arrived in Paarl and stayed as guests of KWV in their country cottage of Laborie. This splendid vineyard was founded in 1699 and still produces one of the finest selections of wine in the area. A tour through the cellars and tasting the following day was very impressive and a whole new experience in South African wines. The most luxurious estate and hotel is the five-star Grande Roche, with their award-winning restaurant Bosmans. Here we enjoyed a six-course farewell dinner from the Cape. The next day we arrived by plane in Durban, in the province of Natal on the Indian Ocean.

It was 1824 when the young British Lieutenant Farewell arrived with his good ship Julia and 40 prospective new settlers. The Zulu King Shaka was surprisingly hospitable to the new arrivals, granting them huge tracts of land and allowing them to collect as much ivory and animal skins as they could trade. Durban, today, is the third largest city in South Africa and has developed into a prosperous industrial city and vacation resort. Once Natal was the vicious battleground between the great Zulu warriors and the British army, then it became the home of the Indian guru Gandhi. Today it is an international city with over 120 hotels on the beachfront, a convention center, and the largest export harbor on the east coast of Africa.

Naturally, we stayed at the still famous and elegant Edward Hotel on the Marine Parade overlooking the lush palm trees, beautiful beaches and Indian Ocean. Looking out from my window, old memories came alive after 40 years. A tour through the kitchen reminded me of the old coal stove and a colonial life style of the past. Africa has changed, some for the better, some for the worse, and I was happy to witness the transformation to democracy.

Durban offers many exciting trips into the countryside. The Valley of the Thousand Hills and the traditional Zulu villages are only a short drive outside of Durban. For day trips there is Shaka Land and several game reserves such as Hluhluwe and Umfolazi, the home of the white rhinos.

The food is spicy with a heritage from the Portuguese and Indian settlers. The most memorable dinner was the evening before our departure at the Royal Grill. It reminded me of the movie "Out of Africa". The wonderful memories of this trip will linger on for the rest of my life. On our long flight home to Houston, I thought about the many nice and gracious people we met, the beauty of the Cape, and also the difficult task of former President Nelson Mandela, and his successors to keep South Africa prosperous. It was nice to visit, but I was happy to land again on familiar Texas soil.

A Return to Pomerania

The summer of 1944 was the last time we played on the beach on the Baltic Sea (Ostsee) and enjoyed the last fond memories of a childhood in Kolberg. At this time, the eastern front was far away and the German high command promised a final victory in the near future. Then came a very cold winter and the fall of Stalingrad. General Paulus' mighty sixth army was defeated and the war took a political turn. The soldiers of Russia were now on the march to the west and closed in on our Kolberg.

In March of 1944, my city faced the Soviet Army and became a mighty fortress. Kolberg was the seat of numerous garrisons of land forces and a base for the Kriegsmarine (Navy). The last phase of war came when Soviet and Polish armies approached the frontiers of the Third Reich, prepared to strike the final blow on the eastern front.

At this time the propaganda machine in Berlin announced the fables concerning the invincibility of the town. Kolberg was once more proclaimed a fortress, which had to be defended to the last soldier. The German headquarters in Berlin gave Festung Kolberg a particular role. The fortress was one of the central points of the system, which protected the line of sea communication, with the German troops cut off in the east. Furthermore, the fortress was to endure a long period of fighting, to weaken the Russian troops on their attack on the German capital, Berlin.

Three rings of fortification surrounded Kolberg. Minefields; anti-tank trenches and the neighboring areas were converted into strong resistance centers. Almost every building was adopted for defense purposes and the streets were also barricaded.

The town had more than 1,000 elite German soldiers with heavy artillery, tanks, an armored train, heavy guns of Kriegsmarine warships, among them the armored battleship Luetzow and also the Admiral Scheer. Powerful aircraft forces were concentrated in nearby airports to support the defense. The fortress was almost inaccessible, but then on the 7th of March, the attack of the Soviet Army began. The heat of the fighting is quite evidently shown by the fact that virtually the whole center of the city was left in ruins. The last desperate act of defense was fought in the nights of the 17th and 18th of March.

After the Russian forces regrouped, the army with 65 tanks and 8,000 troops crashed the third ring of defense and then forced their way to the railroad station and the harbor. Soon a white and red Polish flag started flapping over the lighthouse, which was riddled by artillery bullets. Kolberg was totally destroyed, and at the same time it was also the end of the German presence on the Baltic Sea.

At this time I was six years old, but the heat and the noisy impact of rockets stayed with me for many years. For several weeks, we lived in the cellar of our house. We were without electricity and fresh water, and haunted by the fear of a direct hit. This made the days and nights very long and chilling. At the final hour, a messenger ran through the hail of bullets and fire from cellar to cellar to announce the fall of the city. There was only one way out and that was the open sea on a small fishing boat. In the last minute the German Navy made every effort to evacuate as many women and children as possible. My family was one of the last few to leave the burning city under bombardment out to the Baltic Sea.

A happy couple

large city was very pleasant; we were a little tired from the long journey, but still ready to visit the Kudamm (Kurfürstendamm). We arrived ten minutes later by subway in the center of the city next to the Kaiser-Wilhelm-Gedächtniskirche. This old church never was rebuilt and it is now a monument, but also a reminder of World War Two, a horrible time of total destruction.

Berlin, just like New York, is a very special and very proud city. It never sleeps. The next day, we visited the Reichstag.

In Texas I found happiness, prosperity, peace, and most of all a feeling of belonging, but nevertheless my mind often wandered to a far away place called Kolberg. My life had been very interesting and rewarding, but every time I looked at old or new maps, my eyes always went to a small port by the Baltic Sea. Finally in the fall of 1992, I made plans for a visit to Pomerania.

The day of departure was the 3rd of October on Lufthansa flight 437 to Frankfurt. We arrived on Sunday morning and then left again one hour later for Berlin. The Stiglitz hotel in the outskirts of this

In old-time war movies, this mighty building was the center point of speeches and impressive parades, but today it is empty and waiting to be renovated. The Brandenburg Gate, just two years earlier sealed off with gun towers and barbed wires was now the hub for tourists. The famous Berlin Wall was totally gone, and the only evidence of its dark history could be purchased in small plastic pouches for $2.

Checkpoint Charlie, once the only opening between east and west, is now a museum. The Friedrichstrasse, a well-known name from old spy movies, is now just another busy street in Berlin. Under den Linden, once playground for East

Berliners, is now the place to purchase old Russian uniforms and medals with hammer and sickle. The cold war, the iron curtain, the shooting of humans, who tried to flee to the West, and the unproductive life of the last forty years seem now so very senseless.

Berlin is in the process of being renovated, painted and rebuilt. The traffic is terrible, but soon we found our Autobahn, E 28 to the east. For three hours we traveled through the former DDR, along gray-looking villages with sad looking facades. We crossed the river Oder and soon reached the Polish border. The line for passenger cars was short, a smiling Polish officer looked at our blue passports with the beautiful American eagle, he stamped our documents, wished us a pleasant journey and we were in Poland.

To our left was the former capital of Pomerania called Stettin; now under the new regime it is Szczin. We stayed on E 28 east. this always has been the main road from west to east for hundreds of years and goes up to Gdansk (Danzig) and on into Russia. Now the landscape changed to a thick forest in beautiful fall colors, the sun was shining and it was just a great day. Our little Ford took us through neglected farming communities with strange names like Trzebiatow (Treptow) or Karlino (Köslin) and along huge potato fields. Very few automobiles traveled on E 28, and my thoughts went back to the chilling winter of 1945. Along this very same road came more than a million refugees from East Prussia and Pomerania on wagons to escape the advancing Russian Army.

At that time, tanks, artillery and a fast moving infantry heading for Berlin had priority and only a few refuges survived the trek. Several of my relatives perished on this road and most likely I passed their unmarked graves. Soon we approached a crossing of E 28 and we turned left to our final destination: Kolberg.

The entrance to the small town is a tunnel of the most beautiful chestnut trees. The cathedral, just as 47 years ago, stood on the top of the hill. My heart started pounding, and I knew my trip halfway around the world had come to an end. We passed the old train station, totally destroyed during the last days of the battle, but now rebuilt in the same style and beauty. We crossed the river Persante and on to the old Post Office, built in bright red bricks two hundred years ago. The only change at the City Hall was the Polish Eagle on the tower. We went on to the Orbits Hotel near the beach.

As we unloaded the car, my friend thought he heard the noise from an advancing freight train. This sound was very familiar to me, it was the surf from the Baltic Sea behind the trees. The Polish government operated the hotel: it was not the Plaza in New York, but for $65 including a hearty breakfast, it was a bargain.

We were anxious to visit the beach and naturally the harbor, the place of my tragic departure a half century ago. During dinnertime at the hotel, we had the pleasure to meet several senior citizens from Hamburg. As it turned out, in 1944 the gentlemen were students at the local flying school to be pilots in the German Air-Force, and during this time each of them married a local beauty. It was a reunion after fifty years, and we Texans were delighted to join them in this happy affair. After a short conversation we realized to my greatest surprise, that one of the ladies, Mrs. Metzger, had been a neighbor in the same street where I had once lived. She also had been on my father's swim team and told me stories related to my dad. Soon we exchanged many old, fond memories. Mrs. Metzger made a copy from her old German city map, and the next day we were able to trace the streets and surroundings from the past.

Our house on Kummerstrasse No. 13 was hit in the final days and burned to the ground. It was rebuilt in a more modern style, housing now a small grocery store. The home of my aunt on the Kaiserplatz was still standing, but in horrible shape, with big cracks and no visible paint. Again we returned to the harbor. Very little had changed since 1944. The bomb craters are overgrown with trees, the mighty lighthouse at the entrance is rebuilt, and several old planes, rusty tanks and heavy artillery are now stored in the Polish military museum.

The beautiful Strandschloss (Beach Hotel), once the pride of the Spa City that was Kolberg, was burned out and now housed a hospital for Polish miners. The old bathhouse on the beach, built at the turn of the century, had withstood the war and also the storms from the sea. It reminded me of a precious time with my family.

The village of Wobrow and the farm of my grandfather brought back thoughts of happy days. The memories of the fine horses and beautiful carriages, of the stables with milk cows and my grandmother's Streuselkuchen (Crumb Cake) stayed with me for over fifty years. Now, with the help of the old maps from Mrs. Metzger, we were on our way to Wobrow. First we stopped at the old small chapel on the outskirts of Kolberg. It was built by Katharine the Great of Russia in the thirteenth century. Then, up the hill to the Baron von Eschen estate; once it was a very large farm with thousands of acres planted with corn and potatoes. The Baron had the finest horses and was the richest man in the land. Now after a half century of Communist rule, his house still has the style of a Prussian Nobleman, but it is in shambles. Nine families occupy his house, and the once beautiful flowerbeds are now overgrown with weeds. The carriage house is empty and the stables are caved in. My thoughts pictured it as it once was, a long, long time ago.

Finally we arrived in Wobrow, the birthplace of my mother. To my big surprise little had changed. The community bake oven in the center of the village with the inscription of 1929 survived the war and is used again by its new citizens. The main house, with the proud coats of arms of the Radünz family still in place, awakened many fond memories in me. Sad looking occupants watched us. We looked for the vegetable garden. It, too, was gone. But the fresh apples from the front yard of the house tasted just as delicious at this time of the year as they had a half-century ago.

Everything has come to an end. We returned by car to Berlin and onward by plane to Frankfurt.

The next day we enjoyed a chilled bottle of Champagne on the ship Germania on the river Rhine. We cruised through beautiful old villages from medieval times along old romantic castles. Fast trains, filled with happy travelers, sped north and south, and my thoughts returned to Kolberg, a different time, a different life and land.

I was thinking about the bartender at the Orbits hotel, who without much interest served a few guests in a day for only a few pennies in tips, and about the pretty Polish waitresses, unskilled and trained in a Communist system. I also was thinking about the farmer who sold his crate of apples for ten cents the kilogram and a dozen eggs for 25 cents. The lady in the rest room at the train station sold the toilet paper by the yard, and I also thought about the ugly and shabby apartments of its residents, blessed with so much beautiful land and still living in such close buildings. It is very sad.

I admired the next generation of happy and pretty Polish children, playing just like all the children around the world in well groomed parks. Kolberg, or now Kolobrzek, has only a few busses and no bicycles; everybody walks and walks. Most of the houses need a good coat of paint and the city needs a few hotels with service up to western standards. Only five hours driving time from Berlin to a beautiful beach and a very favorable exchange rate, Kolberg has a great future.

My last thought was the Maikuhle, a very pretty park and also the playground of my childhood. In the center of the park was the cemetery with beautiful marble tombstones and also the last place of rest for many of my forefathers. To my great disappointment, every grave has vanished and it is now only a disarray of wild trees and bushes. Every trace of a German past or history is gone; it is a new land with different ethnic goals and lifestyles.

The circle of my life had closed, my big dream was fulfilled. Again, it was my most happy day once the plane approached Houston Intercontinental Airport and landed on American soil. I can say only: God bless America!